D1212647

10-76

WORKING CLASS YOUTH CULTURE

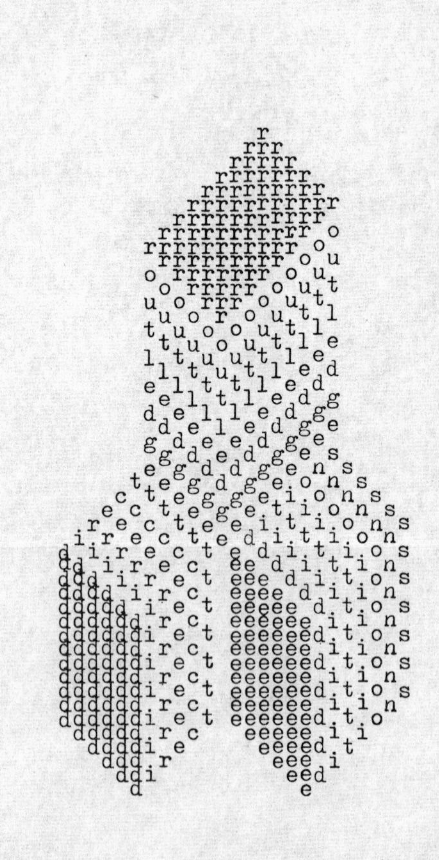

WORKING CLASS YOUTH CULTURE

Edited by
GEOFF MUNGHAM
Department of Sociology
University College, Cardiff

and

GEOFF PEARSON
School of Applied Social Studies
University of Bradford

ROUTLEDGE DIRECT EDITIONS

ROUTLEDGE & KEGAN PAUL
London, Henley and Boston

To our parents

HILDA JONES and GEORGE PEARSON

MARIE JOHNSON and TOM MUNGHAM

First published in 1976
by Routledge & Kegan Paul Ltd
39 Store Street,
London WC1E 7DD,
Broadway House,
Newtown Road,
Henley-on-Thames,
Oxon RG9 1EN and
9 Park Street,
Boston, Mass. 02108, USA
Manuscript typed by Brenda Hutt
Printed in Great Britain
by Unwin Brothers Limited,
The Gresham Press, Old Woking, Surrey
A member of the Staples Printing Group

ISBN 0 7100 8374 2

CONTENTS

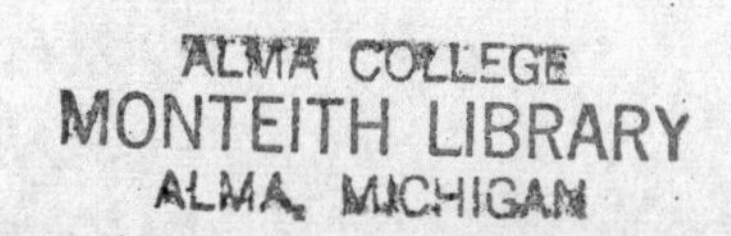

PREFACE

A number of the essays collected here were originally given as papers to a conference on 'Working Class Culture' at University College, Cardiff in November 1973. We owe a debt, therefore, to all those who gave us their support in that venture, read papers, made beds available to visiting speakers, cooked food, made cups of tea, etc. In particular we wish to thank Anne Murcott who organized the conference with us. We have also incurred a heavy debt to Jackie Griffin. The contributors have tolerated revised deadlines, re-thinks and re-writes - all necessary if collective writing is to be a possibility. Peter Hopkins of Routledge & Kegan Paul has been a constant source of encouragement. Finally, the continuing stimulation and friendship of those in the National Deviancy Conference reminds us that we are not working alone.

CARDIFF GM
BRADFORD GP

CONTRIBUTORS

John Clarke	Centre for Contemporary Cultural Studies, University of Birmingham.
Tony Jefferson	Centre for Contemporary Cultural Studies, University of Birmingham.
Robin McCron	Research Assistant, Centre for Mass Communication Research, University of Leicester.
Geoff Mungham	Department of Sociology, University College, Cardiff.
Graham Murdock	Centre for Mass Communication Research, University of Leicester.
Howard Parker	Department of Sociology, University of Liverpool.
Geoff Pearson	School of Applied Social Studies, University of Bradford.
David Reynolds	Department of Social Administration, University College, Cardiff.
Ian Taylor	Criminology Unit, Faculty of Law, University of Sheffield.
Dave Wall	Faculty of Law, Queen's University, Belfast.

'What would you do if you had a million pounds?'
'I'd buy a Bugatti and a Rolls and a Bentley and I'd go two hundred miles an hour on Pendine Sands.'
'I'd buy a harem and keep the girls in the gym.'
'I'd buy a house like Mrs. Cotmore-Richard's, twice as big as hers, and a cricket field and a football field and a proper garage with mechanics and a lift.'
'And a lavatory as big as, as big as the Melba pavilion, with plush seats and a golden chain and ...'
'And I'd smoke cigarettes with real gold tips, better than Morris's Blue Book.'
'I'd buy all the railway trains, and only 4A could travel in them.'
(Dylan Thomas: 'Portrait of the Artist as a Young Dog')

Ah get born, keep warm
Short pants, romance, learn to dance
Get dressed, get blessed
Try to be a success
Please her, please him, buy gifts
Don't steal, don't lift
Twenty years of schoolin'
And they put you on the day shift
Look out kid
They keep it all hid....
(Bob Dylan: 'Subterranean Homesick Blues')

INTRODUCTION: Troubled youth, troubling world

Geoff Mungham and
Geoff Pearson

I

The adolescent boy has perhaps received more than his fair share of attention from sociologists, psychologists, criminologists, psychiatrists and welfare professionals. But the seam is not over-worked. On the contrary: although adolescence has held social scientists spell-bound, it has also seemed to make them lose their heads. Thus, inevitably, youths are portrayed as troublesome and as a problem category. Even when a recent psychiatric text looks at what it calls 'normal' adolescence (Group for the Advancement of Psychiatry, 1974) one is left with the impression of gross abnormality, everywhere and at all times. The familiar platitudes are trotted out: for example, 'all adolescents are particularly vulnerable to the strains of ... rapid social change' (GAP, 1974, p. 17). And later we read: 'It is not surprising that adolescents, driven as they are by the thrust of puberty, often repudiate adult values and at times give way to "orgies" of seemingly meaningless and sometimes destructive behaviour' (GAP, 1974, p. 49).

On the other hand, the young are sometimes seen as being in the vanguard of social progress. Theodore Roszak is such a writer who sees the 'orgies' of youth as a meaningful and life-giving revolt against an over-systematized and over-technicalized social order (Roszak, 1973, p. 252). Writers such as Roszak, in fact, are truly in love with adolescence: 'more and more, it grows to be the common expectation that the young should be those who act, who make things happen, who take the risks, who generally provide the ginger ... the alienated young are giving shape to something that looks like the saving vision our endangered civilization requires' (Roszak, 1971, p. 1). The romanticization of youth, and especially deviant youth, has been very common in recent developments in social enquiry (cf. Pearson, 1975a).

We ask ourselves: just who is this creature? Adolescents are either condemned out of hand as rebellious, ill-fitting members of a well-ordered world; or glorified as potential rebels and revolutionaries who will overturn a world which is sick, lifeless and dull. We search, in fact, through the mountains of words, facts and opinions on the adolescent and inevitably come up against some form or another of gross sentimentality - either negative or positive.

There is, of course, a third position which both has its cake and eats it. More usually associated with social pundits, perhaps, it tells us that 'youth can teach us a lesson or two' and that the criticisms and 'antics' of youth are in some sense salutary for the rest of us. But it also ultimately condemns youth, usually because 'they always end by going too far'. It is thus the language of the Reverend J.C. Flannel in 'Private Eye'. It is our impression, however, that this kind of dithering is less common than the outright celebration or condemnation of youth who have the power to excite the passions of the social commentator.

One of the problems, we think, is that when social scientists and welfare professionals turn their eyes on the adolescent, they somehow forget their own youth. And so their reason falls prey to the recurring moral panics which surround young people: drug orgies, football hooliganism, mugging, mods and rockers, Hell's Angels, rock festivals, truanting, student unrest, ban the bomb, cosh boys, teddy boys, skinheads, drop-outs, venereal disease, glue-sniffing, vandalism, etc., etc., etc. 'Moral panics', as Stanley Cohen has shown, can take on a life of their own which is quite unrelated to what is actually going on. They can amplify public concern over 'troublesome kids'; they can stress what is bad, and the occasional dramatic flare-ups, out of all proportion to their actual significance; they can even generate trouble through over-reaction by the police, social workers and magistrates (cf. Young, 1971). Moral panics, that is, sometimes tell us more about those who panic than about what provokes the panic (cf. S. Cohen, 1972; Lefebvre, 1974; Paul, Jimmy and Mustafa Support Committee, 1973). But also (and this is crucial) there is trouble among youth. All the more reason, then, for clear heads and critical thought when we approach youthfulness. First, let us list some of the things which make for wrong-headedness in the study of youth, and also set out the rationale for this book.

Generation gaps

The first problem is an utter lack of attention to detail. There is endless talk, for example, about a 'generation gap'. But can youth be usefully lumped together simply as one generation which is all alike? Is it really the case that student troubles, for example, and queer-bashing have the same roots? Or the 'gentle hippies' and the 'wild ones'? Are the conditions of life really the same for the middle class kid in the suburb, and the working class youths on council estates, downtown areas or the shop-floor of the factory? We think not.

Classless youth

Behind all the talk of 'generation' and 'generation gap' there is the forgotten question of the class structure of society. It is as if when youth are discussed that social class goes on holiday. But youth are not a classless tribe, and the essays in this book focus specifically on working class youth and the ways in which class structure alters the experience of learning to place oneself in the social, and divided, world.

The Coca Cola generation

Youth are not only thought of as a classless formation, but also as a group without a national identity. The explosion of the popular music industry in the post-war period, specifically since the arrival of rock-and-roll, encourages the belief that through pop music youth have acquired an international vocabulary. Also, the heavy domination of American literature in the field of social science helps to blur real distinctions and real differences between youth of different nation states. However, in addition to re-asserting the banished concept of class in the understanding of youth, this collection of essays refuses to allow itself to be 'transatlantic': our focus, and our interest, is with British youth.

Mindless yobbos

We mentioned at the outset the way in which youth are predominantly seen as a problem. But, if they are thought to be misfits, they are also seen as individual misfits - lonely atoms in a big world. We do not wish to deny that kids can be broken and damaged in childhood. But we are at the same time tired of the unending repetition which blames broken homes, individual psychopathology, dubious hereditary factors, or faulty upbringing for the troubles of youth. Perhaps, as Paul Goodman (1960, p. 11) said, it is not that troublesome youth are under-socialized: perhaps they are socialized perfectly well, 'perhaps the social message has been communicated clearly to the young ... and is unacceptable ... and therefore there is difficulty in growing up.' Correspondingly, our essays do not focus on the adolescent's individual problems, nor on the 'senselessness' of his actions. Instead they look to the meaning and sense of youthful behaviour, and to the shared problems and perspectives of young, working class people in post-war Britain. Although we are not too happy with the word, our focus is with their culture.

Grown-ups

Always, it seems to be assumed, the young and the old are at war. We ask: is it really the case that youth have nothing in common with their parents' generation, or with their grand-parents? In his vital contribution to the study of working class youth cultures in Britain, Phil Cohen (1972) has argued that working class youth do in fact share many experiences and problems with the generation of their parents; and that they are often trying to re-enact and re-create (albeit symbolically and magically) some of the life conditions, work conditions and culture of an earlier generation of working class men and women. Kids, that is, carry on and develop the old traditions; they do not only break away. These connections between the established (but eroded) traditions of working class life, the struggles of youth and the working class community as a whole - connections which cut across generation and relate to the shared experiences of life, work and leisure - are developed in a number of the essays in this volume.

Uni-sex?

Finally, there is an appalling neglect in the considerable literature on adolescence of young women and girls. Youth culture is held to be synonymous with male youth culture, so that girls - when they do appear - appear only as something which boys sometimes fight over, or merely as objects in the gaze of men. Our book is also guilty of this fault, and although some of the essays say a little about girls, it is certainly not enough. We are not happy with this state of affairs, and perhaps our inability (as editors) to recruit someone to write on the life of the working class girl simply underlines the problem. (1)

II

The reader will probably be familiar with the main features of post-war British youth culture and youth style. Nevertheless, we think it might be useful, as an aid to memory if nothing else, to offer a brief sketch of the post-war youth scene.

There is a very definite form to the changes in youth culture in post-war Britain, and the line of descent runs from the teddy boy, through the mod to the skinhead. Each of these styles has its own distinctive flavour. Each of them is specifically the creation of working class districts in London. Each of them is associated with its own 'moral panic'.

In 1953 the teds emerged, as Rock and Cohen (1970, p. 289) put it, 'without much warning'. The most distinctive aspect of their style was their spectacular dress. The teddy boys borrowed a high fashion trend of the early 1950s which had revived (in rather a decadent manner) the dandified cut of Edwardian clothes, and they transformed it into a lavish and aggressive symbol of the new rock-and-roll. Long (incredibly long) jackets with velvet collars, tight drain-pipe trousers, boot-lace ties or 'slim-jim' ties, and thick crepe-soled suede shoes (known as 'brothel creepers') went together to make up a startling uniform. Hair was also worn long with side whiskers, a quiff at the front to hang down like an 'elephant's trunk', and meticulous combing at the back which made a style which was called (and looked like) a 'duck's arse' or DA. The music of the teds was early rock. And the early rock musicians out-dazzled even the most dazzling teddy boys: for example, Wee Willie Harris who wore bold colours and dyed his hair orange, green, violet, or any colour which seemed an unlikely colour for human hair.

The elegant Edwardian suit was soon abandoned as a high fashion style when the teddy boys took it for their own: no fashionable city gent would be seen in what had now become a 'ted suit'. And it is hard to resist the impression that in grabbing high fashion for itself, the teds had scored a remarkable symbolic victory over the upper class. Harry Hopkins (1964, p. 428) refers to the style as 'the badge of a half-formed, inarticulate radicalism': 'A sort of half-conscious thumbing-of-the-nose, it was designed to establish that the lower orders could be as arrogant and as to-the-manner-born as the Toffee-nosed Ones across the River.' Certainly, it was a class-based phenomenon, and sometimes the teddy boys were pretty rough. Some of the teds ripped out seats at the early rock concerts, and some danced in the aisles. Some of them terrorized cafe owners and late-night bus conductors. The rest were probably content to look good in their bold suits of bright pink, deep purple, and electric blue.

The classic teddy boy had probably died his death by the late 1950s, and over the years the dress style underwent a number of modifications and adaptations. The style had emerged from working class areas of South London, and one can do no more than guess about how quickly it spread to other areas of Britain, or how long it survived. We cannot therefore trace its natural history. Indeed, in one sense, such phenomena as these have no 'natural' history because once they emerge they are taken over by the commercial world, marketed, exploited and transformed. We do not know therefore the mechanism by which youth style 'catches on'. We know that smaller boys will imitate bigger boys: in the days of the teds, for example, school blazers were often worn off-the-shoulder to try and create the impression of the long, broad-shouldered ted suit. We also know that in parts of northern England the traditional working man's cloth cap (or 'ratter') was modified by some teds and taken on as a vital part of the uniform. But it is in the nature of popular culture (because this is what youth style is) that it has no written history: we only know that it came out of the blue, and then disappeared. However, we cannot assume that this was merely a 'craze' with no more significance than, say, the hula-hoop. The ted signified something about his culture and he played his part well: as George Melly (1972, p. 36) puts it, 'the whole thing gelled to look undeniably right.'

It is one of the features of post-war British youth culture that it goes into quiet phases when there is no clear-cut, crystallized or dominant style available. The immediate period following the teddy boy is a case in point. There was a brief period in which the so-called 'Italianate' (or 'modernist') style made an impact. The music was still rock, but this was quieter than the hard rock of Bill Haley and the Comets, Little Richard, or the early Presley. Correspondingly, the clothes were quiet: sharp, sombre suits which were buttoned high with narrow lapels. And, apparently, the kids were quiet and the major moral panic of the period concerned the Campaign for Nuclear Disarmament. Working class youth culture was waiting for its next explosion: the mods.

The mods also came out of the blue; or rather, out of London's East End. Hair was worn short and neat; clothes were less distinguishable than the ted suit, but clothes were vitally important to the mods who were always immaculate. The mods, Melly (1972, p. 154) writes, 'were not afraid to look pretty.' They added a form of transport (the scooter) to the necessary equipment of every well-groomed mod, and they were fond of pep-pills (blues, leapers, black bombers, purple hearts). Initially the mod music was 'Blue Beat' (a Caribbean derivation) and rhythm-and-blues. Very quickly, however, with the sudden rise of British rock bands (the Beatles, the Who, the Rolling Stones and the so-called Liverpool Sound) the music of the mods became indistinguishable from the general trend in popular music. One pop group, the Who, were very much a mod group and on the LP 'Quadrophenia' they have set down a musical commentary on what it was to be a young, working class mod (The Who, 1973). The possibility of the young producing their own social commentators adds a new, and complicating, factor to what one means by youth culture.

There was more to being a mod than the outward insignia of clothes, scooters and neat hair. As with the earlier teds and the later skinheads, it also involved a distinct approach to life. As an outraged mod correspondent put it in one of the popular magazines of the period, he was tired of the magazine's stress on clothes and records: 'Mod isn't something you can just walk into a shop and try on. It's an attitude of mind.' In this volume John Clarke and Tony Jefferson develop some of the themes of the mod imagination.

The mod thing first became noticeable as a distinct style in 1963, but it only really burst to life after the riots at holiday towns in 1964 between mods and rockers (cf. S. Cohen, 1972; The Who, 1973). Rockers preferred leather jackets to smart gear, and noisy motor bikes to GS scooters. At least in their appearance rockers were hard, tough, male and hot; mods were soft, peacockish, almost feminine and cool as ice. But appearances could be deceptive. Although mods were despised by rockers because some of them wore make-up on the face and, therefore, were nothing more than 'fairies' or 'bum-boys', the events of Easter 1964 showed the rockers that mods were still young working men who were quite prepared to fight their way out of, and into, trouble.

The mod style was highly complex and contradictory, and one of the difficulties in trying to describe it clearly is that because it rested on visual neatness it was easily commercialized and marketed. Perhaps the pure mod style was never seen outside London; but again we have no way of mapping its dispersal amongst British youth. It arrived in Sheffield (to give just one example) as late as 1965, by which time the style had been drastically transformed by clothing manufacturers. It also quickly evaporated into the highly commercialized period of 'Swinging London' and Carnaby Street fashions, and the mod became lost as a pure style in the glut of trendy gear.

The teddy boy had been and gone; his younger brother the mod also came and went. Both were momentary crystallizations of style which passed away into periods which had no style; both were working class creations; both were phenomena which might be given a voice if we knew how to 'de-code' and 'read' the signs of popular culture (cf. Barthes, 1972b; Clarke, 1973; Jefferson, 1973; Hebdige, 1974a).

We will mention here the imported California style of 'Flower Power' only in order to point out that it hardly took root on British soil. Even so, this 'counter-culture' was more attractive to middle class youth and those undergoing higher education, so that we see relics of vaguely 'hippie' styles nowadays only among university students. The kids who work in the factories did not go for the ragged edges of shaggy coats from Afghanistan, kaftans, bells and beads, the so-called 'progressive' music of Pink Floyd et al., or the mysticisms of the 'I Ching', 'The Tibetan Book of the Dead', or 'acid consciousness'. When working class youth culture emerged in its next crystallized form, in fact, it almost seemed to be a reaction against the quiet, introspective influence of Flower Power; and its most obvious symbol was 'bovver boots'.

The skinheads are the latest style to have dominated post-war British youth culture, and again they come out of the East End of London, and their influence spreads haphazardly to other regions. The skins adopted a uniform which seems to be, at one and the same time, both a caricature and a re-assertion of solid, male, working class toughness. With half-mast trousers, braces, boots, and hair cropped close to the head their aggressive gait smelt of trouble and danger. Their music was adopted from Reggae - black music from the West Indian ghettos. Moral panics associate skinheads with 'queer-bashing', 'paki-bashing' and football hooliganism. In the eyes of 'public opinion' it almost seems inconceivable that the skinhead could find a way of enjoying himself which did not involve offending someone else. Of course, skinheads did not invent racial violence (although the moral panic seemed to suggest that they did) and they were not the first to beat up homosexuals - in West Germany, for example, where there are no skinheads, 'queer-bashing' is well known and is called by the delicate name of 'schwüle tippen'. Nevertheless the opposition between 'us' and 'them' did take a number of forms in the skinhead's way of seeing things. The importance of one's own patch, one's own football team, and the defence of working class territory and neighbourhood loomed large in the skinhead's life-style. Hence the graffiti on the walls where they lived: 'Boot Boys Rule. OK.'

The skinhead style evaporated into groups known as crombies (because of the coats which they wore), smooth-heads and casuals. It is sometimes said that the skinhead is dead. Even so, anyone with eyes can still see skinhead youths around the major British towns and cities. And whether the skinhead is dead, where the next crystallized style will come from, or whether it will come at all, is anyone's guess. In this volume, Ian Taylor and Dave Wall question the possibility that the so-called Glamrock cult may be the successor to the skinheads. If so, then it breaks the pattern of post-war youth culture in Britain. Glamrock - the 'good time music', the glittering rock bands, the bisexuality of some of the stars of 'faggot rock' - is indelibly a commercial product. Teddy boys, mods and skinheads (on the other hand) made themselves, and made their styles. And although we wish neither to glamorize nor to romanticize these 'self-made men', we cannot see them as trivial. The solidarity of the teddy boys, the mods and the skinheads seems to us to be an important, and intriguing, feature of the under-life of post-war British capitalism.

III

Finally, we will say something about ourselves. The authors of this book are, without exception, young men. And this is important. We were born either during the Second World War, or immediately after it: if you like, we were potential (and actual) teddy boys or mods, although we are too old to have been skinheads. It is one of the necessities of reflexive sociology, or critical sociology, to make this clear: the social world is not just something going on 'out there', and those who study society are also participants in society.

Furthermore, a large number of the authors also come from working class families, and we think that this is important in its own way. For although this is our background, we are also (in a formal sociological sense) upwardly socially mobile. Thus, we are part of an upwardly mobile élite within the working class and the lower middle class, unlike the kids who are described in this book: for they are the ones who are reckoned to have failed; they are the ones who have been left behind.

The difficulties of bridging the gap between what one is (a member of a professional élite) and what one was, are spelled out by Raymond Williams in his recent studies of the English tradition in literature. He is discussing Thomas Hardy's novel 'Jude the Obscure', and he is attempting to relate this discussion to his own life; just as we are trying to relate our work to our personal biographical experiences. Jude, it will be remembered, was a working man who longed for education, but who was refused admission to 'Christminster': he was one of those who 'failed'; one of those who were left behind. Williams writes (1974, pp. 80-1):

> The ideas, the values, the educated methods are of course made available to us if we get to a place like Christminster: if we are let in as Jude was not. But with the offer, again and again, comes another idea: that the world of everyday work and of ordinary families is inferior, distant; that now we know this world of the mind we can have no respect - and of course no affection - for that other and still familiar world. If we retain an affection Christminster has a name for it: nostalgia. If we retain respect Christminster has another name: politics or the even more dreaded sociology.... /The problem/ is what happens to us, really happens to us, as we try and mediate those contrasted worlds: as we stand with Jude but a Jude who has been let in; or as we go back to our own places, our own families, and know what is meant, in idea and in feeling, by the return of the native.

Williams adds that: 'This has a special importance to a particular generation, who have gone to the university from ordinary families and have to discover, through a life, what that experience means.' The authors of this book belong to the generation of which Raymond Williams writes. The reader will have to bear with our nostalgia, our sociology and our politics as we attempt to articulate the experience of our class. He will find different styles and different emphases in these essays. Some are heavily flavoured by autobiography and personal experience; others place their emphasis on a theoretical development of the question of youth. The essays also reflect the experience of working class youth in different regions and industries therefore provides a back-cloth to our studies. We do not claim to have covered all the angles; it is only a beginning to the important work of de-mystification in the field of youth culture.

We began by saying that youth are inevitably regarded as a 'problem' and that we reject this emphasis. The reader may therefore wonder why it is that these essays constantly return not to untroublesome youth, but to those who are a trouble and those who are troubled - truants from school, car-radio thieves, paki-bashers, football hooligans, kids who fight, vandals and joy-riders. He may ask: does this not confirm that youth are a problem class? Our answer is that there is no other way. The de-mystification of the youth question must be attacked at its roots, and the roots say that youths are problems and that their problems are senseless and hooligan. The important thing, therefore, must be to understand the sense and the meaning of the troubles of the young members of the working class. In focusing often on the troubled aspects of working class youth culture, however, we are not trying to rescue the young working man's reputation. We are saying, emphatically, that he has got something to say which is critical to our understanding of class society, although sometimes he may say it in a muffled and violent fashion, or at other times he may only mutter incoherently to himself:

> there is something very improbable about there being a whole phase of life which embodies nothing but disadvantage; one would have thought it more likely that the imagination of a boy and of a man each possessed a particular vantage-point, clarifying some things about life and obfuscating others (without the differences merely coming to six of one and half a dozen of the other).... The more open way to come at it is to ask: along with the disabilities and mawkishness of adolescence, what truths about life is the adolescent better stationed to see than either the boy or the man? (Ricks, 1974, pp. 10-11)

Youth is definitely troubled, and working class youth seems to be more of a trouble than most. But there is no smoke without fire.

NOTE

1 Since going to press, a short and illuminating exploration of this problem has emerged from the work of the Centre for Contemporary Cultural Studies in the University of Birmingham. See Angela McRobbie and Jenny Garber, Girls and Subcultures, 'Working Papers in Cultural Studies', no 7/8, Summer 1975, pp. 209-22.

Chapter 1

YOUTH AND CLASS: The career of a confusion

Graham Murdock and Robin McCron

Over the last two decades or so in America and Britain, young people have probably attracted more publicity and theorizing than almost any other social group. This barrage of attention has not developed in a vacuum however. On the contrary, ideas about youth have been intimately bound up with the dominant images of capitalism in change; images of pluralism and openness, of affluence and consumerism and, above all, of increasing classlessness.

Theories of youth have been tied to the withering away of class primarily by the argument that the division between the generations has increasingly replaced class inequalities as the central axis of the social structure, and that this shift has been accentuated and confirmed by the emergence of a classless culture of youth, separated from, and opposed to, the dominant adult culture. Variations of this argument have underpinned a great deal of both the popular and sociological commentary on youth, with the result that in much of the writing, class is seen as largely irrelevant and either evacuated altogether or treated as a residual category. At the same time however, research on youth, including much of the work generated from within the 'youth culture' paradigm itself, has persistently produced evidence which points to the continuing centrality of class inequalities in structuring both the life styles and life chances of adolescents.

This chapter sets out to trace the career of 'youth culture' theory through its successive stages; to highlight the disjunctions between the theory and the accumulating evidence; to suggest how and why the discrepancies were glossed over and explained away; and finally to argue that these confusions can only be resolved by restoring class to the centre of the sociology of youth. It is intended as a ground clearing exercise, offering a point of departure for the subsequent chapters in which some of the elements of an adequate class analysis are outlined and explored.

THE DISCOVERY OF 'YOUTH CULTURE' AND THE EVACUATION OF CLASS

By the mid 1920s, youth was a well established topic among psychologists and educationalists but apart from a few scattered writings, sociologists in America and Britain had paid little attention to it. Towards the end of the decade however, interest began to gather momentum, mainly under the impetus provided by two books.

The first was Margaret Mead's monograph, 'Coming of Age in Samoa', which showed that the stereotypical picture of adolescents as rebellious and anti-adult did not fit the Samoan case, and suggested that these responses were not so much a 'natural' part of maturation as a specific product of modern social conditions. The book which was published in 1928 rapidly became a best-seller and focused attention of the social position of American youth and their reactions to it. One of these reactions had already been exhaustively explored by Frederick Thrasher in his monumental study of Chicago youth gangs, published the year before, in 1927. Thrasher saw the gangs as 'one of the many symptoms of the more or less general disorganisation' of the down-town areas. Faced with the breakdown of family life, inefficient and alienating schooling, and a lack of leisure facilities, he argued, adolescent boys respond by creating 'a world distinctly their own - far removed from the humdrum existence of the average citizen' - the world of the street gang (Thrasher, 1927, p. 3). Two years later the Wall Street Crash and the onset of the Depression dramatically underscored Thrasher's emphasis on social disorganization and the failure of conventional institutions, and reinforced interest in the idea of adolescents filling the gaps by creating self-contained groupings cut off from the mainstream of adult society.

It was against this background that the American Sociological Association organized a conference at Yale in the spring of 1934 to explore directions for future research in the sociology of youth. In his keynote paper, E.B. Reuter took up the gang theme and argued persuasively that future work should concentrate on finding out how far 'adolescents live in a world which is isolated from that of adults' and how far 'they think of themselves as belonging to a "we-group" as opposed to adult groups' (Reuter, 1936, p. 83). Three years later he returned to these questions again, claiming that they were more central than ever, since American adolescents were now actually engaged in the process of creating 'an inclusive social order' separated from adult society and sustained by a distinctive 'system of collective definitions' (Reuter, 1937, p. 421). Reuter's argument that this emerging adolescent culture deserved urgent sociological attention was supported by the eminent anthropologist Ralph Linton, who gave a speech to the American Sociological Society pointing out that the ways in which age groups develop 'a sense of category solidarity based upon community of knowledge and interests' were among the most important but least studied of all social processes. 'We are prone to forget', he added, that children and adolescents 'have their own distinctive culture patterns which are not learned from adults' (Linton, 1942, pp. 590-1). But it was left to Talcott Parsons (1942) to isolate the 'unique and highly distinctive combination of age grading and sex role elements' then supposedly emerging among American adolescents, and to coin the term 'youth culture' to describe them.

In Parsons' formulation 'youth culture' stands opposed to the male role which forms the hub of the adult culture. Instead of stressing productive work, conformity to routine and the acceptance of responsibility, the 'youth culture' emphasizes the inverse values of consumption, hedonistic leisure and irresponsibility. Although he acknowledges that these values are present in muted form in the adult culture, Parsons argues that these continuities are 'probably structurally secondary' to the growing gulf between the mainstream adult culture and the emerging 'youth culture' (Parsons, 1942, pp. 91-3).

At the same time that Parsons was outlining his definition of 'youth culture' an alternative interpretation of the situation was emerting out of the research being conducted by August Hollingshead, one of Reuter's graduate students. The research was based on a detailed study of adolescents in a small mid-west town, 'Elmtown', just before the effects of the Second World War were apparent locally.

Hollingshead began his pilot work in the summer of 1941 with the aim of determining how far the social behaviour of the town's adolescents was attributable to individual maturation and how far to social experience. By the autumn however, his initial observations had convinced him that this formulation was too vague and deflected attention away from what appeared to be the major factor determining the social behaviour of Elmtown's youth - their class situation. The subsequent year of painstaking field-work amply demonstrated the superiority of this more focused formulation, and led Hollingshead to conclude that class position was the main determinant not only of adolescents' social behaviour:

> one of the important things this study highlights is the diversity of behaviour exhibited by adolescents in the different classes.... Commonsense judgements might have inclined us to think that in such a narrowly restricted age group social behaviour would fall into a more or less common pattern in each sex group. That it did not was a surprise (Hollingshead, 1949, p. 441)

but also of their social consciousness:

> the family and neighbourhood sub-cultures ... provide him /the adolescent/ with ways of acting and definitions of action.... Situations ... are defined in a general way by the class and the family cultures, but they are defined explicitly by the cliques /in which adolescents spend their leisure time/ (Hollingshead, 1949, p. 445).

Although Hollingshead finished his fieldwork at the end of 1942 the completion and publication of the final report was delayed by the war and the book did not appear until 1949, by which time the Cold War was gathering momentum.

The Cold War was not only a political but also an ideological struggle. Essentially this struggle centred on the contrast between the image of American society as a pluralist democracy based on individual choice and an open competition for power, and the image of Soviet society as a totalitarian state in which a self-recruiting party élite manipulated a passive and conforming population. Within this dominant definition of the situation, any attempt to develop a class analysis of American society was doubly disadvantaged. Not only did it threaten the pluralist image, but it was also strongly linked to Marxism and therefore with Soviet communism. Consequently, when the 'Elmtown' study was finally published, although it was widely acclaimed for its thoroughness and wealth of detail, the central implication - the centrality of class inequalities in the lives of adolescents - was largely passed over.

Parsons' formulation on the other hand, was entirely consonant with the preoccupations of the period. Returning to the theme of 'youth culture' in 1950, he underscored his earlier emphasis, arguing that the developing 'youth culture' was characterized by a 'compulsive independence of and antagonism to adult expectations and authority' and a 'compulsive conformity within the peer group of age mates' (Parsons, 1950, pp. 342-3). This stress on group conformity fitted well with more general Cold War concerns, and more particularly with fears that the ethos of individualism which formed the basis of the pluralist system was being superseded by a growing emphasis on going along with the crowd. This fear found its most cogent formulation in the analysis of the shift from 'inner' to 'other-directness' which formed the core of David Reissman's 'The Lonely Crowd', also published in 1950. The book made a considerable impact and its preoccupations permeated many areas of sociology, including the developing research on youth.

COLD WAR RESEARCH: IMAGES OF PLURALISM

One of the earliest and largest programmes of post-war American youth research was the Purdue Opinion Panel, which regularly sampled the views of several thousand high school students throughout the country. As the findings of the various surveys accumulated, a consistent picture of youthful conformism began to emerge. Reissman seemed to be right. American adolescents were becoming more and more 'other-directed', with the majority conforming to peer group opinion in their leisure choices and parental opinion in other areas. Conformism also pervaded their wider views. In one poll for example, three-quarters of the sample had endorsed 'obedience and respect for authority' as the most important habit for people to learn. All in all the studies showed individualism at a low ebb, and this, as the poll's principal authors realized, presented something of a problem for America's pluralist image.

> The internal stability of any democratic society, as well as its effectiveness in meeting the challenge of rival ideologies, is dependent on the constant and active exercise of those freedoms that epitomize the democratic orientation. Passive acceptance of choices made by others is actively destructive to the American ideal (Remmers and Radler, 1957, p. 230).

The key to combating this situation, they argued, lay with a school system which provided a working model of the pluralist system rooted firmly in the central values of competitive individualism. The Purdue team never followed this connection through, however, and it was left to James Coleman to explore it empirically.

In common with many other academics of the time, Coleman was committed to the pluralist ideal. As he remarked later, 'I saw the critical political question of the future as one to which socialism is irrelevant: not in whose hands the means of production will rest but in how many independent hands' (Coleman, 1961, p. 185). However, in order to demonstrate that America's pluralism was a concrete reality and not just a matter of public rhetoric, it was necessary to show that pluralism dominated not only the public face of the political system but also the day-to-day workings of social institutions at every level. Institutional studies therefore played an important part in the defence of pluralism. Their value had already been underlined by Seymour Lipset's study of trade union organization, 'Union Democracy', on which Coleman had worked as research assistant. Encouraged by the study's success, he began looking for an institutional domain in which he could develop his own research, and given the relative availability of funds for educational research, high schools offered a convenient choice.

Coleman's main aim was to demonstrate the essential pluralism of the schools by showing the diversity of different status systems that co-existed within them. He saw this as an illustration of his general argument that political pluralism grew out of cultural diversity. In order to attract research funds however, the study needed to be more clearly tied to current educational problems, and so he added the secondary aim of discovering how far informal status systems among the pupils supported or opposed the schools' academic goals. This resonated well with the growing publicity and concern over pupil disruption and violence in schools epitomized in the image of the 'Blackboard Jungle'. The application was successful, and work began in ten Illinois high schools in the spring of 1957.

Coleman's pluralist thesis rested on the assumption that the various informal status systems were all equally open and that a pupil's position was solely the result of individual achievement. As the research results began to accumulate however, it became increasingly apparent that in at least four of the study schools, a pupil's status was determined primarily by the social class position of his family.

These findings placed Coleman in an acute dilemma. Not only did they contradict his central thesis, but they pointed to the importance of a class analysis, an alternative which went against his basic political beliefs. After a year of disorientation he resolved the situation by pushing his original pluralist thesis to one side and developing the study's secondary theme around the notion of 'youth culture'. In the opening chapter of his influential research report therefore, Coleman followed Parsons in stressing the growing separation of adolescents from adults, and the emergence of autonomous youth subcultures. The modern high school pupil, he argued,

> is 'cut off' from the rest of society [and] With his fellows, he comes to constitute a small society, one that ... maintains only a few threads of connection with the outside adult society ... separate subcultures exist right under the very noses of adults - with languages all their own, with special symbols, and, most importantly, with value systems ... that

lead away from those goals established by the larger society (Coleman, 1961, pp. 3, 9).

As he later pointed out, this solution simultaneously provided a comprehensive 'frame of reference for the research results and helped to bring consistency into them' by playing down the contradictions (Coleman, 1961, p. 203). And, most important of all, it offered a plausible alternative to a class analysis.

With this shift in emphasis the study acquired new connotations and resonances. As the image of pluralist democracy receded from the centre of the analysis, so the emergent 'youth culture' theme welded it to another of the central images of American capitalism; the image of the consumer society.

TEENAGERS: HARBINGERS OF CLASSLESS CONSUMERISM

From the time the term first appeared in the early 1950s, the image of the 'teenager' was intimately bound up with the idea of the consumer society. In 1945 for example, an enterprising 18-year-old, Eugene Gilbert, established a commercial research agency, Gil-Bert Teen Age Services, to advise firms on how to exploit the market potential he saw emerging among his peers. Marketing to teenagers he argued, 'is quite unlike marketing to any other portion of the total market.' They were a new consumer group requiring new techniques based on the kind of 'deep insight into their habits, ideas and thoughts' that his agency was in business to provide (Gilbert, 1957, p. 52). But he added, this was a small price to pay for access to a growing market with enormous profit potential.

By the time Coleman came to do his fieldwork in 1957, events had proved Gilbert's point. His agency had become a multi-million dollar concern, and selling to youth had become big business, with a sizeable section of the entertainment industry, mainly centred on the expanding pop music business, catering almost exclusively for teenage tastes. Coleman saw the emergence of this youth market as a decisive factor in further segregating adolescents from adults and in creating a homogeneous culture of youth which dissolved traditional social divisions. His view was shared by the authors of a large scale study of adolescents based on a national survey taken in 1956. On the basis of their results they also conclude that 'the peculiar conflicts of age itself and the force of modern mass communications' had combined to produce a growing 'homogenization of American adolescence across regional boundaries and, by and large across social class lines as well ...' (Douvan and Adelson, 1966, p. 345).

Among the forces of mass communications contributing to this homogenization, pop music was singled out as being particularly important. As Coleman's research assistant put it, 'if one was asked to identify the single cultural trait which best characterises the American youth culture, one would find it difficult to avoid mention of its popular music' (Johnstone, 1961, p. 71). But once again the hypothesis was at odds with the evidence. Far from uniting youth around a shared set of age-specific symbols and values, Coleman's findings clearly indicated that pupils' pop music tastes tended to follow existing social divisions. Despite the fact that Elvis Presley had been insistently publicized as the incarnation of the youth cultural values of sexuality, hedonism and antagonism to adult authority, only a fifth of the sample nominated him as their favourite pop performer, the majority of the rest opting for the adult approved style of Pat Boone. Further, a secondary analysis revealed a clear connection between pop preferences and class background. Presley's brand of rock-and-roll was an almost exclusively working class taste (see Johnstone, 1961, pp. 73-80).

These results undermined the notion of a homogeneous 'youth culture' and pointed to the continuing importance of class situation in determining adolescents' choice of leisure styles. They also pointed to the emergence of an increasingly complex relationship between media-relayed symbol systems and pre-existing class cultures. Coleman however ignored these implications and continued to organize the analysis around the 'youth culture' concept, leaving the underlying contraditions in the data unexplored and unexplained. This systematic myopia on the question of class was not confined to American academics however, it also characterised much of the developing British research on youth.

Eugene Gilbert had come to England in 1954 and again in 1956 with the intention of establishing a permanent London office, but after briefly surveying the situation he had left, concluding that the British youth market lacked the potential for significant growth. Events were soon to prove him wrong however, and by 1959 Mark Abrams was able to publish his pamphlet, 'The Teenage Consumer', announcing that English youth had emerged as a significant consumer grouping and a major market for records and other entertainment goods. Abrams' presentation contained a familiar contradiction. On the one hand he argued that adolescent spending on leisure and entertainment represented 'distinctive teenage spending for distinctive teenage ends in a distinctive teenage world' (Abrams, 1959, p. 10). On the other hand, however, closer analysis revealed that this distinctively teenage market was almost entirely working class, and that many of the commodities usually described as typically teenage were in fact 'typical only of working class teenagers' and 'largely without appeal for middle class boys and girls' (Abrams, 1961, p. 10). Clearly this evidence was at odds with his earlier emphasis on the primacy of age per se. Three years later however, when he came to publish a further study of youthful consumers, he resolved this discrepancy by the simple expedient of treating class as a redundant category.

He developed his argument in three basic stages. First, he stressed the 'more than normal ... sense of alienation' between 'the 16 million young people born and brought up after the defeat of Hitler' and the adult generations who had grown up before the war (Abrams, 1964, pp. 13-14). Second, he emphasized the parallel process of 'embourgeoisement' and the withering away of class. 'In the post-war world', he claimed, 'class barriers have tended to lose their clarity.... Some working class families have incomes as high as some white collar families and there is little to choose between their styles of living' (Abrams, 1964, p. 57). And finally, he linked the two processes, arguing that, 'Under conditions of general prosperity the social study of society in class terms is less and less illuminating. And its place is taken by differences related to age' (Abrams, 1964, pp. 57-8).

In this new formulation, the growth of the youth market no longer appeared as an isolated phenomenon, but as part of a general transition towards a new social order of affluence, in which the class system rooted in the traditional relations of capitalist production was being increasingly superseded by a new system of age stratification based on the emerging relations of consumption. This transition seemed to be well under way in the Britain of 1964. The burgeoning British pop culture spearheaded by the Beatles seemed finally to have created a distinctive and homogeneous teenage culture, dissolving class divisions and uniting youth around a common set of symbols and leisure styles. Hence teenagers appeared as the harbingers of the coming society of spectacular consumption, announcing the imminent arrival of a capitalist society without classes.

Field research such as Peter Willmott's (1966) study of working class boys in Bethnal Green, however, showed a rather more complicated relationship between the youth-oriented culture of pop and pre-existing class cultures. Despite the fact that the main interviews for the study were conducted in the summer of 1964 at the height of the pop explosion, the values, aspirations and life styles of the great majority of respondents emerged as firmly rooted in the culture of the locality. Although the Bethnal Green boys had easy access to the burgeoning discotheques, beat clubs and boutiques of the West End, for example, only a minority made use of them. The rest were more likely to do their dancing to the beat groups provided by the local pubs and to buy their fashion clothes from the local menswear shops. Clearly, the process of change was more uneven and ragged than Abrams allowed for. Rather than replacing class-based cultures, the new teenage leisure culture was being laid over the top, setting up an increasingly complicated interaction between the two.

An alternative version of the changing relations between class and age in the England of the 1960s was provided by Frank Musgrove in a series of influential writings which focused on the changing social position of youth. As modern capitalism developed, he argued, so youth has been increasingly removed from the sphere of production, excluded from positions of status and responsibility and 'consigned to a self contained world of juvenile preoccupations' (Musgrove, 1964, p. 11). Consequently their power and status in relation to adults has been steadily eroded to the point where they now find themselves in a position of almost total dependence, and subordination to adult authority, with the result that they now constitute 'in effect a "social class", a class relatively independent of the stratification system of adults' (Musgrove, 1969, p. 50). In Musgrove's version then, 1960s youth had not so much transcended the class system as become a 'class' in its own right.

By using 'class' here in Ralf Dahrendorf's specifically revisionist sense of groupings based on the differential possession of power and authority, Musgrove is simultaneously able to portray youth as a separate subordinate 'class' and to present economic class divisions as confined to 'the stratification system of adults' and therefore irrelevant to the study of youth. The result is a truncated and distorted analysis. While it is true that young people are largely excluded from central areas of adult life and confined to age-specific institutions, it does not follow that they are cut off from the wider system of class stratification. On the contrary, through the insistent mediations of the family, the neighbourhood and the school, class inequalities penetrate deeply into their everyday lives, structuring both their social experience and their responses to it. Schools provide an obvious case in point. They are institutions not simply of age segregation but also of class domination. They operate not only to delay adolescents' entry onto the labour market and to reinforce their subordination to adult authority, but also to reproduce the existing structure of class inequalities and class relations. Far from uniting youth as a single subordinate 'class' therefore, schools serve to remake and confirm the prevailing patterns of class divisions and antagonisms.

Musgrove was not alone in devaluing the centrality of class inequalities. Indeed, as the previous discussion should have made clear, he was simply adding another variation to an already dominant theme.

Although class analysis was largely evacuated from the mainstream of sociological writings on youth from the mid 1950s onwards, it did not disappear altogether. Rather it was decanted into the specialized area of delinquency research where over the same period it gathered considerable momentum.

SUBTERRANEAN CLASS ANALYSIS: QUESTIONS OF DISADVANTAGE AND DELINQUENCY

The fear that adolescents' 'natural' hedonism and rebelliousness could very quickly tip over into outright deviance had been a long standing theme in the literature of moral concern and social control. Consequently, from its invention in the 1940s, the idea of the teenager was strongly linked to the image of the juvenile delinquent. The punch line of an American joke of the period, for example, has a housewife telling her neighbour, 'My husband was two hours late getting home the other night. Oh, my God, I thought, the teenagers have got him.' Similarly, the notion of the adolescent peer group as self-contained and antagonistic to adult authority found its logical extension in the image of the delinquent street gang cemented in countless news stories, magazine features, movies and books. Books like Harrison Salisbury's best-seller, 'The Shook up Generation', which was subtitled, 'Teen-Age Terror in Slum and Suburb' and came complete with a glossary of 'Street Gang Argot' to enable uninitiated adults to follow the action. This popular image of the gangs as existing outside the dominant social and moral order was endorsed by the prevailing academic formulations which followed Thrasher in describing gangs as a world apart 'far removed from the humdrum existence of the average citizen' (Thrasher, 1927, p. 3). As the 1950s progressed, however, this orthodoxy was increasingly challenged by work which situated delinquent gangs within the wider class system. The principal departure point for this developing class analysis was Albert Cohen's book, 'Delinquent Boys' (1955).

Cohen's analysis was rooted in the recognition that the education system operated primarily to reproduce the prevailing class structure and that consequently schools provide one of the principal means through which class inequalities are mediated into the everyday experience of adolescents. As a result, he argues, the majority of working class adolescents are cumulatively disadvantaged within the school system, and experience education predominantly in terms of cumulative failure and loss of self-esteem. Faced with this situation they disengage themselves from the school's rituals and values and orientate themselves instead around their leisure aciivities. More particularly, argues Cohen, they create an autonomous sub-culture of leisure based on an inversion of the school's core values. Hence hedonistic leisure, immediate excitement and defiance of authority replace hard work, conformity to routine and subordination to adult commands at the centre of their value system. By demonstrating the centrality of class inequalities in structuring both the social situation of youth and their responses to it, Cohen's analysis marks a considerable step forward. At the same time however, it contained important deficiencies. In the first place, by presenting the delinquent subculture as a rejection and inversion of the dominant culture it ignored the continuities between them. Second, by continuing to characterize the culture of the gang as largely self-contained it seriously underestimated the extent of its connections with the wider working class culture. This second set of connections was however explored soon afterwards by Walter Miller (1958) who argued on the basis of extensive field observations that the core values of delinquent subcultures - toughness, excitement, luck, the ability to outsmart the authorities - were not so much inversions of middle class values as versions of the 'focal concerns' of working class culture extended and reworked to fit the specific situation of working class youth. But it was left to David Matza to suggest the possible lines of connection between delinquent sub-cultures and the dominant culture.

According to Matza, delinquents had 'picked up and emphasised' values which are embedded not only in working class culture, but also in 'one part of the dominant culture, namely the subterranean values of leisure' which find their conventionalized expression in the officially approved forms of recreation and consumption (Matza and Sykes, 1961, pp. 717-18). Hence, far from constituting isolated enclaves cut off from the dominant cultures, delinquent subcultures emerge from Matza's analysis as 'stretched' versions of the values of hedonistic consumption which counterpoint the ethos of productive work within the dominant value system. As Matza realized, this formulation carried implications that went beyond the immediate question of delinquent sub-cultures:

> To the objection that much juvenile behaviour other than simply delinquent behaviour would then be analysed as an extension of the adult world rather than as a product of distinctive adolescent subcultures we can only answer that this is precisely our thesis (Matza and Sykes, 1961, p. 718).

In a follow-up paper he extended this point and presented 'youth culture' as a contentionalized version of the delinquent subculture hence as similarly related to the subterranean tradition of hedonism within the dominant culture (Matza, 1961).

Hence, in place of Parsons and Coleman's presentation of 'youth culture' as a self-contained system set over and against the value system of adult society, the analysis of Matza and of Miller directs attention to its connections with the two central configurations of class culture - the dominant culture and the subordinate culture of the working class - and raises the complex questions of triangular relations between them. Apart from an impressionistic attempt by Bennett Berger (1963), however, these relations were left unexplored.

In the absence of a comparable body of home grown theory and conceptualization, American work provided many of the starting points for the British research that began to gather momentum in the 1960s. This was particularly true of themes in the American material which resonated with emerging British concerns. Albert Cohen's emphasis on the school system as a central mediation of class was one such theme.

The system of secondary schooling for all, established by the 1944 Education Act, had been generally hailed as a crucial step towards dissolving class inequalities and initiating a new era of equal opportunity. As the 1950s progressed, however, the familiar contours of class began to show through. A mounting pile of sociological studies and government enquiries, culminating in the Newsom Report of 1963, clearly indicated that class inequalities had not been eradicated under the new system but had simply reappeared in new forms. All the evidence pointed to the fact that the great majority of working class pupils remained cumulatively disadvantaged within the school system. Consequently, the ways in which they responded to this situation became a major focus for research.

In his widely quoted study of London school boys in the mid 1960s, Barry Sugarman (1967) arrived at a modified version of Albert Cohen's formulation. He suggested that pupils were caught between two opposed cultures - the culture of the school and the 'youth culture' sponsored by the teenage leisure and entertainment industry and centred on pop music and fashion clothes. Hence, in his model, the pupils who fail to meet the schools' demands, who are overwhelmingly working class, respond by rejecting the school culture and orientate themselves instead around the 'youth culture'. Consequently, in Sugarman's formulation, 'youth culture' appears primarily as the 'culture of the non-mobile working class' (Sugarman, 1967, p. 160). Although it offers a valuable counter to Abrams' simplistic insistence on the growing classlessness of teenage culture, Sugarman's analysis is itself flawed by over-simplification. By treating 'youth culture' as more or less synonymous with working class culture he obscured the complicated interactions and accommodations between them.

These relations were similarly glossed over in another study conducted at the same time - David Hargreaves' (1967) study of the fourth year at 'Lumley' school, a boys' secondary modern in a deprived area of a northern city. With a wealth of detail,

Hargreaves demonstrates how both the basic structures of educational selection and the pupils' characteristic responses to them were reproduced within the school. Hence the pattern he describes was the familiar one in which the working class pupils at the bottom of the school's formal hierarchy responded to their disadvantaged situation and to the accompanying sense of failure, by rejecting the goals and values of the school and involving themselves in an anti-academic culture centred around the leisure environment. The leisure culture Hargreaves describes, however, could not be simply labelled as 'youth culture'. Rather it emerges as a complex amalgam of age and class based elements. In addition to involvement in pop music and fashion clothes, it included activities rooted in the local culture such as billiards, and delinquent acts of theft and vandalism. In the end Hargreaves settled for labelling the anti-school culture as 'delinquescent', thereby side stepping the complex question of the triangular relations between the 'situated' culture of the working class area, the teenage leisure culture, and the delinquent sub-culture. One version of these relations was however offered in another major study of the mid 1960s - David Downes' (1966) analysis of the 'corner boy' culture of Stepney and Poplar.

Downes extended the range of class analysis by arguing that adolescents' class position not only determined their life chances within the spheres of education and work, but also structured their access to choices and opportunities within the leisure environment. Working class adolescents, he argued, are therefore disadvantaged twice over; once within the school and employment systems and once again within leisure. Faced with monotonous and alienating labour both at school and at work, they concentrate on living in their non-work time, and leisure therefore becomes the all important means through which they attempt to retrieve some sense of enjoyment, excitement and autonomy. But here again Downes argues, they are disadvantaged. They have been caught up in the images of glamour and hedonistic consumption relayed by the teenage entertainment industry, but at the same time they lack either the means or the opportunities to realize their rising leisure expectations. The commercial entertainment facilities available locally seem tatty and second rate; they feel alienated from the youth clubs and organizations sponsored by the middle class do-gooders, and the traditional milieux of the pub and the working men's club can no longer contain their new leisure aspirations. The system has made them a promise it cannot keep, and faced with this contradiction Downes argues that the working class 'corner boy' 'reacts against both middle class and "lower class" culture, and arrives at the "delinquent sub-culture" by pushing the legitimate values of "teenage culture" to their logical conclusion' (Downes, 1966, p. 134).

Although it contained a number of inconsistencies and loose ends Downes' analysis offered a convincing demonstration of the centrality of class inequalities in structuring both the work and leisure situations of adolescents, and pointed once again to the need to restore class to the centre of the sociology of youth. Several factors militated against this restoration, however. First, the fact that this emerging class perspective was confined to the sub-fields of delinquency and educational research meant that it was increasingly fenced off from the mainstream of sociological writing on youth by the growing specialization of sociological labour. In the second place, class theories of youth were almost entirely themes about working class boys. They had little or nothing to say about working class girls or about middle class adolescents. Consequently, their generalizability was severely curtailed. Nor were these gaps filled by a comparable body of work developed elsewhere. In fact, apart from their inclusion in portmanteau surveys and a few scattered studies, middle class adolescents had attracted very little sociological attention. Basically this was because the vast majority appeared quiescent and conformist and therefore presented no particular problem of explanation. Even their non-conformity and deviance took easily containable forms. Certainly compared with the spectre of gangs of delinquent rioting in the streets and classrooms, the beats seemed to offer little serious threat to property and public order. Hence the bohemian undercurrent among middle class youth went almost unresearched. As a result, emergence of the hippie movement in the late 1960s took sociologists almost completely by surprise, and in the absence of developed alternatives commentators turned once again to the preoccupations of mainstream youth theory, and more particularly to the embourgeoisement theme.

'YOUTH CULTURE' AS 'COUNTER CULTURE'

As most commentators saw it the hippie movement marked the transformation of the youth culture into a counter culture in which antagonism to adult institutions and values had turned to outright rejection and hedonistic leisure had become a way of life. They saw the hippies as the vanguard of a bloodless cultural revolution in which 'the economic class struggle' was being 'transcended' (Reich, 1972, p. 259) and the youth generation were being united in 'one electronically based, interconnecting network' (Mead, 1972, p. 89) rooted in the new consciousness carried by 'progressive' rock music. It was a compelling argument and when half a million young people turned up for the Woodstock rock festival in the summer of 1969, it seemed to be beyond dispute. But once again this image of a homogeneous culture of youth was increasingly contradicted by the accumulating research evidence which clearly pointed to the counter culture's class base.

The studies showed first that by and large the counter culture found its main constituency among students, ex-students and college drop-outs, and that consequently, apart from the minority of working class educational survivors its effective social base was almost entirely middle class. Second, a number of studies indicated that far from being 'profoundly, even fanatically alienated from the parental culture' (Roszak, 1971, p. 1) the hippies' core concerns were extensions of themes and values embedded in middle class culture (Young and Crutchley, 1972; Berger et al., 1972). The focal concern with 'doing your own thing' for example, appeared as a 'stretched' version of the central middle class values of individualism and self-expression. Similarly, at the same time that they scorned the consumer durables of 'straight' society, the life style of many hippies centred on the commodities produced by the burgeoning rock industry. But if the research indicated that the gap between the generations was a good deal smaller than the counter culture theorists made out, it also demonstrated that the class divisions within the youth strata were a good deal wider and more permanent.

Despite the insistent publicity given to counter cultural styles and values, the movement gained comparatively few converts among working class youth, the majority of whom continued to regard hippies with attitudes ranging from disinterest and incomprehension (Mills, 1973, p. 25) to outright hostility (Daniel and McGuire, 1972, pp. 71-3). Ironically, it was pop music which provided one of the main means through which this basic class division was expressed and confirmed.

As its title implies, the 'progressive' rock music produced by the counter culture attempted to go beyond the standard pop formulas and to experiment with longer and more complicated musical and lyric structures. Its main vehicle was the stereo LP designed to be listened to through a domestic hi fi system. Mainstream pop on the other hand, remained tied to the basic format of the 45 rpm 'single', and continued to provide the bulk of top twenty hits and the majority of the records played in discotheques and on juke boxes and pop radio shows. This basic technological and stylistic division between 'progressive' rock and mainstream pop largely corresponded to a social division within the youth audience, between those who had left school at the minimum age and those who had stayed on to take up a place in the rapidly expanding higher education sector, a division which in turn largely reflected the class differentials in educational opportunity. Hence, far from dissolving class differences and creating a homogeneous generational culture, the bifurcating cultures of pop and rock became one of the main means through which these divisions were extended into the sphere of leisure (Murdock and McCron, 1973).

The counter cultural theorists could not grasp this situation because like the embourgeoisement theorists whom they succeeded they were convinced that consumption and leisure had replaced production and labour at the centre of social life, and that class differentials in life chances were being wiped away by nominal equality of access to life styles. Both themes rested on the idealist assertion that 'culture controls the economic and political machine, not vice versa' (Reich, 1972, p. 235) and consequently both were fundamentally mistaken. For, as Marx had pointed out, it was exactly vice versa. Hence, as the economic situation began to worsen, so the imagery of youth as the harbingers of classless capitalism started to fade and the contours of the class system once again became starkly visible. As a disillusioned John Lennon put it, 'the class system is exactly the same except that there is a lot of middle class kids with long hair walking around in trendy clothes. But apart from that, nothing happened, it's exactly the same' (Wenner, 1973, pp. 11-12).

This realization that advanced capitalist societies were still at root class societies began to penetrate into the heartland of mainstream sociology. For example, after a sizeable study designed to 'replicate and extend' Coleman's work had failed totally to support his hypothesis, the two authors belatedly realized that their reliance on the 'youth culture' theory had obscured the real dynamics of the situation. Reluctantly they concluded that:

> American society is deeply divided /with/ blue-collar workers against white-collar workers. It may be less threatening to adults to attribute differences to generations when they actually emanate from differences between class or interest lines within adult society itself (Kandel and Lesser, 1972, p. 185).

Even marketing men were beginning to deny the existence of a separate youth market and to restore class to a central place in their calculations (e.g. Clemens, 1973).

TOWARDS A COMPREHENSIVE CLASS ANALYSIS OF CONTEMPORARY YOUTH

The rediscovery of class inequalities finally revealed the conceptual bankruptcy of 'youth culture' theory. Its historical moment had clearly passed along with the notions of affluence an 'embourgeoisement' in which it was embedded, and although it retained a residual currency in both popular and academic discussions, increasing numbers of commentators and researchers recognized the need to restore class to the centre of the sociology of youth. In Britain, this process of reconstruction began initially with the retrieval and extension of the lines of analysis developed within the sociology of education and deviancy theory. While these directions are still being developed, themes derived from cultural studies and communications research have also been added, so that current sociological work on youth is characterized by a considerable range of interests and methodologies. Nevertheless, out of this apparent diversity, the outlines of a comprehensive class analysis of contemporary youth are now beginning to emerge.

Restoring class to the centre of the sociology of youth does not mean evacuating age. Clearly age is an important factor in structuring the social situation of young people. Some experiences, notably compulsory secondary schooling, are youth specific. Similarly, young people just entering the labour market are particularly vulnerable to shifts and uncertainties in the structure of employment. Age also plays a key role in determining the range of options and choices available within the leisure environment. It is not therefore a question of simply substituting class for age at the centre of analysis, but of examining the relations between class and age, and more particularly the way in which age acts as a mediation of class.

This question of mediation is crucial, for young people, along with everyone else, experience class relations primarily in the mediated or filtered form of the concrete social relations which they are involved in at school, on the job, in the family, and in the local area. At the level of everyday life, then, class inequalities are encountered not as some abstract and far-away force, but as specific distributions of opportunity, advantage and control. A class analysis must therefore begin by examining the ways in which class relations are experienced and negotiated within particular work and non-work situations.

The most powerful and pervasive mediations of class occur within the work situation, at the point of maximum articulation to the system of production. Although within the education system this articulation is displaced rather than direct, schools remain basically work situations. For the majority of young people, the experience of both education and work is characterized by varying degrees of monotony, boredom, and alienation. However, since they are not in a position to exercise much control over their work situation, their response to these experiences is largely displaced into the sphere of leisure, where class is mediated in more diffuse forms and where the areas of choice, autonomy and control are correspondingly greater. Leisure behaviour cannot be fully understood therefore without a prior understanding of how the work situation is experienced and negotiated.

Leisure styles are not determined solely by work experience however. Hence, having established this relation, the next step is to examine in detail how specific leisure styles are generated and sustained. Recent work on adolescent leisure has focused primarily on the complex negotiations between the 'situated' class cultures embedded within the family and the local area, and the youth oriented culture relayed by the mass media. Drawing on sub-cultural theory studies have explored the ways in which adolescents in particular class locations, select elements from both the 'situated' and 'mediated' cultures and rework them into a distinctive style which both embodies their view of their situation and represents an attempt to transcend it (e.g. Clarke, 1974). By demonstrating the way in which media-relayed elements are actively selected and invested with sub-cultural meanings, this work provides a valuable corrective to the simplistic view of youth as a homogeneous mass market. But at the same time there are considerable problems with using the sub-cultural approach.

Sub-cultural studies start by taking groups who are already card-carrying members of a particular sub-culture such as skinheads, bike boys or hippies, and working backwards to uncover their class location. The approach therefore excludes adolescents who share the same basic class location but who are not members of the sub-culture. As a result it tends to draw too tight a relation between class location and sub-cultural style and to underestimate the range of alternative responses. The problem is not only to explain why styles such as the mods or the skinheads developed within particular class strata at the times and in the forms that they did, but also to explain why adolescents in essentially the same basic class location adopted other modes of negotiation and resolution. This question can only be answered by going beyond general characterizations of class location and examining the detailed variations in the mediations of class within specific work and non-work situations. The limitations of the sub-cultural work are specific instances of more general gaps in the literature as a whole.

The work done so far has been heavily weighted towards the top and bottom of the class structure. Most of the available studies deal with youth from either the semi-skilled and unskilled manual strata or from the professional and managerial middle classes. There is comparatively little material on youth at the intermediate levels of the class structure. An imbalance also occurs in the treatment of the relations between adults and youth. The adults who appear in the existing literature are primarily either agents of moral entrepreneurship or social control, most notably the police, or agents of commercial exploitation. Clearly these relations are important and studies of labelling and amplification have added a crucial dimension to the developing class analysis. But a comprehensive analysis must consider not only spirals of action and reaction within the specialized spheres of social control and the mass media, but also the more general and routine connections and discontinuities in the relations between adults and youth. More particularly, it must examine the ways in which age mediates the experiences and responses not only of adolescents but also of adults within the same class location, and structures the relations between them.

Although these imbalances are important and need to be corrected, the crucial gaps in the available British literature lie elsewhere in the almost complete absence of studies on girls and the dearth of material on black youth. Both groups pose the crucial question of how far class experience is mediated not simply through age position but also through sexual and ethnic situation. The problem is therefore not only to discover how the class system is experienced and negotiated by adolescents in particular class locations, but also to determine what difference it makes if they are also female and black.

Finding answers to these questions and the others raised above is crucial, not simply to the production of a more adequate and complete description of contemporary youth, but also to the development of a comprehensive analysis which, while starting from the centrality of class inequalities, is sensitive enough to accommodate the complex levels of mediation through which these inequalities are experienced. Such an analysis is in turn essential, not only to the immediate task of reconstructing the sociology of youth, but also, and perhaps more importantly, to the wider enterprise of developing a more complete and coherent understanding of the class structures of advanced capitalist societies and the ways in which they are changing.

Chapter 2

BOYS WILL BE MEN: Brief adolescence in a down-town neighbourhood

Howard Parker

ADOLESCENT FUZZ

The unevenness of our sociological iterature is obvious, some areas are well grounded and carefully researched whilst others lack both theoretical and empirical sophistication. The present pseudo-sociology of youth falls squarely into the latter category. Adolescence is viewed from perspectives which when surveyed (Roberts, White and Parker, 1974) show distinct polarization. Adolescence must seemingly be a period of stress, trauma and malleability (Miller, 1969) or else a complete myth (Elkin and Westley, 1955). Similarly 'youth culture' is taken to be either a quasi-independent value system uniting western youth (Flacks, 1971; Keniston, 1971) or an adult-invented conspiracy aimed at keeping down the challenge of new generations (Musgrove, 1964). None of these polarized positions can be adequately and independently borne out although the creation of 'youth culture' as an alternative to class analysis can, as Graham Murdock points out, be found particularly lacking and in need of demolition before a valid sociological analysis of youth can be developed.

Some of the confusion can be easily cleared since it is a creation of cross-cultural trading. As is so often the case American studies of youth are of little use and perhaps overtly harmful to a study of British youth. Hence the unification and harmony which some academics have claimed exists among large sections of American youth has never been shown to exist amongst British youth except in relatively superficial ways (e.g. most youngsters drink Coca Cola, wear denim wranglers and enjoy listening to Bob Dylan). The all embracing role of the American high school as opposed to the limited functions of the British secondary school would enter a discussion of why this difference occurs (Musgrove, 1964, p. 30).

Focusing on the problems within the British literature most of the confusion, sometimes in the guise of unwarranted clarity, must remain until more elaborate theoretical perspectives are developed and more carefully designed and substantiated research is carried out. The make-up of present statements about youth is itself symptomatic of the conventional wisdom which discusses youth only as a problem. It follows that anyone who has run a youth club, witnessed a gang fight, attended a pop concert or been around during a football riot assumes licence to produce their own treatise on 'Youth Today'. Any of us concerned with youth studies are in danger of perpetuating the 'youth as a problem' syndrome particularly in terms of discussing working class youth. Recent hit and run research whatever its aim ends up inadvertently highlighting the sensational at the expense of a balanced study which probes both the social context and wider social structure in which youth act (see for example, Patrick, 1973).

In many ways efforts towards a sociology of at least working class youth have fallen away rather than built up over recent years. Whatever the faults and limitations of the now dated semi-criminological studies of researchers like Sprott, Mays and Morris, plus the work of Hoggart, their background analysis and general documentation was significantly more substantial than recent attempts. Various typologies of 'youth' largely based on that research era are still referred to (Mays, 1965; Milson, 1972) and they are not without the merit of identifying the obvious diversity of motivation and behaviour among British youth. What such attempts have failed to do in particular and because they lack an adequate structural framework is identify the variables which produce diversity in youthful attitudes and behaviour.

To date very few theoretical frameworks which identify the dialogue between micro and macro structural variables that affect different social groups in general and their young in particular have been developed. Without such analyses the prospects of demolishing the present mystifying stereotypical explanations of youthful activities and substituting any alternative structural frameworks are poor. As yet there are only scattered reference points identifying the monumental problems involved in constructing a substantive sociology of youth. Indeed it may well be that such a compartmentalization will prove invalid, a theme to which I shall return in conclusion when the implications of the case study reported here are considered.

'Brief adolescence' is used here as a purely operational definition. The definition utilized is an implicit working principle which was found operating within a particular social context during a longitudinal participant observation, case study. This report is not directly concerned with 'official' definitions of adolescence such as those found in the psychologist's textbook but with adolescence as it is conceived by residents of Roundhouse, my name for a neighbourhood of tenements situated in down-town Liverpool. In particular a life history of a group of thirty youths - the Boys - who have grown up in this area will be discussed in relation to the significance of their brief and accelerated 'adolescence'. 'Brief adolescence' in this social context takes in the period between school leaving at the age of fifteen (Year One), commencing in April, through to the end of Year Four when in general all the major local definitions of 'manhood' are ascribed or achieved.

In many ways ethnographic work does not lend itself to precise summary and consequently this paper is limited in its utility. It involves asking theoretical questions retrospectively of a study not specifically designed to test hypotheses about adolescence and youth culture. However, accepting this limitation plus the methodological problems of the fuller study (see Parker, 1974b, pp. 214-24) it can be stated from the outset that this particular research project provided almost no support for any discussion which can usefully parade under the youth culture banner. Instead this project forced an engagement with a cluster of perspectives revolving around cultural diversity on class lines and social structural analyses generally. Subsequently this paper addresses itself to competing explanations of working class youth which emphasize on the one hand the significance of subcultural traditions and pathological neighbourhoods as opposed to structural analyses which emphasize the accommodative and rational nature of decision making by actors faced with the constraints of a particular social context.

SUBCULTURAL NEIGHBOURHOODS?

Using 'objective' quantifiers of living standards, to grow up in Roundhouse is to grow up 'deprived'. Roundhouse, that 'slum', that 'ghetto of the less able' with its high indices of core social problems - delinquency, personal sickness, truancy, unemployment, debt, etc., etc., is seen officially as handicapped by social malaise (Amos, 1970). That the Boys had almost all truanted regularly during secondary school and left at the earliest possible moment is not remarkable. That they left without qualifications, without trained skills, without apprenticeships to follow and in the main without particular jobs to go to is not unusual. For aren't these the inevitable dead-end lads? Aren't they the third group in Carter's typology of 'young workers' in terms of their social backgrounds? Don't the Boys come from

> The rough deprived underprivileged type of home and family background where there is little regard for the 'official' norms and values of society. Parents live for the present, spending money quickly as soon as they get it: repudiate the values of the school and have as little to do with them as possible: do not encourage their children to join 'official' youth organizations, which in their view are full of snobs. Where they ask does 'honesty' come in - is not 'dishonesty' rife everywhere? Life is a matter of luck - but you don't get much luck if you are not ready to take a chance when it comes along. From these homes come many 'deprived' youngsters who are ill-equipped but ready-made for 'dead-end' jobs and anti-social in their behaviour (Cater, 1966, p. 40).

Depicting the unskilled early school leaver in such a way does at least accept a basic fact absent in much 'youth culture' literature - that adolescents, adults and children from various social groups to a large extent share the same socio-economic position and general cultural milieu. When considering the families of Roundhouse, and in particular the Boys' delinquent careers, this fundamental starting point takes us back to the well grounded theories of crime and delinquency conceived initially in the 1920s and elaborated in Britain during the 1950s. Discussions about the twilight areas of inner cities have bridged two decades and the main arguments put forward by cultural diversity theorists are now part of the layman's explanatory currency also. Carter's classification basically derives from the 'culture of poverty' school which emphasizes the sub-cultural and insular aspects of many pathological areas.

> Once it comes into existence it tends to perpetuate itself from generation to generation because of its effect on children. By the time slum children are six or seven, they have usually absorbed the basic values and attitudes of their subculture and not psychologically geared to take full advantage of changing conditions or increased opportunities which may occur in their lifetime (Lewis, 1967, p. xiv).

Such a statement is a useful starting point for it highlights the crux of a whole arsenal of conflicting perspectives revolving around issues about the poor and whether they are 'deserving' or 'disreputable'; whether their poverty is a matter of pathology or structural circumstance. Aspects of the Boys' behaviour during their adolescence do much to vindicate Carter's tag. The group regularly breached social standards receiving responses rating from rebuke through to incarceration. Their 'anti-social' behaviour raged from bad language, 'scruffiness', 'laziness' and indifference to work through to breaking drinking laws, traffic laws, drug laws and property laws.

This behaviour does have strong correlations with their 'brief adolescence' and it is also undoubtedly related to their growing up in a down-town neighbourhood where the transmission processes Oscar Lewis identifies do operate. Indeed daily scenarios witnessed around Roundhouse would suggest that youngsters do indeed take over traditional practices behind which it is assumed lie traditional values. Take the two 10 year-olds who had been in a Roundhouse local pub for some crisps. Out of the noisy pub they came, one turfing out the other by his neck sending him sprawling across the pavement. In went the boot to the crutch, the ribs, the face. But somehow the boy on his back got up and butted his opponent, kneeing him in the groin as he fell heavily. In went the boot again ... for a second the attacker stopped to look around ... would someone intervene? But alas the traffic-lights outside the pub had changed and the cars of spectators were moving off. So the two kids called it a day and sat on the pavement to eat their crisps.

Observations throughout the fieldwork period reinforce the view that traditional responses are passed on, that, as the Boys themselves remark, 'the younger kids copy the older ones' and 'they just want to be hard like the older blokes.' Yet what was the meaning of the little scenario described above? Was it simply unsupervised youngsters out late at night hanging around pubs and acting out the goings-on they'd seen or heard about which in a few years they would be indulging in for real? Or was it two talented kids putting on a sophisticated street show aimed at the captive audience stopped at the traffic lights?

Throughout the fieldwork period observation and participation in the social context of Roundhouse these problems of interpretation have been continual. What the researcher was left with in this study was two types of interpretation both with obvious relevance. On the one hand the 'subcultural' aspects of Roundhouse appear frequently, with traditional values daily r inforced and transmitted to the young - data implying the need for some kind of neighbourhood pathology model. On the other mounting evidence that in particular the Boys' behaviour throughout their adolescence was a rational response to the constraints they faced as decisions and factors in the wider society impinged on their lives. Here the need for a structural model becomes obvious. The problem this study has not solved centres around the exact relationship between the two types of explanation, for many of the answers are tied up in long lost historical processes, others are simply beyond the scope of the micro study.

This paper then merely outlines the problematic nature of a micro sociology of one group of working class adolescents. It tries to show how structural factors and social processes in the society impinge into a particular social context and affect the lives of, in this case, the Boys from Roundhouse. Such factors operate on a backcloth of history, tradition and relative insularity. The relationship between traditions and change, transmission and transformation are only partially uncovered. Two examples of this awkward dialogue can be looked at. First, a trip back through the Boys' school days shows that while some of them never achieved well either at primary or secondary school a dozen of the group in fact passed their 11 plus and entered local grammar schools. Yet within two years all but a couple were back in St Patrick's, the local secondary modern, and in retrospect are now abundantly clear of their reasons.

> 'It was when we got back to St Pat's that we realized how bad the teachers were. Like in St Pat's there were a few bastards, but most of them were OK, you could talk to them and joke with them. But at grammar school they seemed just like zombies, they'd come in, do the lesson and go out, you couldn't say a word out of place' (Fatch, taped).

Such a view, which was typical of the former scholarship boys in the network, matches closely Musgrove's (1964, p. 4) conclusion that the typical English grammar school 'firmly insists that they "keep their place" in return for the services it renders. An institution which confers or at least promises high status, it will tolerate no touch of arrogance - or even proper cheerful self-expression - in its pupils.'

It would obviously be quite inadequate to see the school system as inflexible and dogmatic without considering the other side of the issue which returns us to Roundhouse, parental attitudes and neighbourhood ethos. Similarly, if we look at the Boys' first post-school year at work (Year One) problems of interpretation again arise. When the Boys left school (April) the local job market was relatively buoyant and jobs were readily available. However, rather than settle down into a steady job the Boys tended to chop and change. Sometimes they got the sack, sometimes they got laid off, sometimes they simply chucked it in - Carter's typology vindicated again? Or was it the fact that the jobs were butt-end involving work as a fish porter, mopping up in the abattoire, putting dough into tins, pushing around oil drums? And were the wages before stoppages, of between £8 and £16 a week, any real incentive? And what of the phoney apprenticeships which never materialize, the last-in-first-out syndrome? Having spent Year One sampling the jobs, working conditions and pay that were within their reach the Boys concluded within the year that 'work was bad news', that the attitudes and approaches held by older brothers and other adults were correct. Had they come to a set of rational decisions about the value of work, and concluded that unless work was a 'cushy number' which 'makes your wallet fat' then it was a doubtful way of spending one's time? The employer or foreman sees it differently, however. They point to the poor attendance record, the cheek they get, the lack of effort, the 'knocking off'. They complain as the school teacher did that the down-town youngster is impossible, he doesn't give a damn.

Again there is a dialogue between the attitudes to outsiders and work the Boys in part absorb from their immediate social milieu and the limitations and constraints they come up against and rationally reject when they enter the butt-end job market with its poor pay, poor conditions and vulnerability to lay offs.

There is too little space here to consider these issues fully. This paper will limit itself to discussing the Boys' delinquent careers in relation to the theoretical problems it has identified - the effects of transmission of pathological and 'subcultural' values as opposed to the view that delinquency as one 'adolescent' activity is a rational response to constraints and limited opportunities.

A CONTEXT FOR DELINQUENCY

It has not been possible to sum up the cluster of attitudes about delinquency operating amongst Roundhouse residents in a way which does justice to the obvious diversity of opinion and more especially apparent contradictions between public opinions, private beliefs and action. Local adolescents' views of adult opinion are more accessible, however. Nearly all the Boys agreed that any vandalism of neighbourhood property and theft from within the neighbourhood tenements was totally condemned. Petty theft from outsiders on the other hand received less condemnation and indeed implicit condonation from many elders of the neighbourhood. Many people 'knew the score' but 'said nothing'. Parents unless there was conclusive evidence to the contrary always argued that it was not their kids but everybody else's that were 'up to no good' and got 'the place a bad name'.

The extensive and highly functional 'receiving' of stolen goods amongst the majority of Roundhouse residents also suggested a condonation of theft from outsiders (crime without victims) in the eyes of local adolescents. Even the very young kids could go 'round the Block' offering 'knock off' for sale on the doorsteps and, as long as they avoided their relations and their own landing, be sure of either a sale or a polite refusal. 'Grassing' on the activities of neighbours of whatever age is almost completely unknown. The motto of the uninvolved law abider is 'say nothing'. Roundhouse, then, whilst its residents fall across a whole spectrum of attitudes to law breaking, regard local solidarity at all age levels as more virtuous, or at least expedient, than 'legality' and the acting out of the 'correct morality' of the 'respectable' citizen in an ideal world. Residents tend to view Roundhouse as far from ideal and thus see morality and the law as in need of manipulation. Whilst Gerald Suttle's description of a Chicago slum may be valid for a wide variety of settings it is particularly fitting for Roundhouse: 'a social compact in which respectable residents and those not so respectable are both tolerant and protective of one another.'

For the Boys this local condonation of petty theft from outsiders found expression in phrases like 'once you're in the Block you're laughin', no busies'll get you then' and 'no-one round our way is a stooley, not unless they want to move.' A minimal compact operates then not because adults and youngsters all agree amongst or with each other about the ethics of theft but because in general terms they share the same economic and social position in society and receive the same treatment from that society especially in dealings with official control agencies.

Many of the reasons for the Boys becoming 'persistent offenders' reach back much further than their adolescence and cannot be fully discussed here. Certainly growing up in a 'delinquescent' neighbourhood has its impact through how one traces this with any degree of certainty is also problematic. There is, however, a substantial literature on this theme and here the task in hand is to mediate this subcultural perspective by considering the Boys' delinquency in terms of a micro-structural analysis.

Throughout the fieldwork period, the Boys' brief adolescence, there was very little parental influence (see also Willmott, 1966). The reasons for this cannot be fully entered upon here but suffice to say that structural factors again come into play, e.g. small overcrowded flats being up in the air, mothers having to work, etc. Once allowed in the Block to play youngsters may well be influenced by the changing but ever present street corner milieu which can act as a transmitter of delinquent solutions: views of manhood, etc. The interplay of 'opportunity structures' during the Boys' adolescence is of vital significance to understanding their involvement in theft behaviour.

Being close to the city centre with its shops, warehouses and parked cars, opportunities for delinquency of various forms, especially in the absence of alternative legitimate facilities, are monumental. Roundhouse is surrounded by parked cars nearly 24 hours a day. Many of the cars contain property both loose and 'fixed' to the dashboard. Car radios are abundant and valuable on the 'knock off' market. There are fencing activities throughout the city. Roundhouse has its local small time 'villains' who deal profitably in stolen property and readily in stolen car radios. The street corner knows all about such 'middlemen', where they are to be found, what they will buy and how much they are likely to buy for. For those youngsters 'new' to the scene a further link service is provided by older adolescents who will take a cut for acting as further middlemen. The presence of such a distribution service acted as an important stimulus in the Boys' delinquent careers since its perpetual presence could always be relied upon and turned to at critical times.

The discussion above is basically a picture of 'illegitimate opportunity structures' which are relatively slow changing. Indicating the presence of illegal pathways as 'temptation' does not, of course, explain delinquent action since many other factors taboo delinquency and emphasize conformity. Something must be said, therefore, about more basic motivation - about why the Boys chose, for a while at least, to adopt a delinquent rather than a conformist style.

Personal choice about types of behaviour to employ is not simply a matter of expediency, of showing that the illegitimate is an easier route than the legitimate to desired goals. Expediency is an important but not all embracing explanation for, in this case, theft behaviour. In a society pre-occupied with 'socializing', with morality, symbols of good and evil, matters of conscience, etc., nearly everybody restricts their behaviour because of edicts from others. Since I am arguing that the Boys are the same rather than fundamentally different from other people their delinquent behaviour must be explained within a framework which also encompasses the behaviour of those who do not deviate from society's rules despite such deviation being as 'tempting'. Why do not all Roundhouse youngsters become delinquent?

Sociological explanations of delinquent motivation have varied considerably. Merton's explanation of crime and delinquency, Cloward and Ohlin's sophistication of his general thesis and early Albert Cohen explanations of delinquent motivation all rest, to varying degrees on the assumption of the internalization by all sections of the population, including the working class on the goals of the dominant ideology. Strain is caused by a shortage in the supply of legitimate means of achieving these goals and hence the need to engage in available deviant solutions.

The cultural diversity perspective, which includes the work of Walter Miller and the British sub-cultural era of Mays, Morris, Sprott and to some extent Downes on the other hand, whilst still emphasizing the significance of transmission through socialization and internalization divides the population up. A distinctive cultural milieu is transmitted specifically to sections of the working or lower class and is to varying degrees either in conflict with or dissociated from the dominant meaning system of a middle class powered society. There are at times connotations of pathology associated with this perspective as with Carter's classification quoted earlier.

A third or recently rejuvenated perspective belongs to the control theorists. This school of thought revises the 'why delinquent?' question asking instead 'why not delinquent?' and subsequently comes up with different types of answers which move towards a conflict model of society and a morality of expediency rather than commitment. Travis Hirschi (1970, p. 26) for instance states that

> Delinquency is not caused by beliefs that require delinquency but rather is made possible by the absence of (effective) beliefs that forbid delinquency.

This stance at its logical conclusion leads us back to the view that behaviour is simply due to the absence of control and presumably the availability of illegitimate opportunities.

A critique of the various theoretical perspectives cannot be attempted here. Having indulged in the exercise elsewhere, however, I would suggest that delinquent motivation should be presented as an open ended framework since in reality motivation for deviant action is not only diverse amongst populations but changeable in the same person. It is quite possible that Mays' 'predisposed' delinquent, Matza's 'drifting' delinquent and Hirschi's 'anomic' delinquent and Patrick's 'psychopathic' delinquent all exist. A framework should be available to encompass them since their varied motives may well become quite feasible in the context of their situation. In short it is wise to assume that

> delinquent motivations run the whole gamut from total acceptance of social morality through to those cases where deviants are in total opposition to conventional morality and are in large part motivated by their desire to alter or destroy it (Taylor, Walton and Young, 1973, p. 185).

Within such an open ended and flexible framework the motivation to be delinquent for an individual, a social network or a gang can be allowed an authenticity which does justice to the context of delinquency. It is implicit in what follows that such a framework is a realistic starting point for looking at the Boys' delinquent careers first by assessing their general commitment to a wider social morality, then tracing briefly the history of their delinquency of a two year period commenting on how that commitment affected and was affected by experience and rethinks in response to new contingencies.

Both by talking with the Boys in small groups and by being present at numerous discussions they have had during the course of their normal conversation a picture was built up of their general views about law breaking, especially theft behaviour from outsiders. Their views can be related to the street corner milieu, the neighbourhood's general philosophy and the edicts of the wider society and appear to be fluid and, rather than merely insular, based on the wider value system. One way of conceptualizing this dialogue is offered by Frank Parkin (1972, pp. 79-103). He suggests that a local working class 'community' because of the position it holds in society, whilst it does not reject the dominant ideology or 'meaning system' has to accommodate the demands and rules of such an ideology. Roundhouse adults' view of theft from outsiders can be seen as part of the neighbourhood's particular subordinate or accommodative value system. Having grown up in Roundhouse, the Boys obviously take much of their world view from this accommodated meaning system, that is they 'accept' large parts of the dominant value system but make reservations and exceptions in relation to their situation as part of an unskilled and semi-skilled manual worker population receiving, for instance, less than its share of the 'good life'.

The street corner milieu represents the extreme of the neighbourhood's accommodation and 'social compact'. The street corner man goes one clandestine step further rather than walking out of the local value system. Obviously at some point the street corner milieu becomes 'contrary' or in conflict with the neighbourhood since there is a point at which an extension takes on an identity of its own and becomes a subculture of delinquency

(Matza 1964). The 'street corner milieu' is of course a fluid concept resting on the beliefs and actions of the men who give it substance. The Boys obviously formed their views of what is and isn't important and their hierarchy of the components of manhood from many sources. The traditions of the neighbourhood and the 'talk' of their elders around the area provided the main source of information about law breaking, however. Since there is widespread agreement about what is and isn't acceptable, what is or isn't of great social concern in this sphere of influence it is perhaps reasonable to talk of 'the Boys' view' as a homogeneous collectivity in this paper, accepting that in reality they deviate from such a 'collective conscience' to some degree.

The Boys' commitment to the 'correct' morality and a 'christian' type approach to living is spurious. This commitment tends to be neighbourhood bound and extends beyond only in relation to significant others and people or situations which are similar enough to their 'own kind's' predicament to allow an empathy and thus restriction on 'amoral' behaviour. The Boys have certain stereotyped figures drawn from their experience which illustrate and delineate acceptable behaviour. Clepto, a local peer, was condemned and ostracized for instance, and held up as an example of where boundaries must be drawn.

> 'He'd stab his own grandmother in the back for two bob' (Joey).
> 'Stealing from someone in the Block that's different. I couldn t do that. I don't know why, I just couldn't. I could never steal from a mate like that Clepto did. He's the world's number one cunt' (Tommy).

The Boys' social commitment corresponds to that portrayed by the dominant meaning system only where the 'victims' can take on some personal significance. Their restrictions of their 'take what you need' attitudes and consequent egocentric and deviant behaviour do not correspond to the normative expectations of the wider society over theft matters, therefore. There is no simple formula to why the Boys accept some and reject other normative expectations, reasons are complex and historical. The Boys for instance, tend to reject violence for its own sake and 'mugging' as pieces of action. They often show sympathy for the old and down-and-out, the pregnant woman and people in distress in a much more direct and personal way than one would get from other sectors of the population.

Obviously the Boys' views about theft from outsiders vary and cut across the over simplified 'collective conscience' presented here. Confusions and conflicts are conspicuous in their opinions but even apparently contradictory viewpoints, at their essence, show the significance of the relationship between the ideal and the necessary.

> 'Screwing cars is wrong. Someone could have worked hard to get it like. Say someone's worked his way up and he's got a new, shining Rover, it's bad news having it done in' (Streak).
> 'I wouldn't like to rob from someone really poor but these posh twats, I take a real delight in robbing from. Sometimes you go by the Church and you see all these fucking big twats with big cars, big flash cameras and all the gear and you think I'll go and pipe that car and it's got a cassette so you screw it' (Bone).

'Screwing cars is wrong if they can't afford it. But a big percent of the cars we do the people have a good few bob. If they've got the money to pay for Rovers and that they're alright. But you can't say we only rob from the rich can you, we'd screw any car if we thought we could get away with it' (Joey).

'It's not wrong, well I'm against it like, but they must be soft to leave the cars so things can be stole. And the lads have to go out of a weekend and need clothes and that. I'm not saying that's the best way of going about it but they can't get a job, how else do they get poke?'

From the discussion so far we can see the considerable problems of interpretation involved in deciding why the Boys are 'anti-social'. Nevertheless, it must be already clear that perspectives which are based only upon precipitating behaviour - under-achievement at school, indifference to work, rejection of certain property rules, are liable to mislead. This point can be made more effectively by a detailed analysis of the Boys' delinquency. For here we see that only when delinquent action is viewed within the micro-structural context in which it takes place can justice be done to explaining the Boys' behaviour.

THE BOYS AS THE CATSEYE KINGS

So if we move into Year Two and return to the Boys' 'becoming' we are now in a better position to understand their moral position in relation to the car radio thieving that followed to the extent that they become the Catseye Kings (a title the Boys gave themselves derived from 'catseyes' a local term for 'fixed' car radios with two big shiny buttons). The group's real interest in car radios began in the autumn (mid Year Two). Nearly all the network were on the dole at this time having packed in any jobs they'd had to enjoy the summer holidays only to find that by autumn the job market had closed up considerably, especially with a new batch of school leavers chasing those jobs which were available.

Delinquent escapades during Year One had, as previously, been occasional and opportunistic, involving breaking into cars for saleable articles, breaking into a sweet shop, the same record shop three times and an 'empty' house. A few of the network were convicted of shoplifting during the year but as a group and in general their delinquent activities had been of little significance.

Year One had seen several symbols of manhood chalked up. Simply leaving school had been significant. It meant you were no longer a 'Kid' who was subject to routine authority when in school and mockery when you were truanting around the block. Leaving school signified a new freedom, for the first time you could 'spew it' if it got bad. Schools you couldn't leave, employment you could. Sequentially being old enough to work triggered off other processes revolving around the wage packet and its purchasing power. New clothes especially expensive leather jackets appeared. Further, unless one was particularly young looking the dominant view - old enough to work, old enough to drink - allowed entry into local pubs. Being old enough to go 'on the ale' without any embarrassing trouble was a major landmark, the passing of which was greatly savoured. Access to all down-town pubs was acquired over this year for majority of the network so that by the end of Year Two going on the ale and going for a night down-town became the leisure pursuit par excellence and a crucial factor in understanding the group's extensive theft behaviour.

The dynamics of the network's increasing involvement in the catseye business cannot be fully elaborated here (but see Parker, 1974b). Very basically it saw about twenty of the network becoming extensively involved in breaking into cars and yanking out car radios to the extent that many of the Boys were making around £35 a week, selling the goods on the local black market. What this paper is concerned with is the style which such proceeds allowed the group to adopt and their fate when heavy policing was introduced into the Roundhouse area, for both aspects relate to the significance of adolescence.

Initially things went well for the group and they continued their theft activities with only the occasional apprehensions. Throughout the spring (end of Year Two) they indulged in the pleasures of having a 'roll of notes' in their pocket. They got up late, spent a few hours in the pub drinking, smoking and playing cards. They'd have a good meal, go home for tea, meet on the corner and go back to the pub. After closing time they'd go on the cars again. Even a year later the hedonism of these days was recalled vividly.

> 'They were the best days of my life. They were fuckin great. We were loaded the whole time. I'd spend 30 quid just like that. I'd buy a pair of shoes for 6 quid just like that peel them (pound notes) off. If you were skint in those days you'd just go on the cars for a couple of hours' (Fosser).

THE GOOD TIMES

This affluent, street-corner boy style which the group adopted might appear peculiarly adolescent in itself. This, however, is not the case. The Boys' preoccupation with cash and its ability to purchase the good times of smoking, drinking, having plenty of money, plenty of time, the chance to be smart, generous and cool is a priority not just widely held by down-town adolescents and men but, as Matza (1961) points out, by most males even if at a 'subterranean' level. What the catseye business allowed the Boys was an access card to the good times which as men they will continue to enthuse over almost as their fathers did. What the group was eventually to learn was that the good times must be earned legitimately and that if this is not possible there have to be less good times. At this time the group's hedonism was a striving towards manhood, towards being the same as rather than different from local men.

Going down-town in search of the good times most nights a week led the Boys into a leisure style which in official terms added to their damnation. For once in the crowded down-town pubs and wine lodges trouble, particularly in the form of fighting, became a possibility. Very rarely did the Boys look for trouble and indeed in relation to the number of times they frequented the pubs trouble was a rare occurrence. The problem with down-town drinking is that it only needs 'one bloke with a nark on' and all hell is let loose. Take a Sunday night down-town during Year Three.

Six of us were sitting in a bar when a rather drunk bloke on the other side of the room started 'eyeing' Colly. Colly looked back and asked the bloke what he was looking at. The reply was a beer glass which smashed on the seat right next to Colly. It was with some disbelief that I watched this, for there were six of us including Fosser and Arno whose very appearance convinces me that I'm lucky to be on their side, sitting down quietly, whilst the glass thrower had only one mate with him. Only Colly got up at first, obviously not sure whether the bloke was looking for trouble or simply 'out of his head' and thus to be excused. A second glass broke all over his head, which convinced everybody, even me, that retaliatory action was needed. What ensued was later aptly described by Murky as 'a real cowboy fight'. The two aggressors had chairs cracked over their heads, and if Arno had actually managed to get it high enough a table would have landed on them also. Colly who'd been sitting down examining his wounds whilst the fight was in progress, picked up a Guinness bottle and broke it over the glass-thrower's head: this was a signal for retreat, and everybody left quickly amidst an uproar as the bar staff and others became increasingly hysterical.

Although uncommon such fights are always possible in the down-town situation. Throughout the fieldwork period the lesson was repeated many times, trouble is not something you have to look for but something you find yourself in.

The Boys' involvement in drug use constitutes a further facet of their deviant behaviour. Again this aspect of their style cannot be fully elaborated here. Basically the Boys were the first generation of Roundhouse adolescents to use soft drugs regularly: in many ways they took on marijuana use and institutionalized it as a permanent aspect of the good times. Pot smoking, although occasional pill taking and acid trips have occurred, is not seen in Roundhouse as a mind stretching 'spacing out' unifying experience (see Auld, 1973), but as a simple pleasure device to be used with or instead of alcohol. During nights out down-town marijuana joints were used to add to the general euphoria aimed at getting one 'pissed out of me head and stoned out of me mind'.

It is significant that in Year Four a few of the Boys have become informal sources of supply for older men who have become attracted to marijuana because of the Boys' use. This further reinforces the validity of the universality rather than age specificity of the Boys' leisure style.

THE CONTEST WITH AUTHORITY

Having outlined some aspects of the good times we must now return to the conflict of the latter part of the catseye business for the Boys were not allowed to continue their theft behaviour unchecked.

A retrospective look at the number of reported offences involving theft from unattended vehicles from the Roundhouse area during Years Two and Three shows that some 2,500 incidents were recorded. This is approximately 80 per cent more than the next highest one square mile grid in the Liverpool police area. Hardly, surprising, therefore, that the police entered the fray in order to 'clear up' the crime rate.

The Boys, who had always been aware of the risks they were taking, now found that the odds were changing and that the charge of excitement involved in working on a car park was reaching a dangerously high voltage. Their chances of apprehension were not only increasing due to the greater time exposure of simply being 'on the cars' more often but also due to likely areas being heavily policed. Conversation pieces continued to change in emphasis. The Boys pondered over whether they were being 'greedy': as they sounded each other during a lunchtime drink.

Colly 'Ay, Ay, here comes greedy arse. You can get the bevvies in today lad, four catseyes last night.'

Fatch 'Three man, three. All on me own as well no trouble.'

Colly 'You're just greedy lad, you want to save a few for everyone else.'

Emo 'I couldn't screw a car on my own I'd fuckin shit meself.'

Fatch 'Easy lad, easy ... anyway who's talking, Colly, you've whizzed more than me this week.'

Colly 'Who me? I don't screw cars, I'm a good boy.'

Colly did 'screw' cars, however, and he was up in court two weeks later having walked around a corner into the arms of a police sergeant who, remarking 'you're looking fat sonny', removed a car radio from Colly's coat.

The early summer (Year Three) saw a whole series of warnings that going on the cars was not as easy as it used to be. The risks were rapidly increasing as catseye talk revealed during numerous poolings of experiences.

The use of a plain clothes Task Force team in the area created new contingencies. Routine stops and 'slaggins' from the police, though not new, became more numerous. A widening of definitions of delinquent behaviour occurred with 'suspicious personal loitering' and 'equipped for theft' becoming regular charges pinned on any adolescents suspected of car radio thieving. Since most Roundhouse adolescents walked across car parks and waste ground near their area a lot of 'mistakes' were made and resentment and fear built up as being under 'methodical suspicion' left its mark in the form of keenly felt hatred of the policeman. 'Lucky escapes' multiplied and became a daily talking point. Jimbo and Colly appeared on the corner where several of us were standing one afternoon. They were both shaken and out of breath.

> 'Me and Jimbo have just had a fuckin lucky escape. We were just going to do this Rover and a big red Cortina pulled up. Two plain clothes dived out. This cunt with a sheepskin on says - against the wall you two. Colly had a punch (for opening windows) down the back of his kecks but this feller must have thought it was his backbone or something coz he missed it. He couldn't do us for nothing so he says "If I

see you around here again I'll run you off your fuckin feet, now beat it." We walked away dead lucky.'

'Lucky escapes' were not the only signs of authority's assertion of ban. Task Force as its understanding of the situation increased resorted to more devious methods of detection although the 'hard front' intimidation of likely looking adolescents continued. The number of false arrests and 'negotiation of reality' (Young, 1971) to secure otherwise ambiguous situations as convictions increased rapidly. I personally witnessed two false arrests one of which led to a conviction.

Crime was being committed, however, and large numbers of successful convictions accumulated as most of the Catseye Kings got shot down in action. Task Force by using plain clothes policemen and women and unmarked cars were able to patrol the area more effectively. Look outs situated on high buildings with binoculars and presumably (though I cannot verify this) radio contact aided arrests also.

Joey, Colly, Arno, Jimbo, Emo, Fatch and Tommy were all convicted at least twice for car offences or 'loitering' within six months (early Year Three). Tank was sent to approved school, Tuck was in borstal. Fosser spent ten traumatic days in a remand centre. Many had been fined, been on probation and done 'scrubs' at attendance centres. Fines were outstanding and 'final warnings' repeated. Catseye talk centred around police behaviour, police misbehaviour and court. Things were no longer so good and going on the cars was considered more critically. Motives, for instance, were discussed in some detail and the necessity of radio thieving questioned to the extent that many of the network considered opting out.

THE END OF ADOLESCENCE

A related but separately identifiable factor in the Boys' retreat from the catseye business involved the whole process of moving into manhood. Throughout the four years since their school leaving a whole series of landmarks had been passed and symbols acquired which gave credence to the arrival of their manhood. By the age of 19 and 20 local definitions of adulthood are satisfied and the end of adolescence has arrived. During their brief adolescence the Boys have moved on from being old enough to leave school and 'sign on' or work through to receiving adult rates of pay or unemployment benefit. They have moved on from being accepted drinkers in local pubs, through to all city pubs, local clubs and then down-town clubs. Similarly they now play football for open age teams not the Under 17s or 18s, etc.

Particularly during Year Four the Boys as a group have splintered. Many have left their parents' homes and moved towards setting up a domestic unit of their own. Some have obtained flats out of the area and others have married and achieved fatherhood and have taken up or await a flat in the block. So what was a battle for loyalties between the Boys and the steady girlfriends for their feller's time has now been largely settled. Joey is married and a father, so are Streak, Pablo, Jimbo and Des with Fatch and Mocky both recently involved in pregnant marriages. Almost without exception these men were courting their girlfriends for long periods before the pregnancy and marriage and these new responsibilities have emerged steadily rather than overnight. Now there are the rent, the HP payments, the housekeeping money, the baby, the wife - all new responsibilities, new contingencies, new talking points.

For some of the group the girlfriends or wives acted as a further pressure against the catseye business. With many of their blokes on the threshold of the institution the female partners resorted to strong tactics to discourage their man from going on the cars once too often.

> 'Me old man says he can get him a job in a few weeks. I've told him to take it or find someone else. He thinks I'm only messin' but we'll see' (Fatch's girlfriend, Anita).

Joey's dilemma summed it up

> 'You can't go on robbing when you've got a tart and babe to keep, like, it's not right.'

Even for those of the network not directly involved in these new responsibilities of marriage and fatherhood the indirect pressures of having on the one hand mates who weren't 'robbing no more' or were 'not going near a catseye' and on the other less social solidarity with regards delinquency generally from other mates, were considerable. Continuing doing the cars under all these circumstances was queried as a potentially alienating activity in a similar way to that which Monod (1967) described it for Paris street gangs where alienation revolved around 'the issue of a social process depriving an individual or a group of the meaning of his action, thus condemning his action to self destruction'. Those like Tuck, Arno and Colly who carried on regardless, whatever their own views were seen by the rest as 'mad fuckers' or 'divvies' for leaving themselves open to such a process.

Looking back, 'brief adolescence' is now increasingly falling into place for the Boys. It was that period when they had only themselves to look after, when they could go wild, break out and lay themselves on the line with nothing to lose by doing so.

> 'We were fuckin mad then boy, the things we'd do for a few bob' (Fosser).

But now things have changed and the constraints have moved in closer. Many are now on their 'last chance' and can afford no further brush with the law. Many can no longer 'spew it' when the job gets them down. They now have others to consider not just in the wife and the baby but the wider family who expect men to give support in other ways such as lending a few bob, looking after granny and child minding for other parts of the family.

The Boys have never lacked realism, even from their early secondary school days they knew the odds against things changing to the extent that they have always celebrated what they have and ignored rather than fantasized about what they won't have. Now as men they have the scars to prove that they have discovered what they always suspected - that work, when you can get it, is bad news and that if you try to change things in an illegitimate way the chances are you'll end up a loser.

So the Boys are no longer that special entity, most have left the street as if to make way for the next generation. They will still meet to enjoy the good times in much the same way, but much less often, for now one must save for the big nights out, in practice reserved for weekends. The good times are still vital for they are dialectically related to the not-so-good and bad times (see Blumensteil, 1973). Not that adulthood has simply closed various doors, it has to some extent opened others. It allows privacy for instance - a place of one's own hidden from the policeman's gaze. Here one can smoke in peace, entertain one's mates and escape from those occasional bad days when even hanging around on the corner was torturous. Also by simply being and looking older the new Roundhouse men largely pass out of the policeman's stereotype of who is up to no good. There are less routine stops although locally the explanation for this change relates to the policeman's fear of tangling with men who are tougher than he.

CAPITULATION

Whilst the various pressures and commitments culminating in the end of adolescence have undoubtedly affected the Boys' theft behaviour the prime and immediate reason for their capitulation was the ban imposed by authority. Although in the short run some continued to go on the cars despite everything the majority opted out. Certainly at first verbal comments like, 'I'm not robbing no more' were only statements of intent forgotten after a few pints and late at night, but they were the first stage of a real withdrawal in the face of unfavourable odds.

It has been argued throughout that the Boys at all times choose their solutions rationally and based on a life style which achieves an optimum balance from the possibilities available. Their stance in terms of social morality which allowed such direct problem solving has been indicated already. It was expedient to utilize delinquent tactics during Years Two and Three not least because the Boys had nothing to lose in the way of job, reputation, status, etc., by laying it on the line. Indeed whilst their freedom was not threatened the network in the main regarded the prosecution process as an occupational hazard (although personal 'coolness' and parental reaction to court proceedings affected continuation considerably).

As the Boys came into contact with authority, the various officials of the prosecution process, their 'memory file' started to collect a whole series of injustices. A large catalogue of police mistakes, police brutality, negotiations of reality, solicitor inefficiency, probation officer indifference, magistrate bias, built up. The realization and continuous reinforcement of the fact that these social control agencies that claimed the right and moral superiority to judge and punish the Boys were also devious and corrupt was an important talking point. Such an awareness only increased the Boys' view that life was a contest of wits, deviousness and power and may have acted as a 'neutralizer' of what little guilt some of them may have felt.

This view of authority summarized by the phrase 'the law's on the law's fuckin side' should not indicate that the down-town adolescent sees society totally in conspiratorial or conflict terms, however. It is authority rather than the society that employs social control agencies which alienates the Boys and receives their resentment. They do not have a comprehension of social structure which leads them to a revolutionary praxis or a bitter alienation towards the society in which they live. There is some resentment certainly towards some employers, some 'toffee nose' rich and the middle class 'poser' but in the main the Boys dissociate (Downes, 1966, pp. 257-88) from the wider, middle class society and celebrate staying close to the social space in which they are welcome.

In the same way the Boys did not start attacking policemen for their unfair treatment - they retreated. They retreated through fear. They were afraid not of the policemen but their awareness of his ability in the long run, to turn the odds against them. Jimbo for a time at the end of Year Three would not walk across car parks in case he got picked up simply because 'they know my face'. The Boys would not go to Court as witnesses for each other even if they felt a miscarriage of justice would ensue. They feared that,

> 'If the coppers see you down there trying to get your mates off they'll make trouble for you' (Murky).

And when your freedom is threatened you avoid trouble. You don't 'have your say' in court because it causes you trouble. You avoid certain department stores because the security staff cause you trouble. And so on. Trouble is something you tempt only if you've got a reasonable chance. The Boys' concern is that authority is part of the facticity with which they have to come to terms. For most of them this means capitulation. As Sartre (1960) puts it:

> 'I am obedient because I can do nothing else and that gives pseudo-legitimacy ... to the sovereign.'

As far as the majority of the group were concerned their continuation of the catseye business became irrational and 'asking for trouble' at the end of Year Three when so many of them were on the threshold of the institution. This re-orientation in relation to social reaction should not indicate a 'spoiled identity' in the Boys. Their celebration of the life style of their own kind and their denial of authority's moral right to act as judge protected them from such identity crises. The end of the story is one of a compliance of acceptance of the bad deal because little can be done when 'you've got no fuckin chance ... what's the point?'

TOWARDS A STRUCTURAL ANALYSIS

A micro case study basically appreciative in nature, can only measure the impact of macro structural issues in a fairly impressionistic way by documenting how they impinge on a particular social context and affect the actions of people within. This paper has tried to indicate the complexities in studying one group of adolescents as they grow up in a down-town neighbourhood. The conclusions drawn from this study relate to meanings of adolescence in that they illustrate the limited utility, if not futility, of 'youth culture' perspectives in studying some sections of British working class youth. Devising alternative perspectives is no mean task and this longitudinal study has thrown up many imponderables. A particularly problematic issue at neighbourhood level involves discovering the exact relationship between subcultural perspectives emphasizing cultural diversity, pathology and transmission and a social action approach which emphasizes the need for a structural analysis in turn connecting micro social constraints with their origins in wider social processes.

Accepting that this discussion does not deal satisfactorily with these difficulties it does nevertheless identify a large number of constraints encountered by the Boys during their adolescence and suggest how their contingency plans led to particular styles of anti social behaviour which through various stereotyping mechanisms become part of the lay ideology's definition of adolescence (Smith, 1970).

Whilst accepting that a good deal of the Boys' behaviour is influenced by the transmission of 'traditional' attitudes, such as those involving race and the place of women, and that the well documented subcultural processes operate in Roundhouse this paper suggests a vital point of mediation. It suggests that through their brief adolescence the Boys were continuously reacting to constraining influences which limited their range of choice and freedom. These factors did not emerge simply from within the neighbourhood or even the city but from processes quite outside the Boys' control and at times symptomatically their comprehension. At a physical level the lack of space, facility and suitable housing in a depressed city with 20,000 on its public housing list acts as a potent stress factor on families and the way children can be brought up. Many Roundhouse youngsters have to grow up on the street. Likewise élitist educational policies, inflamed further by religious sectarianism, which demand bourgeois standards discriminate unfairly against youngsters from down-town areas even if they make it, as many of the Boys did, to selective secondary schools. Nor can the rigidity of Catholic teaching be ignored in its impact on escalating unwanted pregnancies, early marriage and the resentment that young parents at times cannot help feeling against their kids.

Most of all, however, the employment scene restricts the down-town adolescent both by limiting his choices and preventing him from achieving what he is sure he wants - purchasing power. Year Two in particular saw the number of young people registered as unemployed at nearly 2,000 with that figure well exceeded during Year Three. The availability of jobs which pay well and which are other than butt-end has never been a prerogative of the Boys. In fact the availability of jobs of any nature ebb and flow with economic policy. Deflation hits depressed areas hardest and cyclical unemployment hits the casual labour market first. And when these jobs are in short supply they go to older or married men in preference to adolescents.

Quite apart from its high permanent unemployment and low total employment (see Cunningham and Lawton, 1970, p. 49) Merseyside catches cold as the first draught blows, invariably it is the city adolescent who suffers most. The Boys' delinquency was intimately tied up in the local job situation, for given their desire for the good times the balance between legitimate and illegitimate pathways to cash was fundamental to decisions both about getting involved in and getting out of the catseye business.

As Sheila Allen (1968, p. 327) points out, taken within such a structural framework:

> the explanation of the behaviour of unemployed youth or those who leave school early would not be presented in terms of 'a lack of achievement motivation' or inadequate socialization to 'common values' (or heritage), but would first assess the behaviour in terms of the realities of the socio-economic situation. The realism or lack of it could then be related systematically to the total social situation in which young people enter work.

Years Two and Three, given the goals the Boys were striving for, saw the catseye business as an available and in context a rational strategy, almost 'praxis', allowing an immediate termination of the bad times and the celebration of the good times. The persecution the Boys received was not something they'd failed to anticipate but merely something that they were willing to tolerate until their freedom was threatened and the scales tilted the wrong way. The catseye business was a choice made from limited alternatives and whilst some aspects of the Boys' behaviour are best seen in terms of a form of cultural diversity theory the catseye business was a product of their immediate situation and here it is more fruitful to see their behaviour as a reaction to their relative isolation and powerlessness rather than the imperatives of a culture of poverty.

Turning to the facets of an adolescent culture there is very little evidence that anything more than superficial and ritualistic elements found in pop music, fashion and aspects of the media affect the Roundhouse adolescent. This is not to suggest Roundhouse adolescents are insulated from the wider society but rather, as was argued earlier, that they will only take on those features of the 'frantically' changing world of the young which are meaningful. The introduction of illegal joyriding into Roundhouse by youngsters (see Parker, 1974a) several years the Boys' junior for instance illustrates the creation of a new delinquent solution never entertained by the Boys' contemporaries when they were entering their teens. For the youngsters involved in this new activity the meaning of the car is taken from a whole variety of sources and created into a realistic proposition which is feasible and attainable within the city context - joyriding. Similarly the Boys' institutionalization of soft drug use into the neighbourhood suggests an on-going re-creation of the good times whereby activities in the wider society are taken on and accommodated. Hence the meaning of marijuana for the Boys differs from the youthful 'hippy' ideology with which it is most often associated and in both these innovations the motivation has been tied up with aspects of manhood, the desire to be like men, to be daring, hard, and capable of really enjoying oneself.

One justification for a study such as this which reviews the dilemmas of the young unskilled manual worker in a down-town situation is not the novelty or originality of the findings but the basic unnewness of them. Rather than be swept into a new technology, an expanding and effective educational system: rather than be 'saved' by progressive youth policies or 'got together' by a unifying of adolescent culture, rejecting adult values and cutting across class boundaries, the down-town adolescent has stayed where he is. He is as isolated and dissociated from his contemporaries in other social groups as he ever was.

Certainly there has been stylistic change both in leisure patterns and delinquent solutions and relatively the city adolescent is probably better off. But in the end the crunch is that in Roundhouse as in many other city neighbourhoods parents, kids and adolescents basically share so many of the basic structural constraints and social inequalities forced on them that their world views are consistent and in harmony much more than they are in opposition. Such neighbourhood unity, however, whilst it suggests insularity and contrariness in relation to the wider society can be seen to be to a large extent an accommodation to a particular structural situation rather than a perpetuating rejection of dominant values and life styles.

Chapter 3

'PAKI-BASHING' IN A NORTH EAST LANCASHIRE COTTON TOWN: A case study and its history

Geoff Pearson

We reach a special kind of knowledge about a town by studying it scientifically. There is a different - but equally special - kind of knowledge from living in the town. But it is a whole world to us if we are brought up there.

Our knowledge of a town and its people then becomes autobiography, and easy scientific generalization must be hedged about with reservations (and also illuminations) based on reminiscence, hear-say and gossip. Dilthey was a social scientist who recognized the particularly rich value of autobiographical data for social scientific enquiry. Yet now a position such as his sits uneasily against the technical preoccupation with objectivity and neutrality, and we live in a scientific culture where it has become necessary to apologize for autobiography. If the reader requires them, he can have my apologies.

What follows is an attempt to elucidate some aspects of youthful hooliganism, based on my observations of what is thought of as a specific youth problem - 'paki-bashing'. This essay makes no attempt, however, to encompass the whole field of racial violence. Instead it fixes its attention on Accrington, a small town in North East Lancashire, and it relates the racial question and the question of hooliganism to the social and economic life of the town. I was brought up in Accrington, and the reader should therefore recognize that this essay has a distinctly personal quality. And rather than trying to disengage myself 'scientifically' from those personal roots, in what follows I have tried to picture for the reader how 'paki-bashing' makes itself felt, and finds its place, in the everyday, working class world of this part of Lancashire. You could say that I claim the 'special' knowledge of autobiography in this essay. Even so, the accumulated folklore and common-sense knowledge of the people of a locality is so dense that I must admit to only an imperfect knowledge. For I was not born in Accrington, but in Manchester where my parents were also born. We are therefore cut off from some of the common sense of Accrington where, to this day and after thirty years of residence, my parents will still be known to some of the locals as 'foreigners'. They therefore carried with them not the traditions of the small town, the mill, the local dialect and 'wakes' week, but the traditions of city folk. And it is interesting (and important) that they also carried with them a mistrust of the Irish Catholic population which arrived in waves to parts of Manchester, which are now themselves only a memory, as long ago as the 1820s. What is the nature of this mistrust between the local and the migrant worker? This is the question which first encouraged this study, for my imperfect credentials for autobiography are complete in one sense: by the time I left Accrington in 1961 I had learned to mistrust the Pakistanis who were arriving in the town - 'in waves'. Here are deep divisions within the working class which set worker against worker, and a comment by Karl Marx (1974 edn, p. 169) in a letter of 1870 states the matter well, and offers a starting point:

> All English industrial and commercial centres now possess a working class split into two hostile camps: English proletarians and Irish proletarians. The ordinary English worker hates the Irish worker because he sees in him a competitor who lowers his standard of life. Compared with the Irish worker he feels himself a member of the ruling nation and for this very reason he makes himself into a tool of the aristocrats and capitalists against Ireland and thus strengthens their domination over himself. He cherishes religious, social and national prejudices against the Irish worker. His attitude is much the same as that of the 'poor whites' towards the 'niggers' in the former slave states of the American Union....
>
> This antagonism is artificially sustained and intensified by the press, the pulpit, the comic papers, in short, by all the means at the disposal of the ruling classes. This antagonism is the secret of the impotence of the English working class, despite its organization. It is the secret which enables the capitalist class to maintain its power, as this class is perfectly aware.

WHAT IS 'PAKI-BASHING'?

> When you get some long stick in your 'and an you are bashing some Paki's face in, you don't think about it (Daniel and McGuire, 1972, p. 84).

This comment, from the member of a gang (or 'mob') in East End London, sums up the accumulated wisdom of what paki-bashing is about. This skinhead youth appears to have reached some agreement with officialdom: attacks on immigrants are reckless, spur-of-the-moment efforts to bash the living daylights out of someone who, for some reason or another which is not clear, is disliked. It is a 'gut reaction', we are told. It is the act of a mindless vandal. It is something which gives vent to animal emotions. It is uncivilized.

'Paki-bashing' emerged as a social problem at some point in 1969 or 1970. (1) The precise date is in one sense unimportant. It is not when attacks on immigrants began in the UK, although it signals the emergence of a 'moral panic' when the official and semi-official view of 'public opinion', the mass media, the courts and the police found a new word to describe acts of 'unprovoked assault' on people who are said to be racially inferior. Paki-bashing became associated with skinheads - those boney-headed yobs with boots and braces and half-mast trousers whose appearance was 'senseless' enough to justify anything. Liberal consciences might ask: 'Why on earth do kids beat up immigrants?' But Liberal consciences had seen nothing on earth like the skinhead: the senselessness of his football hooliganism, his violence, and his clothing forced a neat closure to any critical thought. Anyone dressed like that would do anything: it stood to reason.

Thus we are left with one of those self-evident truths of a media-induced hypnosis, and there is no longer any reason left to search for the reason why people attack immigrants. The result of all this is not surprising: we are left with no worthwhile attempt to understand what is called 'paki-bashing'. The wheels of reason are oiled instead by a remote sense of scandal, panic, and a knowledgeless 'knowing' disapproval.

The very phrase 'paki-bashing', however, shows that the phenomenon is more discriminating than any piece of uncontrolled animality could ever be. It suggests a distinction between Pakistanis and other black immigrants. The distinction is probably best described as that between Asians (that is, Indians and Pakistanis) and West Indians. The West Indian is 'more like us'. He speaks our language (or so we tell ourselves) and he is of our culture - or so we fool ourselves. 'Pakis' (that is, Indians and Pakistanies) on the other hand are not like us at all, or so the distinction says: they speak a different language, they eat peculiar food which does not smell like our food, and they keep to themselves. Daniel Lawrence's study of race relations in Nottingham finds that these distinctions are expressed within the immigrant population itself. A West Indian says of Asians: 'They're clannish. Their way of thinking and behaving is entirely different from ours. I've known a few but it's hard to get through to them' (Lawrence, 1974, p. 155). Surprisingly, perhaps, Lawrence finds that both West Indians and Asians think that they are more like the English than each other. Nevertheless, he holds that West Indians 'are closest to the whites in terms of culture and sense of identity' (Lawrence, 1974, p. 157).

Gerry Stimson's (1969) report on working class youth finds a similar discriminating discrimination among London skinheads who hate hippies, weirdos, students, Greeks and Pakistanis: 'We can't stand the Pakkis - we all went down Drummond Street one night, down the road that is, like its all infested with Pakkis. About fifty of us went down fucking putting bottles through their restaurants and that was a good laugh that was. It got in all the papers, how the Pakkis were asking the police if they could arm themselves and form vigilante groups.' Stimson writes that: 'Strangely they don't dislike West Indians. It might be because they dig West Indian music and dance their dances.... The Blacks are admired by the gangs. "Like they were the first with the short hair. They're alright the Rude boys. Rudies hang about with Rudies mostly, and with white girls, and Blacks fight Blacks and Whites fight Whites and that's it."' And a young working class man in a Cardiff pub, having described to me how he is not racially prejudiced and actually likes the blacks, because they do a fair day's work for a fair day's pay, goes on: 'Pakis? Oh no! I don't like them, like. They're right cunts. Cover themselves all over with grease and hair-oil ... it makes me sick to think of 'em.'

The Pakistani is no ordinary black man. One of Stimson's informants talks of 'them Black Irishmen from the North - Pakkis'. And in the north, in his study of Blackburn people, Jeremy Seabrook (1973, p. 122) takes his tape-recorder to a young rocker who is sitting beneath Queen Victoria's statue in a public square:

> What are you doing here?
> NEB: Sitting.
> Where is there for young people to go in Blackburn?
> NEB: Nowhere.
> Where do you spend most of your free time?
> NEB: Here. Things I like doing are against the law.
> Like what?
> NEB: Screwing.
> There's no law against that is there?
> NEB: Not that sort of screwing.
> Get into many fights?
> NEB: When we have to. Fight the Pakistans.
> Don't you like them?
> NEB: Do we like the Pakistans? Piss off. If I told you what I thought of Pakistans it'd bust your machine.

'THEY FLICKED MATCHES AT US': TROUBLE

> And you get beaten up by blacks
> Who though they worked still got the sack
> (The Who, 1973)

Blackburn is a few miles from Accrington; they are part of the same straggling conurbation of industrial towns which stretches between the moors of North East Lancashire. The major towns are Darwen, Blackburn, Accrington, Burnley, Nelson, Colne, Haslingden, Rawtenstall and Bacup; and there are smaller centres such as those around Accrington itself - Rishton, Clayton-le-Moors, Great Harwood, Hapton, Padiham, Huncoat, Badenden, Church, and Oswaldtwistle. In the summer of 1964 there was a sudden, brief outburst of paki-bashing in Accrington. The purpose of this section is to describe the trouble. The sections which imeediately follow will set the trouble in the context of Accrington's social and economic life, and alongside the peculiar place which the Pakistani migrant worker assumes in the drama of the collapse and transformation of the industrial base of the locality.

On 21 July 1964 a man was killed in a brawl outside a small coffee bar in Accrington. An argument had broken out between a group of Pakistanis and a group of white youths and men. According to one version, a Pakistani had flicked matches and cigarette ends at the whites, cracks had been made about white women, a fight broke out which spread into the street, a knife (or knives) were pulled and a white man died, allegedly stabbed by a Pakistani. It is the same kind of incident which sparked off the race riot in Leeds (cf. Hartley, 1973).

It is difficult to say, but this kind of bother may have been fairly common at the time. In one instance which finished in court, a Pakistani had asked a white girl in a cafe to go out with him. When she refused, he swore. When he swore, she fainted: trouble. On 21 July trouble turned into manslaughter.

That was in the afternoon. I knew immediately that there had been trouble of some sort because my workplace overlooked the street in which the fight took place and workmates had seen some, if not all, of the action. They had called other people over to have a look, but from a distance it was difficult to see what had happened, although someone said there was blood on the road. There was a mild excitement: something had happened which didn't happen yesterday, and wouldn't happen tomorrow. It had helped to break up the boredom of the working day. After a brief chat about what all the fuss might be about, we drifted back to our various jobs. When news reached us that there had been a murder, some of the men grumbled about 'pakis' being trouble-makers. 'There's been trouble in this town ever since they came here.' 'I knew it would come to this.'

In the early evening, on my way home from work, I met with a large gang of about 100-200 white youths and men, ages ranging from 15 to 30. They were moving down the main street of the town in search of 'pakis' and many of the gang carried chains, belts and sticks. They also had some large, menacing dogs with them most of which seemed to be alsations. It was not clear where they had gathered, or how they had come together, but they were coming from the direction of the same coffee bar which was also close to a pub and a small dance-hall which was well known for minor trouble and toughness. Their appearance suggested that they were 'the lads'. But these were not skinheads: this was long before the days of the skinhead, in the time of the mod. But nor were they mods: mod fashions and styles had not yet reached this part of Britain, and it is doubtful whether they ever really did. The style of the gang was that of the latter-day teddy boy.

The mob, if it was a mob, moved down the street. It sometimes moved into the road, but kept mainly to the wide pavements. A couple of police cars hovered about, but made no attempt to interfere, and as the gang went along a few Pakistanis who were standing at bus queues were knocked down, beaten and trampled on.

I was walking a few yards behind the mob by now, not too sure what to do, going in the same direction. On one occasion as the gang passed a bus-stop, a 'paki' who had not been visible from within their ranks, emerged from under their feet - as if he had been 'heeled' from a rugby pack. 'The lads' were literally walking on 'the pakis'. Whites at the same bus queue stood by watching this. The 'paki' lay on the floor, bleeding from the head and face, dazed and struggling to get off the floor. No one moved to help him, and I felt at the time that nobody wanted to help him. It is possible, however, that people were afraid of confronting the lads as nigger-lovers: that was the thought which crossed my own mind.

It was only a hundred yards to the town hall, and here the gang moved into another thoroughfare, the police cars shadowing them. Apart from the rioters there were only a few people about, on their way home from work. There was no excitement, and the lads moved quietly and even sluggishly. When the mob moved into another street, I carried on my way. I was anxious to eat my evening meal - a meal which is called 'tea' in these parts. Also, I was not then a sociologist filled with the spirit of participant observation. And it should not go unmentioned that I was afraid.

What happened after this is not clear. Local accounts vary, and newspaper coverage of the trouble was over-shadowed by a local flood which had wrecked houses and mills in a near-by town. The 'Accrington Observer' (a twice weekly newspaper) carried a heavy coverage of the flood damage, including a number of front-page headlines. On Saturday, 25 July there was also a subsidiary headline: '"WE WILL STAMP OUT MOB RULE AND HOOLIGANISM" Bench tells gaoled three. Gang of 30 in street. Pakistanis attacked.' The police had eventually moved in on a smaller crowd who had rushed some Pakistanis in a bus shelter. A handful of men were arrested and charged with being drunk and disorderly, and behaviour likely to cause a breach of the peace. But the peace had already been breached, and for a couple of weeks there was a new flood hitting Accrington: 'paki-bashing'.

The trouble erupted from arguments about girls, flicking matches and pulling knives. In the next few days there were sporadic attacks on immigrants, the streets in which they lived were invaded, windows broken, the curtains of their houses set on fire, Moslem food-shops were wrecked and vandalized, and men were arrested when they appeared in the centre of the town with a double-barrelled shot-gun. They shouted: 'Black bastards. Stop or we will shoot you.' The gun was stuck into the ribs of one Pakistani, police intervened, there was a struggle and (in the words of the 'Accrington Observer') the police were told: 'You --- nigger lover. They all want shooting.' 'The lads' were charged and gaoled for everything conceivable: threatening behaviour; behaviour likely to cause a breach of the peace; possession of an offensive weapon; assaulting a police officer; and damage to the door of a police cell. But they were not charged with assaulting the Pakistanis, and nor was anyone else charged with assault during the brief season of paki-bashing. Why? I will attempt an answer to that awkward question in the final section.

The response of the community was definitely ambivalent. Only the shot-gun incident jolted the local newspaper out of its low-key coverage of the trouble, when it carried a banner headline: 'DISTURBANCES. "UGLY TURN"'. Altogether only eight men appeared in court over the few weeks, and about half of them were gaoled. There was a moment of almost comic relief when a man was arrested for carrying an offensive weapon - a large piece of concrete. He shouted something insulting about 'blacks' and then threw his piece of concrete at an Italian who was passing by. He is alleged to have said, 'This Pakistani is not going to knife me', and he got two months for his trouble.

Shortly after this incident a Pakistani who was arrested for carrying a knife was told by a magistrate: 'It is a thing we will not stand in this country.' And in the same week a West Indian, whose problems were completely unrelated to the disturbances, was given the same message: 'If you are going to live in this country you have got to conform to the laws, and you have got to behave yourself properly.' The Pakistani community did not see things in the same way, and perhaps they thought the 'mother country' was not setting a very good example. The Pakistani who had been arrested for carrying a knife, for example, at first claimed that it was for peeling onions. He later coughed up: 'There is trouble in the town. I not want trouble. If a man comes to hit me, I use it.'

It was 8 August, and the trouble was more or less over. It was also business as usual, and blacks could be told to get back where they came from. On 1 August, hidden away on the back page of the 'Observer' along with the local cricket news, a report of an Asian friendship meeting was headed: 'We want to live in peace say Accrington Pakistanis'. The local Asians wondered whether they should take steps to defend themselves. Some of them had fought for Britain in the war, they said, and so they knew how to fight. And it was there that we also learned that the great tidal wave of the black menace, which was described as 'the Pakistani "colony" in Accrington' was 250 strong. Accrington had a population of about 37,000 in 1964.

INDUSTRY: UP AGAINST THE OLD MILL WALL

A'wm a poor cotton-wayver as mony a one knaws,
Aw've nowt t'ate i'th' heawse, un'aw've worn eawt my cloas.
Yo'd hardly gie sixpence fur o'aw've got on,
Meh clogs ur'boath baws'n, un' stockins aw've none;
Yo'd think it wur hard to be sent into th' ward
To clem un' do best 'ot yo' con'.
(Jone o'Grinfilt Junior, circa 1815; Harland, 1882, p. 169)

There are different ways of obtaining an impression of a town. The statistics of a census, or a study of industrial development and decline, will paint a picture in numbers. Maps and charts in a library will also let you know what your legs will tell you if you walk about the towns in North East Lancashire: namely, that they are built on the steep sides of valleys which restrict the growth of urban and industrial re-development. These are little towns, neither country nor city - an urban density over several fields. Even from their industrial depths it is possible to look up and see a moor or a farm. But they are not picturesque, and some think of them as grim little towns. Certainly, they provide a firm impression of what life is about. For example, if you stand on the moors above Accrington you can count about thirty mill chimneys. From the hillside overlooking Oswaldtwistle the number is more than forty. Local opinion will tell you, and maps and charts will confirm it, that at one time there were many more. Cotton waste lying outside the loading bays of some of the mills will tell you that some of them are still working at weaving, spinning or finishing. Local opinion will confirm that in

Accrington it is no more than a couple, and the absence of smoke from so many of the chimneys will confirm that. These are just some of the ways of obtaining an impression of a town.

But there is no way of mistaking what Accrington, and towns like it, are there for and why they were built. Houses are laid out in a grid-iron lattice development, and they are grouped around cotton mills. Sometimes workers' cottages are even built inside the boundaries of the mills. The pattern was set in the nineteenth century: Elizabeth Gaskell (1970 edn, p. 96) wrote of Manchester (which she called Milton in Darkshire) that among the 'long, straight, hopeless streets of regularly built houses' the factories 'stood up, like a hen among her chickens'. These are the houses built for what were called 'the Hands'. Even inter-war years council housing developments were often built around a new mill, and after forty years of life so many of those developments are now being gutted and renovated: they are not 'fit' dwellings. The landscape is thus dominated by the houses built for the Hands, the chapels, and the mills which Charles Dickens (1969 edn, p. 103) in a cruel joke said looked like 'Fairy Palaces' when their lights came on at night; but he added that it was only from a distance. Some of the mills have ornamental flourishes and thus try to disguise themselves as places of worship, whereas the chapels are as utilitarian as factories. The confusion between life, work and worship is total. Houses stand against mills, and mills lean against chapels. In one small street (which is aptly called Cotton Street) in Accrington, for example, the Unsectarian Mission School, the houses and the mill fight for space. Two mill chimneys actually sprout from the Mission's back wall, and while I was photographing them one day a woman passed by and looking at the camera (which might have been a gun) she said: 'I thought you were going to blow it up.... I wish you had done.' She added, 'It's an eyesore. My husband and me we've lived in this street forty year and it were there then ... it's so big', and then she walked on. Adam Smith remarked that the economy was ruled by an 'invisible hand': it has left its visible marks on these towns, and there is no mistaking what they were built for.

In the immediate post-war years the town council of Accrington made plans to give their industrial wasteland a face-lift. A report was commissioned from planning specialists which took for its title the town's motto: 'Industry and Prudence'. These efforts were finally squashed, but the report nevertheless stands as an intelligent and far-sighted document of the town's problems and prospects. Even so, it is a grim comment on the town that the planning report identified the massive railway viaduct which strides through its centre as the principle feature of architectural interest around which to organize the proposed transformation of the landscape.

However, as 'Industry and Prudence' recognized, Accrington required more than cosmetic beautification, for its industry was also in a critical state: 'Accrington's roaring days of expansion, based on nineteenth century economics, are over: the Lancashire cotton trade no longer dominates the world's markets. Both industrially and physically, the evidence suggests, the town is entering a period of stabilization and internal reorganization' (Allen and Mattocks, 1950, p. 39). Perhaps the report did not, however, see just how total this transformation would be. So that by the 1970s, very few trains would run across its striking architectural feature, the mills would have closed down, and the railway line to Manchester - commercial heart of the cotton towns - would have been ripped out. By the 1970s Accrington had become, like many of the surrounding towns, a cotton town only in its sentiments, its ideology and its memories.

The cotton trade, which is the raison d'être of North East Lancashire, had gone through many slumps and recessions in its history, and the possible threat of unemployment and short-time working was never very far away. Accrington has one peculiar aspect which is that since the mid-nineteenth century it has had a major industrial base in engineering - producing, for the large part, textile machinery. And although this does not change the overall character of the focus of its industry and community, it has enabled the town sometimes to ride these slumps with less catastrophic results than in some surrounding towns. In the depression of the 1930s, for example, unemployment never went higher than 37 per cent. This may sound high enough, but it should be compared with Darwen, for example, where the figure was 50 per cent, or Great Harwood where unemployment reached a peak of 60 per cent. These variations are reflected in the occupational structure of the towns at this time. In 1931, 82 per cent of the labouring population of Great Harwood were dependent on cotton, whereas in Accrington the figure was only about 40 per cent - although that too represents a sizeable monopoly over wage levels and working conditions. A further 25 per cent of Accrington's labour force relied on textile engineering, and engineering firms were able to diversify production away from an almost total reliance on the manufacture of textile machinery, thus weathering the storm of the 1930s. Overall in the immediate post-war period, unemployment levelled off at something in excess of 30 per cent. For Accrington the figure was 20 per cent and in 1937, which was admittedly a freak year, it dropped as low as 10 per cent.

The experiences of the working class in the 1920s and 1930s are important in two respects. First because they supply the local communities with a basic structure of experience founded on austerity and hard work, memories which lie deep in the communities' consciousness. Second, because they signal the beginning of the general economic decline of the area. For although Accrington - unlike other towns - had achieved a measure of industrial diversification, this must be set against the continuing specialization in cotton manufacture, as the authors of 'Industry and Prudence' note: 'The truth was that the degree of diversification attained by the town was not nearly great enough, and that the very specialization which had paid such handsome dividends in an expanding economy proved, after 1919, an increasing liability' (Allen and Mattocks, 1950, p. 149).

From the 1920s onwards the message was clear: North East Lancashire was up against the old mill wall. Between 1929 and

1939 the Blackburn region lost 17,538 people through emigration to other areas - 14 per cent of its labour force. In Accrington the figure was very high in this period - 18 per cent of its population, and 22 per cent of its male workers. The industrial revolution was now passing the area by, and British capitalism would work its miracles in other fields.

The population decline in this region over the period from 1921 onwards is quite dramatic, and only reaches a measure of stabilization in the late 1960s (cf. Table 3.1). Between 1921 and 1966 the conurbation as a whole suffered a population collapse which varied from a fifth to a quarter: the overall figure is 22.2 per cent, and for Accrington it is 18.4 per cent. The most dramatic decreases were in the 1930s and 1940s, although the trend continues well into the 1960s. Between 1951 and 1966 - the years of 'booming prosperity' in Britain as a whole - the area lost nearly a tenth of its post-war population. And the cumulative extent of the population fall from the 1920s was as if a city of the size of Blackburn (that is, more than 110,000 people) had simply disappeared. The only bright note is that those who were leaving the area to find work elsewhere relieved the pressure on the available jobs in the region. Estimating that 1,600 people per year were still leaving the region throughout the 1960s, a Department of the Environment report (1971, p. 13) comments that 'otherwise the present level of recorded unemployment would be a great deal higher'.

TABLE 3.1 Census returns by town

	1921	1931	1951	1961	1966	1971
Accrington	44,975	42,991	40,685	39,018	36,390	36,840
Burnley	103,186	98,258	84,987	80,559	76,320	76,480
Blackburn	126,950	122,791	111,218	106,242	100,920	101,655
Nelson	39,815	38,227	34,384	32,292	31,770	31,215
Colne	24,871	23,918	20,670	19,430	19,640	18,865
Oswaldtwistle	15,125	14,218	12,130	11,918	-	-
Rishton	7,013	6,609	5,800	5,433	-	-
Clayton	8,579	7,909	6,825	6,421	-	-
Church	6,746	6,187	5,200	5,888	-	-
Padiham	12,477	11,636	10,041	9,899	-	-
Haslingden	17,486	16,639	14,513	14,360	-	-
Rawtenstall	28,376	28,587	25,437	23,890	21,900	21,395
Bacup	21,263	20,590	18,374	17,308	15,990	15,085
Great Harwood	13,605	12,789	10,739	10,718	-	-
Darwen	37,906	36,012	30,827	29,475	28,570	28,875
Approx. total	508,500	487,200	431,700	412,900	396,600	393,900
Population loss		21,300	55,500	18,800	c16,300	c2,700
Cumulative population loss			76,800	95,600	c111,900	c114,600

(Sources: Census for 1951 and 1961; the figures for 1966 and 1971 are taken from the sample census of 1966 and the advanced analysis of the 1971 census, which is why data are not available for the smaller towns)

TABLE 3.2 The decline of the cotton industry

	Average number of looms running		Numbers employed in the whole of the UK				Amalgamated Weavers' Assoc.n Membership
	UK	Lancs.	Spinning	Doubling	Weaving	Total	
1951	311,700	285,300	116,310	29,120	140,320	285,750	86,259
1952	249,700	228,400	92,840	21,250	118,390	232,480	39,465
1953	270,600	249,000	102,860	22,860	124,190	249,910	87,617
1954	280,700	258,100	106,720	23,550	127,060	257,330	85,288
1955	252,600	231,000	97,570	20,810	117,970	236,350	84,073
1956	229,400	210,000	92,590	19,370	108,340	220,300	80,748
1957	222,700	205,400	93,860	18,760	103,510	216,130	66,030
1958	192,000	177,200	84,000	15,590	92,710	192,390	64,592
1959	172,100	158,900	77,320	14,670	84,870	176,860	59,719
1960	149,400	134,400	69,230	14,900	81,260	165,390	55,647
1961	150,200	134,600	61,560	13,340	70,660	145,560	53,709
1962	131,000	117,800	52,310	11,910	66,250	130,470	50,398
1963	119,800	108,900	49,630	11,940	68,340	129,910	45,483
1964	116,500	105,600	47,780	11,640	66,400	125,820	44,463
1965	113,700	101,700	43,770	10,620	64,220	118,610	43,113
1966	107,200	95,600	41,380	10,050	54,360	106,790	41,701
1967	83,100	75,200	34,580	8,600	49,360	92,540	36,586
1968	-	-	-	-	-	-	33,066

(Source: Hopwood, 1969)

The population decline is largely attributable to the collapse and reorganization of the area's industrial base. Again numbers spell out the bare bones of this transformation: the numbers of people employed in the cotton industry, the number of trade union members, and the average number of looms in operation each year (see Table 3.2).

These are only post-war statistics, and it should be held in mind that before its general decline roughly 620,000 people were employed in the British cotton manufacture. It should also be remembered that these figures relate to the whole of the British cotton industry, thus giving an overall picture of the collapse which finds its reflection in the cotton towns of northern Lancashire. However, as the statistics on loom operation show, Lancashire is (more or less) the whole of the British cotton industry (see Table 3.2).

The problems of the cotton industry in the post-war period can be summarized as follows. In the immediate post-war years the industry was in a state of recovery as mills which had been closed under the Essential Work Order of the war years were re-opened. From that hopeful start the decline of the cotton industry intensified through the 1950s, and it was eventually urged along by government intervention. Trade unionists had hoped that the Cotton Industry Act (1959) would save jobs, but the Act (which compensated employers who scrapped surplus machinery) only accelerated mill closures. Between 1958 and 1962 the labour force was reduced by nearly 30 per cent and it was the end of the road for the traditional economic base of those localities which depended on cotton manufacture. Trade union membership spells out just how gross these changes were. In 1884 when the trade union (which is only one of many for the textile industry) which was strongest in Lancashire first amalgamated, its membership was 37,000. Union membership reached its peak in 1921 at a figure of 224,219 when one district alone had 27,000 members. By the late 1960s union membership had fallen below the figure of 1884: the industrial revolution had turned full circle, leaving behind the debris of the empty Fairy Palaces. Thus, Hopwood's 'The Lancashire Weavers' Story', published in 1969 by the Amalgamated Weavers' Association, ends its history of labour organization and struggle with an account of the trade union's attempts to get the best conditions of discharge, and the best terms for redundancy payments, in the face of the inevitable closure.

The collapse of the cotton industry in Britain, and in other industrialized countries, takes place in the face of intensifying competition from low-cost cotton imports - predominantly from India, Hong Kong and Pakistan. The irony of this development, which was eroding the industrial base of North East Lancashire, is spelled out in 'Industry and Prudence' where Allen and Mattocks (1950, p. 149) write that Asian cotton production was mounted 'with the starting advantage of modern machinery - machinery supplied, in many cases, by Accrington's own engineering shops'. The history of economic competition between British and Asian cotton manufacture is a long one, and it is associated with the depression of wages in the British industry over many years, and with attempts to assert tariff controls on imported cotton goods. This history, which can be traced back to the eighteenth century, has periodic moments of resurgence and we can mention as an instance of this a pamphlet by J. Whittaker - published in Accrington in 1909 - titled 'Tariff Reform in Relation to the Cotton Trade' which rehearses the familiar enough arguments about price war and cuts in the wages of local cotton operatives. The issue of Asian competition - popularly thought of as the cotton produce of 'coolies' in sweat shops, and unscrupulous foreign traders - is, however, by no means only of historical interest. Although their specific origins are obscure, there were similar movements in Accrington in the 1950s. Cars toured the streets calling for the banning of Asian imports, and posters appeared in the windows of houses. The campaign was unsuccessful, but it seemed to excite a great deal of local sympathy, and what is important is that this sympathy was often edged with a sort of racism.

It is difficult to say just where demands for tariff control end and racism begins, but they often have that undertone: what right did these foreign coolies have to take away the livelihood of honest Lancashire mill-workers? Had not the British Empire ruled the sea, stamped half the map of the world with imperial red, and dragged the 'wogs' out of their jungle slumbers? Who did these primitives think they were? The arguments of tariff reform thus provided a sort of economic rationality to suspicion of, and hostility towards, Asians. Prideaux (1972) has also commented on the way in which trade union agitation on textile tariffs can attract and encourage, in an embarrassing fashion, racist sympathies and racist fellow-travellers.

The roots of racial anxiety are therefore already laid in the economic troubles of the cotton towns. It is also worth noting that according to Paul Foot (1965, p. 166) it was Harry Hynd - Member of Parliament for Accrington throughout the post-war period - who agitated for immigration control in the 1950s and 'led the Labour "control" lobby in the Commons for some years'. This was at a time when the Labour Party was officially opposed to immigration controls, a position which was to change in the early 1960s (cf. Foot, 1965). And it was precisely at the time of the final evaporation of the cotton industry that Britain witnessed the panic which preceded, and culminated in, the immigration controls of the Commonwealth Immigration Act of 1962. The arrival, for the first time, of Pakistanis in Lancashire cotton towns in this period provided a concrete and visible manifestation of the economic issue of import control. Thus, the importation of low-cost cotton goods and low-cost labour merge, and the Pakistani migrant worker takes his place in the drama of the 'poor cotton weaver' - in a crude, commonsense form of economic rationality - as a symbol of the problems of a troubled working class community.

PRUDENCE: COTTON CULTURE AND THE MIGRANT WORKER

On Stanley on Boys!
On Stanley on!
We'll cheer you on Boys,
When you get
That ball into the net....
(Fragment of Accrington Stanley supporters' song, circa 1953)

The economic life of a town is not its only life. Statistics can only scratch the broadest outline of the experience of industrial upheaval, decline and partial renewal. A community's economic base is, when all is said and done, only a base. The way in which the economic base realizes itself in the lives of working people we can call the 'culture' of their community, and it is to the working class culture of the mill-town that we must now turn.

Traditionally working class culture is described in terms of the closely-knit extended kinship group, the corner shop, the pub, the Saturday football match, the bowling green, the brass band, the cloth cap, the local dialect, the rattle of clogs on cobbled streets, neighbours sitting out on the door-step on summer evenings sharing local gossip. The picture is often presented as one of a golden age of working class community, where poverty and cramped dwellings had positive, as well as negative aspects, throwing people into contact with each other in an intimacy in which joys and sorrows could be felt as a collective experience.

The concept of 'golden age' - or, although it is not quite the same thing, the 'good old days' - is always one which invites suspicion (cf. Pearson, 1975a, ch. 7). Even so, it has a certain rationality and a capacity to evoke strong feelings - especially perhaps among the elderly. The idea of a 'golden age', for example, constantly re-asserts itself in Jeremy Seabrook's 'City Close-Up' which is built out of interviews with people in Blackburn. It is enough to say that there is a certain amount of truth in such notions, but also a certain amount of nonsense - the 'good old days' were, after all, also the 'bad old days'. But that too has its significance, for the golden age of the cotton towns was an age of prudence, thrift and discipline.

Even the most superficial observation shows how the concept of a lost golden age can appear as a compelling one in this region of Lancashire. Take, for example, one of the traditional working class sports of the area -football. In the immediate post-war period the region supplied and supported a number of First Division football teams: Preston North End, Blackburn Rovers, Bolton Wanderers, Blackpool FC and Burnley. These clubs are scattered over a wide area, but fixtures between them were rightly regarded as 'derby' games and special occasions. Some of the greatest players of the golden age of English football - Tom Finney, Nat Lofthouse, Stanley Matthews - belonged to these clubs and their supporters. But football has gone into decline in this area, and only Burnley remains in the First Division of the Football League: even so, most football commentators agree that by all the laws of economic rationality it has no business there. Accrington Stanley was a less illustrious club, although it too had its moments. But after constantly threatening through the 1950s to escape from the Third Division North into the big-time of the Second Division, it struggled out its last years in the lower reaches of the Fo rth Division. A founder member of the Football League, Accrington Stanley went bankrupt in the 1960s - just another economic casualty in the region.

The Lancashire Cricket League (founded in 1892) is another important local institution which provided a focus of popular entertainment. Although it is nothing more than the amateur cricket league of North East Lancashire, it is perhaps one of the most celebrated of the amateur leagues. By the league rules, each team is allowed one professional player whose job is both to play and coach, and the league has attracted most of the big names in international cricket at one time or another - Bobbie Simpson, Wes Hall, Gary Sobers, and so many others. Before the immigration of the 1960s, if a coloured man was seen in the street it could be safely assumed that he was a cricketer.

At the time of writing, the Accrington Cricket Club is passing through severe financial difficulties. It can no longer support a star professional and relies on a local player, and its fine cricket ground is in a state of chronic disrepair. Some blame the motor car which takes people out of town on Saturday afternoons; some blame television; some just blame 'modern life'. But the golden age of Saturday afternoon cricket has passed away.

A similar cultural transformation is reflected in the religious sphere. Traditionally a stronghold of Nonconformism - Methodism, Baptism and Congregationalism - the chapel, the Sunday school, the men's institutes are no longer the thriving centres of community which they once were (cf. Blackwell, 1974). Where these institutions have survived the cultural deformation, and not all of them have, they live on in an altered and impoverished form. One Primitive Baptist Chapel in the area, which has given itself a face-lift in the direction of up-tempo evangelism, has also almost shamefacedly erased the word 'primitive' from its nineteenth century foundation stone. A further indication of change is that the Accrington Labour Party found it necessary to relinquish their spacious premises some years ago. Possibly (there are rumours) this had something to do with a reluctance to take a licence for the sale of alcohol: a critical instance of how closely the traditions of Socialism and Methodism are interwoven in the mill-town. And at the back of these changes is the most dramatic of all: successive generations of emigration from the area have skewed the age-structure of the population, so that the elderly are very much over-represented in some localities (Department of the Environment, 1971, p. 61).

Jane Morton (1973) has even gone so far as to suggest that this area of Lancashire is going 'back to nature'. She writes also: 'At best North East Lancashire has a future as a dormitory area for those working elsewhere - and they'll only move if the rural charm they are looking for shows through a bit more than it does at present' (Morton, 1972). It is difficult, perhaps, to avoid over-stating the problems of the region. One should not imagine, however, that these towns are mere ghost towns. But they have, nevertheless, been radically altered (and are still undergoing alteration) by a profound economic and cultural disfiguration which has reached through to the many, sometimes conflicting, traditions of working class life.

A weakness in traditional accounts of working class culture is that they tend to miss out one vital dimension, namely work itself. Sometimes these accounts go about their business as if only leisure activities were of any consequence. But this is a drastic mistake if one is trying to understand the changes in the mill-towns in the post-war period. The cotton mill, its tempo and its mechanical rhythm, exacted a high price in terms of discipline and orderliness from the 'Hands' who worked it. For cotton manufacture required workers to do more than passively 'mind' the machinery: it also necessitated a high level of attention and skill if the product was not to be snagged and flawed, and traditionally there were harsh systems of fines and humiliations for workers who allowed shoddy work to pass through. Jeremy Seabrook has suggested that this disciplined conformity to the external and relentless rhythms of production found its way back into the home, and into the character structure of the labouring population: 'These social disciplines were internalized by individuals, who then dutifully reflected them in authoritarian family structures: parents were unwittingly united in blind complicity with the owners of mills and money to ensure that the personalities of their children were sytematically deformed and repressed, in order to provide an unceasing stream of unskilled labour' (Seabrook, 1973, p. 32). And again: 'The patterns of marriage and the upbringing of a further generation of mill-hands were determined by the mills themselves: the process was mechanical, rigid and efficient. They internalized the social discipline, and reflected the tyranny of the economic structure in every aspect of their lives' (Seabrook, 1973, p. 128).

Thus Seabrook describes the process of child-rearing - the process by which a community reproduces itself - as a reflection of the cotton operative's watchful custody of the machine: children, too, must be guarded carefully in order to prevent the development of snags and flaws. He takes as a symbol of this disciplined socialization the eternal vigilance of housewives over the stone door-step and the stretch of flagstone pavement outside it, which would often be scrubbed with a 'Donkey Stone' and pumiced and bleached into a milky smoothness: 'They [the women] exulted in their custodial role, all the sharp-eyed wives and mothers, the permanent unflagging doorstep tribunals, watching, reproving, admonishing, castigating. Their husbands were bound to them indissolubly, and every house in the street was a house of correction' (Seabrook, 1973, p. 128). Perhaps Seabrook overdraws the picture, but it must be allowed that the culture of the cotton mill reproduced itself in many of the traditional aspects of working class life. Even the local dialect, for example, with its broad, round, full-mouthed articulation - ideally suited to communication in the mill where the noise of machinery could make anything more than lip-reading an impossibility. Or, to take a further example, the reorganization of the cotton industry produced a severe dislocation in the strong tradition of female employment in cotton mills - a development, we must assume, which disturbed more than the balance of the family economy.

We can say, therefore, that in the post-war period the cotton culture was in a state of crisis: crisis, that is, in the sense that old, established ways of doing things and understanding one's place in the world, were having to be discarded and replaced by new tactics for the resolution of the problems of everyday life. The economic base of the required reorganization of life was that new industry should be introduced to replace the cotton trade. In January 1961 the 'Accrington Observer' ran a congratulatory editorial which reported that different kinds of industry were slowly being attracted to the area. A key economic possibility was that new firms could adapt the vacated mill buildings for their own purposes, and the newspaper linked these developments to the fact that cotton workers - 'Lancashire folk' as it called them - were not as stubborn and unchangeable as they were popularly thought to be, and that they too could adapt to new ways, along with the Fairy Palaces.

It must be remembered that we are not describing a great metropolis with a constantly changing, bumping, jostling pace of life; but small towns with familiar sights, faces, smells and rhythms. Towns where it is possible to walk from the outskirts to the centre without too much difficulty, and where it is difficult to walk through the town without bumping into someone that you know. Not, like a city, a place where you can get lost, or lose yourself.

It is not surprising, therefore, that the local response to the new 'prosperity' and the new 'permissiveness', when they finally arrived, was ambivalent. We can gather this either from Seabrook's interviews, or from the frequent sermonizing in the 'Accrington Observer'. By the mid-1960s there were signs that economic reorganization was beginning to pay dividends. In the latter part of 1964, the newspaper repeatedly reported - with banner headlines - the drop in unemployment to its lowest level for many years, and the success which local engineering firms were having in securing contracts. Two headlines, almost ecstatic, ran: 'IT'S A BOOM TOWN NOW!' and 'NOW IT'S "MONEYBAGS" ACCRINGTON!' But the ecstasy was tinged with anxiety. Cotton culture was forged not only within the work routines of the mill, but also in the face of the constant threat of foreign competition, overproduction, slump and the depression of wages. In editorials which seemed almost overawed by the return of a sort of prosperity, the image of the 1920s and the 1930s constantly returned - almost as if one were talking about yesterday. The 'Observer' also dithered in its editorial celebrations of the emerging prosperity, because of the apparent lack of thrift which this signified: cotton culture was, after all, a culture of both industry and prudence. Seabrook (1973, p. 131) writes that the new prosperity required people to change, so that their attitudes towards life would be 'not of rewardless toilers, but of diligent and conscientious consumers'. The 'Observer' in an editorial on 21 November 1964 worried about the same change from thrift to consumption: but, it concluded, 'This is the new era.' However, when the newspaper discovered that the people of

Accrington were saving money as well as spending it, another headline splashed the news. And laborious calculations described just how much was being saved - so much a week, so much a day, so much an hour, so much a minute. In conclusion, we can say that the crisis of cotton culture produced a continuing preoccupation and anxiety about the stability of life; of work, worship and thrift - which in cotton culture amount to the same thing.

It is against the background of this cultural and economic crisis that we must set the arrival of the immigrant worker. The Pakistanis started coming to Accrington in 1960 or 1961. At first they were all men, and only later did they bring over their girl friends and wives - by one account probably as late as 1966 or 1967. They worked in one or two smaller engineering shops, and in the remaining textile spinning factories where they worked mainly on night shifts in the ring spinning room. There were only a few of them, but they were highly visible. They provided a strange sight in the streets: for example, they moved about in small groups and seldom, it seemed, alone; and they walked along the pavement in a crocodile line which struck the locals as odd. Their appearance was of men who were confused. They were, after all, migrant workers who, like the Turks and the Italians in northern Europe, were plunged into a strange new world. An enormous mythology quickly surrounded their presence, and we must be careful to distinguish reality from phantasy. It is convenient, in fact, to think of the realities of their lives as the life circumstances of 'Pakistanis', and to think of the mythology of their condition as the problem of the 'paki'.

The stereotype of the 'paki', which is as contradictory as many stereotypes, finds him sitting down at home (where he lives in filth with at least a dozen others in a couple of rooms) to a meal of tinned cat-food or dog-meat, weary from his day of labour at the dole office. He is dirty and promiscuous and cheeky, but he also keeps himself to himself and he does not mix at all. He is a 'homo', but he is nevertheless always sneaking up to white girls in search of 'jig-a-jig'. He is a layabout and an idler who threatens to put other men out of work. Working every hour that he isn't sleeping (and when he isn't sleeping another 'paki' is sleeping in his bed) and with more money than sense, the 'paki' is always, inevitably, out of work ans scrounging on social security. In short, he is a thrifty spendthrift, a secretive show-off, a rampantly heterosexual homosexual, a social security scrounger on the night shift in the spinning room, a randy man with an exotic religion which forbids sexuality, a workshy layabout with the strength of a horse who is only too happy to take the lowest, butt-end jobs which a white man would only laugh at (cf. Wright, 1968, pp. 112-20). How can he encompass all these conflicting projects? Quite simply, because he is not an ordinary man, but a 'paki' - that is to say, a figment of the collective imagination.

Seabrook has filled in the career of the 'paki' - or 'Packie Stan' as he prefers to call him - as he was to be found in the summer of 1969 in Blackburn. By then his dozens of children and his multiple wives have arrived, although these do not depress his sexual appetites; he is still eating cat-food, and sleeping in the rafters above other people's houses or in the belts above looms in the mill. 'He kills goats and chickens in the back yard, his children pee on the flagstones, he has a large family, and he depresses the price of property wherever he goes. He contrives to filch people's jobs and yet batten on Social Security at the same time. The police are on his side and he has been granted immunity from the laws of the land by the Race Relations Act' (Seabrook, 1972; 1973, p. 44). Seabrook describes 'Packie Stan' as a 'folk ogre', sneaking off to collect his dole. In this, we can note, he is unlike the stereotypical 'West Indian' who drives there in a flash car.

Many stories, rumours and jokes surround the 'paki'. According to one rumour in Accrington in 1962 'they' were taking over the mills. It was said that textile factories in the Rossendale valley were no longer bothering to employ white labour, and notices of vacant jobs were always in Urdu. Mills 'all over the place', the story went out, just had a card in the office window which read 'Naggi Jah': which was said to be Urdu for 'No Work'. There were also many rumours - to which there may have been some substance - that white workers in factories employing Pakistanis were demanding separate toilets. Some of the jokes were not particularly nice. A man in a car, for example, runs out of control and has the choice of hitting either a women with a pram or a 'bus queue' of Pakistanis. (We have already seen how 'everyone knows' that 'pakis' always walk in the street in a straight line.) The man swerves to miss the pram and kills seven of the 'pakis' outright, leaving only one. He gets out of his car and says to the woman with the pram, 'I'm sorry lady. Shall I go back and have another try?' Other jokes were less ill-humoured. Just as Birmingham has its bus route to immigrant areas known as the 'Bombay Express', so Seabrook reports that in Blackburn bus conductors would periodically shout, on approaching areas where Pakistanis lived, 'Khyber Pass!' or 'Next stop, Casbah!'

The liberal imagination, of course, is scandalized by all this fictitious, larded, ignorant tap-room gossip. It insists that such racial stereotypes are 'pure phantasy' and it goes on, with a kind of impotent vigour, to insist that 'all men are equal' - despite the glaring contradition that all men are not equal in class society. It follows, of course, that if 'all men are equal' then paki-bashing is a senseless and insensible hooliganism, and paki-jokes are a sort of arm-chair hooliganism. If we wish to understand, however, what paki-bashing is, then we must recognize that the 'paki' and the 'Pakistani' are not entirely separate men, and that the stereotype of the 'paki' has points of contact with the reality of the life conditions of Pakistani workers. Principally, these points of contact are in relation to the struggle over housing conditions, women and jobs; and a further point of contact is found in relation to the work ethic.

The place of the work ethic in the local population's appreciation of Pakistani immigrant workers is as important as it is complex. The ethos of dutiful work and 'paying your way' is, of course, strong in cotton culture, and one of the attributes of the 'paki' is that he is thought to be a relentless skiver who hops off the boat straight into the dole office. The fact that Pakistanis could so often be seen around the town in the day-time (they often worked the night shift) lent support to the popular belief that 'they' were all on the scrounge. In his study of working class community in Huddersfield Brian Jackson notes that discipline (or the lack of it) was an issue between local and migrant workers who were either thought to work too hard, or to be lazy. And it is in such innocuous situations as a bus queue that friction might start about the issue of discipline. Jackson (1972, p. 91) writes that immigrant workers 'had not yet submitted to the habit of queueing. They made nothing of this line of English workmen and tended to join the queue where any friend was standing. There were always arguments between white and coloured workers, who were told to "get to the back of the queue, that's your rightful place".' But this question of discipline provides another, contradictory, tension in the life of cotton culture which is less direct, but equally vital. Cotton culture was, as I have shown, under pressure from the early 1960s to adapt away from the ideology of the work ethic, thrift and prudence towards the 'new era' of the 'consumer society'. And if it was prudence which was being left behind, then it is Seabrook (1973, p. 49) who notices that what is so often reviled in the Pakistani is his own prudent life-style:

> It was ironical that the very things which the townspeople object to in the immigrants are precisely those aspects of the old communal working-class way of life that used to be considered so valuable - the sense of community, the system of mutual help, the sense of duty to kinsfolk, and the extended family structure. In their often vengeful and punitive attitude towards the immigrants, it is as though the working class were confronted by a spectre of their own past, which they are anxious to banish.

Seabrook goes on to make a useful statement about the nature of these strong feelings about immigrants. The hatred felt for the 'paki', he argues, is not a race prejudice, but an expression of the mutilation of the local community's life-style by the arbitrary movements of an economic system over which they had no control: 'It is an expression of their pain and powerlessness confronted by the decay and dereliction, not only of the familiar environment, but of their own lives, too - an expression for which our society provides no outlet. Certainly it is something more complex and deep-rooted than what the metropolitan liberal evasively and easily dismisses as prejudice' (Seabrook, 1973, p. 57).

If we accept this position, then we can also be more specific. And by attending to the other major areas of conflict between locals and migrants, we can understand how the ground-roots to paki-bashing are laid in the circumstances of working class life. In relation to housing, girls and jobs the roots of conflict are certainly as complex as in the case of discipline, prudence and tradition; but they are also more direct. I will first consider housing.

The fact is that when Pakistanis arrived in Lancashire in the early 1960s they were an isolated community, cut off from the surrounding world by language, religion and custom. The fact, also, is that they did tend to live in the same cluster of streets (cf. Department of the Environment, 1971, p. 60). Rex and Moore (1967, ch. 12) have described the forces of economy, housing conditions and culture which tend towards the 'ghettoization' of certain districts by migrant workers. It has also been argued that John Rex's model for this process (developed out of research in Birmingham) is not universally applicable to all towns and cities (cf. Davies and Taylor, 1973). What we can say is that the relationship between the migrant worker's ghetto and the local community, and the struggle over accommodation and house prices, will take a different form according to the specific housing conditions of the locality. In North East Lancashire the most important of these is that the tradition of owning your own home - even though it might only be a small terraced cottage - is particularly strong (Department of the Environment, 1971). Another significant point is that the region is dominated by very small houses, about two-thirds of them built before 1911, with little scope for multiple occupation and sub-letting. Partly this is attributable to the resistance in Lancashire to workers' flats and tenements (cf. Gaskell, 1974). Housing competition between locals and migrants is, therefore, very direct. And the established tradition within cotton culture of owner-occupation made the housing problem of the migrant worker into an intense and lively one: it twitched a cultural nerve of the local community.

The second focus for both bother and gossip concerned women and girls. It is to be expected that without women in their own community Pakistanis would look for girl friends within the local population of available girls. Sometimes this was frowned upon by the migrant worker's compatriots because it was taken to signal a break with the migrant community, and with the folks back home (cf. Dahya, 1973, p. 273). But it is not an unreasonable guess that it would still go on. It is also to be expected that migrant workers would not search for girl friends in 'respectable' society, but in the kinds of places which get defined as 'low dives'; which, in turn, explains why Accrington's paki-bashing started outside a coffee bar and near a dance-hall for teds, and not outside the Conservative Club which is maybe a hundred yards around the corner. Girls, it must be remembered, are a focus for trouble and fighting in the world of the young, unmarried working man without the help of Pakistanis. And girls were in very short supply in the migrant community. The census for Blackburn shows that in 1961 only one-sixth of the Indian and Pakistani communities were women; the figure for the Pakistani commnnity is as low as one-twentieth. By 1966 two-thirds of all 'total commonwealth immigrants' (the 1966 sample census does not make fine distinctions) were still men. Girls were the spark which led to arguments and fights which in turn led to attacks on Pakistani houses and streets.

The third area of conflict concerns jobs. The job opportunities for Pakistanis were again specifically limited, and Pakistani workers were likely to find work in those textile factories which had survived the decline of the cotton industry. There were a number of reasons for this. Survival would probably have meant new production methods, either in terms of capital investment and/or the introduction of shift-working. In the intensified competition from overseas, textile firms were turning towards a system of production which would involve long or inconvenient hours - that is, working conditions which would only be congenial to single, unmarried men. Migrant workers were ideally suited to fill these jobs, especially in this locality where shift-working was unpopular. Cohen and Jenner (1968) find a similar state of affairs in the wool industry. Their research shows that the employment of Pakistani labour was closely related to issues of capital investment in new machinery, night shifts and double-shift working. The tendency was for firms to be more likely to employ Pakistani workers if they had undertaken a measure of capital investment, in which case Pakistanis were employed as machine operatives. Firms which had not undertaken capital investment either did not employ Pakistanis at all, or only employed them as labourers (Cohen and Jenner, 1968, p. 44). There is a further possibility, although this is doubtful, that migrant workers contributed to the depression of wages in both the surviving wool and cotton industries (Cohen and Jenner, 1968, pp. 49-50). Given that wages were generally depressed in the cotton grade over a long period, however, this speculation is not well founded. But it had enough sense about it to make for lively rumour and, as we know, some tricky trade union disputes (cf. Daniel, 1968, pp. 132ff.; Castles and Kosack, 1973, pp. 127-52; Castles and Kosack, 1974, p. 503; Wright, 1968, pp. 145ff.).

In general we can say that the life conditions of Pakistanis in North East Lancashire confirmed, and were subject to, the predictable cultural and economic role of migrant workers. In Holland and other parts of Europe it is the Turkish migrant worker who gets bashed. In Lancashire the Pakistani migrant became an object of gossip and ill-tempered humour, and when the mood took itself into the streets - as it did for a few weeks in 1964 - he was the victim of 'paki-bashing'. Only if we enter into the heart of working class life can we understand these beliefs and actions. 'Paki-bashing' is a primitive form of political and economic struggle. It is an inarticulate and finally impotent attempt to act directly on the conditions of the market - whether the exchange value which is contested concerns housing, labour power or girls. When it is understood at an eye-to-eye level -which is where the local worker confronts the migrant - and not from the lofty distance of social policy makers, it can be seen for what it is: a rudimentary form of political action, and a sad and hopeless rage, which finds its specific location and rationality in the changing industrial base of the community.

A HISTORY FROM BELOW: TROUBLE AT T' MILL

Come all you cotton weavers, your looms you may pull down;
You must get employ'd in factories, in country or in town;
For our cotton-masters have found out a wonderful new scheme,
These calico goods now wove by hand they're going to weave by steam....

So, come all you cotton-weavers, you must rise up very soon,
For you must work in factories from morning until noon:
You mustn't walk in your gardens for two or three hours a-day.
For you must stand at their command, and keep your shuttles in play

(Nineteenth century ballad by John Grimshaw of Gorton: cf. Harland, 1882, pp. 188-9)

I have described paki-bashing in North East Lancashire as a response to cultural and economic change, and as an attempt to stamp a hold on the world. If so, then it must be located firmly as part of the history of working class life in the mill-towns. This history is not peaceful, and we can obtain a better grasp of the nature of working class hooliganism if we compare paki-bashing with the violent eruptions which brought the cotton towns to life.

There is no substantial written history of Accrington, and so we must reconstruct what we can out of the fragments and reminiscences which are available. (2) In the eighteenth century the few people who were scattered over North East Lancashire lived and worked by a combination of farming and weaving. The quickest glance at the dramatic growth of the towns from the beginning of the nineteenth century reminds us, once again, that they were built for King Cotton (see Table 3.3).

TABLE 3.3 Population and Housing in Accrington

	Population	Number of houses
1801	3,077	605
1831	6,283	1,206
1841	8,719	1,666
1851	10,376	-
1861	17,688	3,404
1878	c.28,650	5,729
1891	38,603	-
1911	45,000	-
1918	c.47,130	11,234
1928	43,190	11,851

(Sources: Singleton, 1928; Allen and Mattocks, 1950)

There are two kinds of history which can describe such periods of industrial expansion: the distinction is made by George Lefebvre. The first is a 'history from above', from the elevation of the committee room and the conference chamber. It tells the story of the founding fathers and captains of industry bringing factories, work, churches and civilized life to the area of

Accrington. It is the story of the men who 'built' the town - not with their hands, but with their money, their inventions and their business acumen. For example, the Hargreaves family who established Broad Oak Mill in 1837 also sponsored the building of a number of churches and schools, and built several impressive mansions for themselves. In the mid-nineteenth century, Benjamin Hargreaves employed nearly 2,000 workers at a time when the town was only 10,000 strong. In smaller towns it was not unknown for a mill-owner to be the sole employer - and the proprietor of a truck shop, and local magistrate into the bargain (cf. Aspin, 1969, p. 74). The Peel family was another dominant influence in Accrington - landowners, semi-official squires and factory owners, they were the family of Sir Robert Peel, Prime Minister of England. The Peels are also remembered in a 'history from above' as benefactors of the community. They established the Mechanics' Institute, churches and schools, and donated to the townspeople a hill called the Coppice, known as Peel Park. Although even that much is not true, and there are many holes which can be punched through a 'history from above'. The Peels had been an absent squirearchy for many years in the late nineteenth century, and in fact they gave only thirty-five acres of the Coppice to the town council, who bought a further sixty-five acres. And this was only a remnant of their estate. Before that, in 1889, the Peel family had leased their estate to James Bullock who demolished their family residence, Accrington House, and built grid-iron streets up to the point where the hill rises too sharply to make building easy. Crossley (1930, p. 13) writes that 'many monotonous rows of houses, and ugly streets took the place of what was once a beautiful park.' Even so, on 29 September 1909, 5,000 day scholars made a procession to the Coppice where one of the Peels presented each of them with a medal to commemorate the event. A 'history from above' is not unlike the history of a colonized people, written by the colonizers and not the colonized.

The second kind of history is a 'history from below' (cf. Lefebvre, 1974; Rudé, 1970). It tells of the changes which the mechanization of work, and the factory system of labour, forced onto the local people. In the eighteenth century a man would work for himself, or in his own home at pieces of cloth supplied by a master-clothier. His life-style is sometimes romanticized, and although the romantic picture of the small, independent family economy probably misses the truth, nevertheless the handloom weaver did have a certain independence of status and livelihood. Industrialization changed all this. From 1770 the land was enclosed, the number of landless artisans grew, and the life of the handloom weaver was placed under a series of threats (cf. Tupling, 1927, p. 201; Wadsworth and Mann, 1931, p. 321). The old trades lingered on for many years, but the mechanized factories finally displaced the handloom weaver. A history from above will probably forget to tell us this, and it will only say that it was from this area of Lancashire that the great inventors arrived - James Hargreaves, Richard Arkwright, Samuel Crompton and their spinning jennies, water-frames, mules, and carding machines.

If we simplify matters and telescope history, then as the cotton industry centralized and organized around machinery and mills, the handloom weaver was forced into an unthinkable poverty. Historians from above squabble about the extent of this poverty, and go so far as to suggest that the workers may not have been poor at all. The weight of the evidence, although the calculations are admittedly not easy in this 'standard of living' debate, is not on their side (cf. Hobsbawm, 1964, chs 5-7; Bythell, 1969, chs 5 and 6). The immiseration of the labouring population in Lancashire was, in fact, as much cultural as it was economic; and it was such that the myth of a 'golden age' grew among the people. The golden age of industrial cotton culture was still in the future, of course, and this golden age celebrated the poor handloom weaver - independent, learned, skilled and hard-working. Songs and ballads described his struggles over piece-rates with harsh masters, the threat of the new machines, and the lifeless disciplines of the new production processes (Craig, 1973, ch 3). As E.P. Thompson (1968, p. 316) has written, the conditions of the weavers from 1820 to 1840 are either said to be 'indescribable' or 'well known'; he adds that 'they deserve, however, to be described and to be better known.'

A history from below shows that men and women did not take easily to the new conditions of life and labour in the factories and towns. Men were fined for singing, swearing and whistling at their work. They started work at the sound of a bell, and stopped work at the sound of a bell. Their lives were no longer geared to the rhythms of the domestic economy, but to the external pace of the power-driven looms which Dickens (1969 edn, p. 65) called the 'Mad Elephants': the mills, he writes, were 'vast piles of building full of windows where there was a rattling and a trembling all day long, and where the piston of the steam-engine worked monotonously up and down, like the head of an elephant in a state of melancholy madness.' Men were tied to the machines in some cases by seven year contracts, and some were imprisoned for breaks of contract (cf. Aspin, 1963, p. 80). But perhaps the most alien domination in the factory was the domination of time. The factory clock ruled everything. Sometimes the clocks were crooked; they ran too slowly; or the hands were shifted to extract unpaid labour out of the workers; and some employers rigged up factory clocks to the looms so that if the loom ran slowly, the clock would go slowly, and the 'Hands' would stay at their work until the 'day' was properly finished (British Parliamentary Papers, 1968, 1st Report, pp. 17, 141-2, 2nd Report, pp. 2ff., 15-16; Aspin, 1969, pp. 68, 73; Engels, 1969 edn, pp. 207-8). It is not surprising, if one reflects on the changing conditions of life, that men rebelled against the industrial system which forced them into alien, external rhythms of life and work. What is only surprising is that they did not rebel more often, although they rebelled often enough.

The great power-loom smashings of 1826 began in Accrington. Accounts of what happened vary a little, but on 24 April a mob which had gathered at Enfield or at Whinny Hill marched on Sykes' Mill in Accrington with the intention of destroying it. Benjamin Hargreaves' brother, Robert, saw what happened by hiding behind a chimney (Hargreaves, 1882, p. 42). The first thing to go was the clock which hung in the passage, smashed by a woman.

There had been trouble at the mill, which used power-looms, for some days. William Varley of Higham, a country calico weaver, wrote in his diary on 18 April 1826: 'There is a great disturbance at Accrington; they break the windows where the steam looms are; the country is all of an uproar for the poor weaver has neither work nor bread' (Bennett, 1948, appendix; cf. Bythell, 1969, p. 200). Benjamin Hargreaves, who fancied himself as a writer, says that after breaking the clock there was 'an onslaught on the looms with crowbars and sledge-hammers. These disappeared like pottery ware, and all was finished in the way of destruction.' Hargreaves (1882, p. 42) described the events as 'one of those wild theorisms that overhwelm all reason, like the out-pourings of a volcano, that the power-loom (then just coming into use) was destroying the handloom weaver.' The wild theorism moved off in the direction of Blackburn, having destroyed 158 looms in Accrington, where two mills were completely destroyed and troops killed some men. According to Bennett (1948, p. 286) 'by nightfall, there was not a single power-loom left standing within six miles of Blackburn.' The uprising continued for three days throughout most of North East Lancashire and more than a thousand looms were destroyed.

We must place these events in a firm political perspective. The machine-smashers of 1826 were no more inspired by a coherent political philosophy than the paki-bashers of 1964: what their action signified, in both instances, was the most rudimentary from of resistance from below to the forces which they imagined were changing their lives. Such resistance had a strong, if fitful, career in the cotton industry from the late eighteenth century until the 1840s. The earliest signs of resistance came against James Hargreaves who invented the spinning-jenny in the mid-1760s at Stanhill, Oswaldtwistle. The early history of the jenny is surrounded in obscurity, and Hargreaves was probably attacked (together with his machines) on more than one occasion (cf. Aspin and Chapman, 1964, ch. 1). However, in 1768 his house was ransacked and the jennies destroyed, and Hargreaves - according to some accounts - was forced to run away to Nottingham . His patron, Robert 'Parsley' Peel, had established Brookside Mill nearby in 1760 and, because he had begun to use the jenny in his factory, it was also attacked and destroyed in 1768. Peel rebuilt the mill, and in 1770 he built another at Altham. In 1779 the Altham mill was attacked, burnt to the ground, and the jennies thrown into the river. Mills could have short lives in the early industrial revolution: Sykes' Mill, where the 1826 riots began, had been established in 1821. After the destruction of the Altham mill, 'Parsley' Peel reckoned he had had enough and 'retired in disgust to Burton-upon-Trent, where he built a large mill', hoping that things were quieter in the midlands (W. Cooke Taylor, n.d., vol. 1, p. 8).

Lofty judgments that these outbursts (and there were many more) were the acts of ignorant and deluded hooligans rest uneasily against the fact that the rioters were most discriminating in their attacks on machinery. According to Chapman (1904, p. 76) jennies with less than twenty spindles were spared, because they were thought to be a 'fair machine' which could be used in cottages. In some cases jennies with more than twenty spindles were not wrecked, but were simply cut down to size.

Trouble continued through and beyond the 1826 power-loom smashings. The 'golden age' of the handloom weaver took a long time dying. As late as the 1840s, for example, Chartists around Burnley (full of another 'wild theorism' that each working man should have a small-holding) were staking out Pendle Hill for just that purpose; thus resistance to the machine took many forms. But in one sense the handloom weaver had probably got it quite wrong. Thompson (1968, p. 309) writes, for example, that 'it is an oversimplification to ascribe the cause of the weaver's conditions to the power looms.' Trade slumps were more likely to be the causes of his distress and the outbreaks of violence, in some cases, follow closely to the periods of slump.

It is not enough, however, to say that the new looms would eventually benefit the weavers, or that they were misguided in their choice of targets against which to express their resistance. The Hammonds (1919, p. 53) express the problem particularly well when they write: 'Men and women who see their livelihood taken away from them or threatened by some new invention, can hardly be expected to grow enthusiastic over the public benefits of inventive genius. A larger view and a vivid imagination may teach them that the loss to their particular occupation may be temporary only; but, then, as it has been remarked, man's life is temporary also.'

Eric Hobsbawm (1971, 1972) calls those men who resist from below in an inarticulate, sometimes hooligan fashion, 'primitive rebels' - men who have not yet found, or who are only beginning to find, a mature political voice in which to express and act upon their grievances. The background to the hooliganism of the early nineteenth century was, in fact, a growing sense of political strategy; and a new identity among men who perhaps had been jolted into awareness by industrial capitalism. Out of this locality emerged an astonishing number of social, political, religious and educational movements - the political radicalism of the Chartists, model employers with their model factories and schools, Wesleyan Methodism, mechanics' institutes and free libraries, and the co-operative movement. The family was also involved in a massive re-structuring during this time (cf. Smelser, 1959). In fact we can say that the whole basis of cotton culture was established in this period of transformation in which the golden age of the handloom weaver was pushed aside by the power of wealth and industry. Cotton culture, of course, was to enter its own crisis later and regret its own golden age: thus machine-smashing and paki-bashing both emerge at points of cultural and economic dislocation as a primitive resistance by men (as often as not young men) who cannot define what it is that they are resisting.

Just as the industrial upheavals of the post-war period produced a need for immigrant labour in the cotton industry, waves of Irish immigration to Lancashire from the 1820s onwards reproduced the familiar enough pattern of the migrant worker (cf. Redford, 1926). Many of the growing cotton towns had a 'Little Ireland' - a ghetto of the poorest and the most downtrodden. The place of the Irish was hotly contested, and for a number of reasons. Irish migrant workers were feared and hated by locals as potential (and actual) strike-breakers, and employers used the Irish to 'equalize' (that is, lower) wages. Elizabeth Gaskell's account in 'North and South' of the importation of Irish workers as blacklegs (or knobsticks) to break a cotton strike is thus accurate social history, and not the imagining of a novelist (cf. Redford, 1926, pp. 139-40). It was also widely held that Irish weavers, who were accustomed to a lower standard of living, were dragging down the English labourer towards a state of bestiality (cf. Carlyle, 1840, ch 4; Kay-Shuttleworth, 1970 edn, p. 21; Engels, 1969 edn, pp. 122ff.). The alien dress and language of the Irish further marked them out. Once more in keeping with the role of the migrant worker, the Irish were used in the lowest grades of employment. Redford (1926, p. 131) records, for example, that there were not more than 100 Irish working as spinners (a well paid job) in all Lancashire, although there were thousands of Irish in the county. Thus prejudice built out of religion, race and economics was at a high pitch against the Irish throughout the nineteenth century (cf. Curtis, 1968, 1971). At the time of the massive immigration to the Lancashire cotton towns, Thomas Carlyle (1840, p. 29) passed a bitter judgment on the management of the Irish question: 'The Irish population must either be improved a little, or else exterminated', and we find little record of any sympathy existing between the English and Irish workers. Where employed together, they often had to be kept apart. There were frequent fights and riots with the Irish (Jackson, 1963, ch 8; Redford, 1926; O'Connor, 1972, pp. 11-19, 31ff.). The streets in which they lived were sometimes attacked by gangs of youths, and some instances sound very much like nineteenth century 'paddy-bashings' (e.g., Aspin, 1963, pp. 132-3).

Thus different forms of working class hooliganism surround, and are responses to, moments of cultural and economic dislocation. The interpretations of such events from 'above' or 'below' clash fiercely. From 'above' things tend to look senseless, and elevated judgments will also sometimes try and define as 'hooliganism', 'riotous behaviour' or 'mob law' even the most rational forms of working class resistance - for example, the strike. The last widespread outburst of industrial hooliganism in Lancashire, the Plug Riots of 1842, are a case in point. The 'Plug Riots' were so named because striking workers entered factories and withdrew the plugs from the boilers, thus extinguishing the boiler fires and stopping all work at the factory. Sporadic rioting and fighting took place over a few weeks of the hot summer of 1842 and reached most of the industrial towns of Lancashire and Cheshire. Young boys and men were often the chief troublemakers, although their elders looked on with approval. As a strike, the affair was an almost total failure (cf. Rose, 1957).

Benjamin Hargreaves, whose Broad Oak Mill at Accrington was visited by rioters, had to admit that it was an ingenious and effective way of stopping work and enforcing a strike - he called it a 'handicraftsman sort of work'. But he also wrote in his memoirs: 'I have never heard the true cause of this "plug-drawing"', and added 'but, no doubt, it was distress' (Hargreaves, 1882, p. 61). At the time there were frequent meetings on Sundays on the moors outside the towns. According to an estimate in the 'Liverpool Mercury', at one such meeting outside Accrington 26,000 people had gathered, and 'they say they may as well die by the sword as by hunger' (Newbigging, 1893, p. 325). There had been disturbances for some time in the locality, and the Chartists only a couple of years earlier had routed the police at Colne on more than one occasion (cf. Bennett, 1948, p. 288). And in Accrington, where Benjamin Hargreaves from the elevation of Oak Hill House, Broad Oak House, Arden Hall and Bank House had 'never heard the true cause of this "plug-drawing"', Fay (1920, p. 178) reports that of its population of 9,000 no more than 100 were fully employed in 1842, and that 'numbers kept themselves alive by collecting nettles and boiling them down'. W. Cooke Taylor (1968 edn, p. 107) also found on his tour of the cotton towns at this time that Accrington was badly depressed.

Benjamin Hargreaves was described in the 'Accrington Guardian' of 29 November 1879 as 'a patron saint of the poor'. The issue of the 'Journal of Design and Manufactures' of 1850 in which Hargreaves had described the great success of his manufacturing principles, also closed with an editorial comment on the man's fine character and thanked him for his enterprise. In the copy of the original publication which is kept in Accrington Public Library, the eulogy has been carefully and deliberately obliterated in ruled ink which is now fading: an anonymous hand, an obscure message, in a 'history from above' just another mindless act of vandalism smudging the glorious history of the cotton trade.

THE TOWN TALKS TO ITSELF IN ITS SLEEP

Eawr parish-church pa'son's kept tellin' us lung,
We'st see better toimes, if aw'd but howd my tung;
Aw've howden my tung, till aw con hardly draw breoth
Aw think i' my heart he meons t' clem me to deoth;
Aw knaw he lives weel, wi' backbitin' the de'il,
But he never pick'd o'er in his loife
(Jone O'Grinfilt Junior, circa 1815; Harland, 1882, p. 169)

In response to an outbreak of machine-smashing in 1812 the 'Manchester Mercury' reached for what has become a familiar enough phrase for slapping down and shrugging off the implications of working-class hooliganism: it compared it with 'the very Goths and Vandals of antiquity' (Bythell, 1969, p. 198). From a position of elevation, paki-bashing and machine-smashing are senseless, wanton, pointless acts of vandalism - a pest to be exterminated. They are also the kind of acts which cause a compassionate liberalism to forget its compassion, and to view them as ignorant social nuisances which interrupt the steady progress of race relations, industrial development, or whatever. This is the language of the policy-maker and the preacher, and if ignorance is what is at issue it is they who are ignorant: as the old song 'Jone O'Grinfilt Junior' puts it, it is the language of someone who never 'pick'd o'er' (worked the shuttle) in his life, a language which is both ignorant and distant from the realities of the mass of working people.

I have tried to give a voice to the working-class paki-basher of North East Lancashire, to give that voice a critical bearing, and place his activity alongside some of the working class hooliganism of an earlier industrial era. He is a 'primitive rebel', and the primitive rebel directs his fury against culturally prescribed symbols of cultural and economic decay. Traditional criminological and psychiatric viewpoints, however, think of him as a man cursed by a chromosome defect, or warped by a quirk in his personality. But those are useless ways to grasp his biography which do not even explain why he is beating up Pakistanis, and not throwing milk bottles at cats. In a similar manner, Neil Smelser (1959, pp. 227, 246) is content to put machine-breaking down as 'a relaxation of the most basic controls over socialized behaviour' and 'violent and bizarre symptoms of disturbance'. But we must ask, 'un-socialized' according to whose standards? The machine-smashers sometimes carefully avoided what they defined as 'fair' machines, and by the standards of their own culture they were acting in accordance with a scheme of heroism and in defence of a golden age which led them to risk life and limb in order to protect life as they knew it. If machines appear to threaten the lives of working men, we must not be surprised if men knock them about a bit; and if migrant workers become the culture's symbol of industrial malaise, we should not be surprised if they suffer a similar fate: the logic is the same in both cases, although it is a primitive logic which fails to get at the roots of the problem.

The official response to paki-bashing and machine-smashing is not only wholesale condemnation, however, and the 'societal reaction' contains an awkward tension. The point about such primitive resistance from below is that it finds its rationality in the culture which is under threat, and the official response to this sort of hooliganism (although not other sorts) is therefore not directly repressive, but confused and embarrassed. Primitive rebellion is embarrassing and perplexing precisely because it says something which reasonable men might feel, but not want to hear.

We must try and imagine the town talking to itself in its sleep in the summer of 1964: were these paki-bashing thugs the children of cotton culture? And yet, at the same time, who could blame them? Various solutions to this embarrassing dilemma were peddled about: it was all the work of outside rowdies, boisterous youngsters who had nothing better to do, or yobboes who found it amusing. The very direct form of resistance which paki-bashing represents, of course, is not the form of resistance preferred by the respectable citizen of cotton culture. His resistance can be violently felt, as Seabrook's (1973) study emply shows, but it remains a verbal response. Paki-bashing belongs instead to the 'rough' element of the working class. This is also the cultural milieu of the migrant worker himself, and it comes as no surprise therefore to find that the man who was killed in the initial brawl (the one which sparked off Accrington's troubles) was a white migrant worker - from Scotland. Arrests and convictions amplified matters, and two of the three men arrested on the first night of trouble were also Scottish migrant workers. These 'foreigners' both received prison sentences, while the local lad was sent home, and the magistrate took the opportunity to make a speech about how 'we are not having you people coming here and upsetting this town, not for anything.' He also made two other significant, and embarrassing, statements. First, about Pakistanis who had been attacked: 'We must protect people, whoever they may be....' And, then, to the convicted migrant workers in the dock: 'If you cannot stop this kind of behaviour, get back to where you came from.' In a small town, puzzled and confused by black faces which it had never seen before except as mascot cricketers, there was little doubt about who it was who should 'go back where they came from' and who needed protecting from what.

My impression is that Accrington has tried to forget its embarrassing culture leak which caused cotton culture to look into itself, its own suspicion of the Pakistani as a symbol of new times and low-cost import goods, and the common-sense knowledge of the community that 'pakis' were an odd lot and troublemakers. This was coupled (embarrassment always implies a contradiction, a blushing sense of being in two places at the same time) with a knowledge that paki-bashing was ugly, dangerous and very, very immoral. But who knows how many people in Accrington had thought much about the Pakistanis, or of how they were taking our houses, stealing our jobs and pinching our women? The census certainly does not show it. My impression, for what it is worth, is that in 1964 there was a low-key suspicion of Pakistanis in the town, just a ripple of modest confusion, and about twenty different jokes in circulation which took the 'paki' as the butt, the villain and the clown. There was a current of feeling, and paki-bashing was an awkward realization of some of the worst jokes. I did not find paki-bashing a terribly odd thing to meet on my way home from work in the summer of 1964: I would have found a battle between two rival gangs of white youths in the street something much more exceptional.

The societal reaction to machine-smashing shows the same awkward, ambivalent features. After each outbreak of resistance there were, of course, directly preventive and repressive measures: garrisons were built, roads and prisons were improved, and factories were sometimes defended with cannon and in one instance with a moat. But repression was not the main feature of social reaction. Repeatedly, either light sentences were passed on offenders, or no action was taken at all. There was considerable sympathy for the handloom weaver and it was possible to openly defend the principle of eliminating machinery, without fear of arrest or punishment. On one occasion (although it was only one) a magistrate took an official position against machinery and in favour of hand-work. The government, however, ruled on the side of the masters who introduced the machines. Even so, not all the masters supported the machines and some of the small masters feared them as much as the handloom weaver himself (cf. Hobsbawm, 1964, ch 2). W. Cooke Taylor, Peel's biographer, complained bitterly about 'those who ought to have known better' who egged on 'ignorant operatives' to break Parsley Peel's spinning jennies and destroy his mills. Not only the fear of competition was at work here: in that day there was also a fear that machinery would cause what we would now call redundancies, and send up the cost of what they called the Poor Rates (W. Cooke Taylor, n.d., p. 8). After the 1826 power-loom riots Robert Peel also had to rebuke local magistrates for their reluctance to take prompt action against the weavers - whether he was motivated as a politician, or as a man with capital and estates in cotton towns, is just another embarrassment in this complex web of politicking. The point about primitive rebels is that they do represent the interests of certain fractions within the community and its culture and economic organization, and consequently they embarrass the authorities.

The debate over the machine raged for many years. Long-winded utilitarians such as Dr Andrew Ure (1861) defended machinery and factories as a fine economic and moral principle; whereas Gaskell (1836) condemned machinery as demoralizing and dehumanizing. Volumes of Blue Books and parliamentary reports made their appearance, some of them very fine documents. But it was Charles Dickens (1969 edn, pp. 222, 238), predictably and to his credit, whose critical eye saw the human dimension of what he called this 'parliamentary cinder-heap': 'sifting and sifting ... without being observed to turn up many precious articles among the rubbish', diligent reformers 'hard at it in the national dust-yard ... the national dust-men ... entertaining one another with a great many noisy little fights among themselves'. The sense of outrage which we feel in Dickens' writing found a non-literary expression among the people, and periodically the machine-smashers entered the debate with their direct line of attack. In the 'Accrington Observer' of 20 December 1890 an old man is reported to have kept as an heirloom an instrument said to have been used in the earliest attacks on the jennies: 'a cross between a big drumstick and a huge sledge hammer, consisting of an iron ball of ten pounds weight, perforated so as to admit an ash bough four feet long and two inches thick ... manufactured for the purpose of smashing spinning jenny wherever she could be found.' These were not gentle men by any means. A local form of prize-fighting, known as 'purring', is said by Aspin (1969, p. 103) to have involved fighting almost naked with specially made 'bovver boots' which were 'heavily toed with iron and studded with jagged nails so as to tear skin and flesh away at every kick'. And a man who had lost an ear (which he kept in his waistcoat pocket) in a fight, when advised to take legal action against the man who injured him, is reported to have said: 'Noa, noa, aw'st do nowt at soart; it was a fair gradely stand-up battle, un aw want nother law nor warrant' (Aspin, 1969, p. 104).

If we can call machine-smashing a form of direct-action hooliganism, however, we can also call it a form of heroism. On the way to Sykes' Mill at Accrington in 1826, before they committed what Bythell (1969, p. 198) calls their 'blind act of vandalism', the rioters were stopped by troops - the most concrete embodiment of the social control apparatus. The story is told by a 16 year-old handloom weaver from Haslingden - one of the rowdies from out of town - who is said to have 'turned the grindstone on which the rioters sharpened their pikes' (Aspin, 1969, p. 48). The troops did not turn back the mob. When they heard the weavers' complaints and sufferings, they opened their knapsacks and gave their food to the rioters. 'Then the soldiers left and there was another meeting. Were the power-looms to be broken or not? Yes, it was decided, they must be broken at all costs.'

I have described the young hooligan of 1826 as a hooligan who was also a hero. No doubt he would have told a diligent sociologist of 'youth culture' that, 'When you get some long stick in your 'and, and you're smashing a loom in, you don't think about it much.' What of the paki-basher? The story would be different outside North East Lancashire - in East London, Birmingham, or Bradford. It has been my intention to bring alive the mood of what the mis-directed heroism of the paki-basher speaks to his culture about, and to show how 'paki-bashing', the crisis of cotton culture in North East Lancashire, the evaporation of its industrial base, and the disappearance of Accrington's football team should be understood as different elements of the same dislocation of the lives of working men, both young and old. We can hardly describe paki-bashing as a 'youth problem'. But whenever there was bother, Edwin Chadwick (1842, p. 202) noted in his 'Report on the Sanitary Conditions of the Labouring Population', in the form of riots, hooliganism and mobism, the greatest havoc was always caused by 'mere boys'.

ACKNOWLEDGMENTS

I owe thanks to Joseph King, General Secretary of the Amalgamated Textile Workers' Union, the staff of Accrington Public Library, my parents and numerous friends in North East Lancashire. Without their help, suggestions and memories this study would have missed a great deal.

NOTES

1 The best coverage of paki-bashing incidents in the 1969-71 period is found in 'Race Today' from the vol. 2, no. 5 (1970) issue, through to vol. 3, no. 10 (1971). The journal includes both comment and a break-down of newspaper coverage across the UK.
2 There is a rich jumble of sources in Accrington Public Library, some of which I have used: a social survey of 'New Accrington' conducted in 1790; the 'Manual of the Oak Street Congregational Church' from 1880 onwards; T. Hargreaves, 'The Rise and Progress of Wesleyan Methodism in Accrington' (Hepworth, Accrington, 1883); B. Hargreaves, The Rise and Progress of Great Manufactories, by the Proprietors: Messrs. Hargreaves' Calico Print Works at Broad Oak, Accrington, 'Journal of Design and Manufactures', vol. 13, 1850; Hargreaves (1882); Whittaker (1909); J.T. Lawrence, 'A Short History of St. James's Church and Parish, Accrington' (Hepworth, Accrington, 1903). There are also histories of neighbouring towns and localities, for example: D. Hogg, 'A History of Church and Oswaldtwistle' (2 vols: 1760-1860; 1860-1914) (Accrington and

District Local History Society, 1971 and 1973); Aspin (1963); Bennett (1948); Crossley (1930); Newbigging (1893); R. Trappes-Lomax, 'A History of the Township and Manor of Clayton-le-Moors' (Chetham Society, Manchester, 1926); Tupling (1927). Finally, there are more general texts which touch on the experiences of the working class in the early industrial revolution in Lancashire. These are cited in the text and can be found in the full bibliography. The most obvious are Aspin (1969) which is less well-known and particularly recommended, the Hammonds (1919), Chapman (1904), Wadsworth and Mann (1931), Redford (1926), Fay (1920), Thompson (1968), Hobsbawm (1964, 1969), Bythell (1969), Smelser (1959) and Craig (1973).

Chapter 4

YOUTH IN PURSUIT OF ITSELF

Geoff Mungham

INTRODUCTION

Youth In Pursuit Of Itself is a study of youth and of the regulation of youth at the dance-hall. The study is not of dancing as such; nor is it about any one dance-hall in particular. It is, instead, about a particular type of dance-hall and that segment of youth which patronizes them. What we are concerned with here is the scenario of the 'mass-dance', the youth who frequent them and with some of those who manage and supervise the halls. In Britain, the typical purveyors of the mass-dance are the Rank Organisation (with its 'Top Rank Suites') and the Mecca Group (represented by the 'Mecca Ballrooms'). Under their auspieces the organization of the dance is - especially in the case of Rank - merely a single branch of a more general corporate activity.

There is no doubt that the mass-dance scene is big business even today, despite the drift of some of their youth clientele to other kinds of dance and club centres (a movement I try and explain later). The youth who are drawn to the mass-dance do not really go to soak up a particular kind of music - other than that which goes under the generic label of 'popular' - or because their friends go there, but in order to 'meet people', the usual euphemism, in this context, for a chance to chat-up or be chatted-up by a member of the opposite sex. More than anything else, the mass-dance is the forum for what might be called 'mainstream' working class youth. Their convergence on Friday or Saturday nights in the 'suite' or 'ballroom' resembles a sort of ersatz community characterized by what Riesman (1954) has called a 'compulsive conformity', defined in terms of an intolerance of deviations in dress, appearance, personal mannerisms or musical experimentation. This fetishism of solidarity is reinforced at every turn by the management of the halls who, to paraphrase Seabrook (1973) assume that everyone is the same, socially, emotionally, sexually, and subject to precisely the same desires and wants, which can be satisfied in a fixed and identical way. And as we shall see, those who do not fit or who try to resist this moral calculus are either excluded or ejected.

It has been argued that the mass-dance has seen its best days as a popular phenomenon, but there would seem to be no agreement about the time of death or its causes. Some have sought its peak years in the 1920s; others have insisted upon the period immediately after the Second World War, and there have been those who have located the summit of its achievements in the early 1960s, when the Rank and Mecca Organisations were building suites and ballrooms all over Britain. My interpretation is rather different; it is not that I consider these obituaries are premature but that they have to be regarded as highly misleading, if not actually irrelevant. This is principally because the comment about 'peaks' has been of the kind where those concerned have been talking about very different dance phenomena. But for the moment we can note the continuing popularity of the mass-dance; most people still meet their eventual marriage partner at one, moreover very few dance-halls are ever closed (unlike cinemas) and never find it necessary to ask for subsidies (unlike the theatre) in order to operate.

In the course of this paper I will come to endorse some of the major theoretical themes in the book (e.g. the importance of retaining the concept of 'class' when studying youth culture, the deeply ingrained conservatism of youth, the need to look at conforming youth as a counter-balance to that work which has taken up the more conspicuous and 'pathological' aspects of youth behaviour), but this support only emerges incidentally. I test no hypotheses in this essay, preferring instead to give an account of a significant piece of popular cultural activity of our time. Finally, the methodology of this work should hold no fears for the reader, although as researcher I was more than once terrorized by my sample of 'respondents'. The fieldwork was a combination of participant observation at the dance itself, and talks with various members of dance-hall staff (managers, bar-staff and bouncers) past and present. The interviewing was easily done, but talking to youth itself - at the dance - was a more hazardous project. The reasons for this were elemental; first, it's difficult to hear anything anybody says in a dance-hall where the music and the crush is relentless; second, conversation is anyway heavily circumscribed by conventions about what may be properly talked about; third, the setting up of any contacts has to be elaborately stage managed. Thus unless some preparatory work is done, trying to strike up a conversation with a girl you've never seen before may result in your being physically assaulted by her boyfriend and his mates. On the other side, attempts at conversation with blokes is made difficult by the fact that they tend to arrive and spend the evenings in groups - only splitting off if they manage to find a girl who is willing to be taken home by them. Consequently, attempts to break into these cliques is most likely to be met by threats ('why don't you piss off') or ridicule ('what d'you want then? You a fucking queer or somethin'?') The last difficulty was of a different order. Establishing a contact under these conditions was only the beginning of it. As Seabrook pointed out when he was collecting accounts of life and work from working class people in Blackburn, 'If people are asked about their opinions, they assume that they ought to have some, and obligingly evolve them on the spot' (1973, p. 47). In the event, the dance-hall never became my graveyard and it did prove possible to get accounts that seemed genuine and authentic. If anybody doubts this claim, then I can only suggest some replication studies are done. While I doubt if it will prove feasible to construct a better methodology I can, at least, quite safely predict that any who follow on will have a good time in trying to go one better. This, in itself, is no small recommendation, so long as those who do it are not of the kind who feel guilty if they start to enjoy their work.

In this next section I look at some of the literature on participation in dancing. This is followed by the presentation of 'field' observations and the paper closes with some general remarks on how this piece of empirical work bears upon some of the theoretical controversies in the study of youth culture.

IMAGES OF THE DANCE

While various histories of dancing have been written, the majority of these dwell upon the form of the dance and say little about the context of the dance as a social event. Similarly few books on either 'leisure' or working class culture have much to say concerning the social significance of dancing and dance-halls. Books dealing with 'leisure', for example, usually remain silent about dance activity unless this comes in the guise of 'folk' dancing, where comment - always favourable - may help serve as a preservation order, rather than as a critique of culture. The uncritical attention given to the folk dance - and to the 'folk' music that aids in sustaining it - is ironical. Both effectively parody their origins, becoming increasingly limp maneouvres around an absent centre, namely the notion of 'folk' itself. As Adorno has written of its music: 'Folk music /is/ no longer alive, because the spontaneous 'Volk' /has/ been consumed in a process that left popular music, like all popular culture, the creature of manipulation and imposition from above' (Jay, 1974, p. 185). Propped up by every kind of artificial device the folk-dance too becomes part of the urban junk shop. The only other gesture made towards dancing as an activity by authors of books on leisure, is to sometimes categorize it as a 'pursuit' favoured by X per cent in a table listing teenage leisure interests. Such books typically tell us about leisure patterns, but provide few clues as to why people do the things they do. Hence for dancing we can find data on numbers who do it, at what age, of what sex - but we are no nearer to finding out what actually happens inside a dance-hall and why people flock to them.

Not that books and articles on youth culture or working class culture, specifically, do very much better in this respect. Where the two themes are fused as they are in studies of working class youth culture, descriptions of the dance appear only fleetingly as 'background' material. The phenomenon of the dance is commonly regarded as of no interest in its own right. Not surprisingly perhaps, references - no matter how brief - to dancing, which are inserted into more general accounts of working class youth culture, are often the only way that girls get introduced into these surveys. As we pointed out before (cf. Introduction) those fragmentary studies of working class youth culture have made the term 'youth' practically synonymous with male activity. If nothing else, this equation tells us a lot about the general orientation of such studies in British culture. An orientation, that is, towards the extreme, the conspicuous, the pathological and the bizarre. This is a theme I shall return to in the closing section of this paper, but for the moment we can note that the sympathetic orientation with the 'rebel', the 'resister', with those who try to 'break out' in some way - which leads writers on working class youth culture in the direction of gang activity and the more visible 'trouble' phenomena such as soccer hooliganism - will always effectively exclude the study of working class girls. They, to use Rowbotham's (1974) term, still remain hidden from history; the study of working class youth culture so far has done little to balance accounts.

The neglect of the dance sits strangely at odds with the fact of its evident popularity among working class youth. Kerr, for example, in her study of a slice of working class culture, noted how

> Dancing is extremely popular with the girls until marriage, when it is dropped at once. Sometimes when Marian, aged 22, sees her sister getting ready to go to a dance she is envious ... Marian used to be very keen on dancing too, but she and her husband never go dancing now they are married (1958, p. 32).

How can we account for this interest? In the introduction to this book we wrote 'when social scientists and welfare professionals turn their eyes on the adolescent, they somehow forget their own youth.' Only by delving into those old memories can we hope to come up with something approximating to the plausible. So far, the most inspired guesses for the popularity of the dance comes from the 'litterateur'. W.B. Yeats once wrote, 'I am still of the opinion that only two topics can be of least interest to a serious and studious mind - sex and death.' The activity of the dance-hall is to a large extent a play upon the former. Youth in pursuit of itself turns the dance into a convention of courtship, dating and sexual bargaining. The mass-dance is electric with it, and we can measure the obsession through the amount of time given over to preparing for the dance, the peculiar drama and tension in the dance-hall which is ubiquitous.

Very little of this comes through from the standard social science account of the dance. While some scraps about dancing as a 'social activity' appear in studies of working class culture, such as those by Dennis (1956), Jackson (1972) and Kerr, undoubtedly the best - even if fictionalized - descriptions have come from novelist-observers of the working class scene like Barstow (1962) and Sillitoe (1970). Perhaps the only exceptions to this judgment are to be found in the work of authors represented by Roberts (1973) and Tom Wolfe (1969) who, in very different ways - which I shall refer to again later - have tried to link their analysis of dance activity with wider structural and cultural changes in society. Roberts, in particular, puts forward what might be termed a kind of 'market model' for explaining changes in the organization of the dance and of the behaviour of youth who went to them. For Roberts, the 'market' was defined by the search for a marriage partner. The dance-hall was the forum where initial bargains were most likely to be struck. Roberts wrote of the 'explosive dancing boom' that followed the First World War, in Britain. One result of the war, apart from throwing up the dance boom, was also to create a strained social situation for its practice. The key factor which 'distorted' the 'market' was the demography of death, the price of the war itself. (1) As Roberts put it:

> Nowhere in the land were Great Britain's 1¾ million surplus women more in evidence than at the dance halls. There, when every available male had found a partner, blocs of girls either still flowered the walls or had paired themselves off in resignation to dance with each other ... plenty of working-class girls, in their efforts to 'beat the market', went well beyond the tenets laid down by mothers. Some, we knew, dared all and failed: others got their man with a pregnancy.... And the wise boys with their 'self-protectors' went on happily dancing in a city littered with 'common' halls (1971, pp. 233-5).

Finally, we can note these studies which have explored the institutional and symbolic functions of the dance and dance activity. There have been those who, like Halmos (1969), have seen in the decline of particular modes of dancing a sign of the withering away of certain core social values. Others, following writers such as Dennis have viewed the dance, in their studies of communities, as a totem of community celebration, as another tangible expression of the vitality of community. At the same time, various anthropologists and ethnographers, including Mitchell (1956) and Oliver (1972), have discussed the use of the dance among colonial peoples as a form of symbolic resistance and protest, or as a device for subtly ridiculing the appropriator and oppressor. (2) But this takes us a long way from our present concern, and it is to the observation of the 'mass-dance' in British working class youth culture that I now turn.

THE DANCE: STEP ONE - REGULATION

The spontaneity of the mass-dance is closely guarded. Any small claim to individuality on the dance floor, is discouraged by those who guard the halls. Spontaneity is regarded by managers and their staff - principally the bouncers - as the potential hand-maiden of rebellion. For this reason, the history of the mass-dance is characterized by a tightening of its conformist elements. This insistence, by the staff, on propriety and 'respectability', is captured in the following two descriptive moments of a popular dance in process. It is worth noting that the two accounts are separated by more than thirty years, but the mood they suggest is the same.

> In his way our MC (backed by two large chuckers-out) was a stickler for decorum. All dancers had to perform in a seemly manner: the standard of the habitues was high indeed. He ... came down heavily on any males gyrating as they

> smoked, or with their hats on. That, he felt, lowered the tone (Roberts, 1973, p. 234).

> The place is chock full like Willy said and there's a big crowd just inside the door. I work my way through and edge across the corner of the floor, nearly getting bowled over by a couple prancing about in a kind of private war-dance.... They don't like jiving and rock n' roll and whatnot at the Gala Rooms and they have notices up saying so. Sure enough, while I'm still there, the M.C. comes up and taps the cove on the shoulder and says something to him. They both give him a killing look and switch to a straightforward quickstep, Gala Rooms style (Barstow, 1962, p. 33).

The clinging to order and, above all, respectability - the touchstone of the entire enterprise - is mirrored best of all in the peculiar packaging of the 'front-line' dance hall staff, the bouncers or chuckers-out. These vergers of the dance, usually with arms like fire-hydrants and built hugely out of proportion to the average sized working class youth, were always referred to as 'ballroom attendants' by the dance hall managers I spoke to. Their immediate supervisor also carried a title that had a slight Ruritanian flavour to it, namely 'Chief-of-Staff' and was responsible for co-ordinating the activities of the 'attendants' (the attempt to dignify the world of the dance is further suggested by the adoption of terms like 'suite' and 'ballroom', never 'dance-hall'). All of them - supervisor and staff - were obliged to wear a dinner suit when on duty, or at least a neat dark outfit topped off with a bow-tie. Together, their task was to scrutinize those coming into the dance and keep a general eye on them once they were inside.

Deciding who was to be let in and who was not, always posed difficulties. In the first place, the management insists that male youth wear suits. The theory here being that those who take the trouble to put one on, will be the kind of nice lads who won't start fighting and causing trouble once inside, but instead will spend the time admiring themselves and peacably pursuing girls. This interpretation was fiercely defended to me, despite the mountain of evidence that seemed, weekly, to contradict it. When enflamed by a few brown ales or whatever it did not seem to matter whether male youth wore a suit or battle-dress in terms of their willingness to have a go at anyone deemed to have caused them offence. The usual flash-points for conflict being either the competition for a girl, or arising out of the 'challenge' of being 'looked at'. (3) In this context (and elsewhere, too) one male who catches the eye of another, or who is conscious of being stared at by another male, will not infrequently abuse or threaten the looker. This invasion of what is taken to be personal space can provoke some of the most violent sentiments of machismo. As a result, men in these situations learn to avoid these kind of eye contacts, as they also learn to avoid looking at a girl who 'belongs' to another man, unless they want to deliberately cause conflict. Normally, as we know, to catch the eye of a stranger often causes momentary embarrassment or discomfort, but the 'offender' will quickly turn away and the incident is forgotten as soon as possible. Not so, often, at the mass-dance. With the result that elaborate and in a sense incongruous - given the large numbers and limited space of the dance-hall - avoidance mechanisms are evolved by those who understand the language and cues of the culture of the dance floor. On the other side, fights between girls are very rare; partly because they are usually outnumbered by men and therefore are more competed for, than competing. And partly because physical conflict between them is heavily proscribed by respectable working class male youth. Their condemnation also extended to the use of 'strong' language by girls at the dance. Many of the males were genuinely shocked and disgusted by girls who swore strongly. Their reaction was uniform and strict on this point; 'it's not decent', 'it's common', 'you lose your respect for them', 'it's alright for fellas, but I dunno, it's not very nice when you hear it from birds is it?' There was a lot more in this vein; the intolerance of working class youth on this issue is, to a large extent, a product of strong matriarchical family structures, where the women - especially the mother - are simultaneously patronized and revered. Two other points remain to be mentioned about their attitudes; in the first place, they were taken up and defended by the girls themselves, who happily accepted the dominant definition of 'common decency' and 'niceness'. Second, that this complex of attitudes is deeply rooted in working class culture generally, is shown in the large number of studies which have mentioned its persistence.

Returning more specifically to the regulation of the dance, perhaps the major problem for the 'Chief-of-Staff' and his retinue, lies in deciding who, from the general crush on a Friday or Saturday night, should be granted entry to the dance-hall. Clearly, a process of self-selection operates, which means that most of the youth who are prepared to present themselves to regulation 'smartness' are let in. Most, that is, but not all. Like all custodians of the respectable, the management draw upon various folk stereotypes as well as their own prejudices when making a distinction between the respectable and the 'rough', in isolating and excluding those who were 'likely to cause trouble'. The following quotation makes it clear that the management of the mass-dance have, over the years, at different times, put together a fairly inclusive list of those they saw - or experienced - as breakers of the peace. Thus,

> It was Mecca's policy to refuse admission to persons identified with a group which had recently been involved in trouble at one of their establishments. In the past it had banned such groups as coloured youth, sailors, Jews, teddy boys and deaf and dumb mutes as a result of disturbances. (4)

The dances I observed were in cities with large coloured populations. 'Coloureds' were not welcome. This was explained to me in terms of a variant on 'it's-not-me-but-the-neighbours' thesis. In this instance, the staff claimed that they, of course, had no objection to them, but that any 'unrestricted' admittance of blacks would only antagonize racially prejudiced white working class youth, and in this way cause trouble. Their categorization of white youth, in this respect, was quite accurate so the exclusion of black youth was, in this context, popular. The basis of this generalized 'schadenfreude' towards blacks was, unquestionably, rooted in fantasies about black sexuality and in sexual politics, where the bargaining was for girls. And although the most virulent anti-black invective came from white male youth, white girls gave a feebler echo to it. To continue with this subject for a little longer, their readily aired racial prejudice, as expressive of part of their general view of the world, is an apt reminder of a comment of Seabrook's about the character of the world-view of the white working class youth he observed:

> Their social and political opinions are often perfunctory and cruel. These are simply not seen as having any importance, and are consigned to a peripheral area of their concern. They were not slow to give their views on such topics - it's simply that they were casual and perspectiveless, often echoing the views of their parent in a fractionally less restrained and more savage way (1973, p. 153).

The immediate problem for the managements, if we return now to the halls I studied, was how to 'regulate' the entry of black youth without provoking any political protest. By and large this was achieved in two ways; one, by employing black 'Chief-of-Staff' and black 'ballroom attendants' wherever possible. Employing enough, that is, to cool-out and manage any black youth who might otherwise become 'stroppy'; and, second, by allowing in a token quota of black youth - just to show the others that they could get in, that the management 'had nothing against coloureds as such'.

In the halls I observed, this particular tactic of 'exclusion-acceptance' has been used ever since they had started up in the late 1950s. This historical point is important, because it means that by the time the 1968 Race Relations Act reached the statute book (I was tempted to say 'become effective' - but this the Act has never really been) it was largely irrelevant to this problem. In the meantime, most black youth had moved on, or rather retreated, to setting up their own clubs, in the predominantly black areas of the cities.

One way of keeping out, or deterring, the 'lumpen' white youth, was to set the price levels of entrance and of drinks inside the dance-hall at a high level. This was done specifically to keep a 'certain element' out, according to several of the supervisory staff I talked to. There could be no doubt that the mass-dance was an expensive place for male youth to go - every bit as pricey as the private clubs elsewhere in the cities. I put the stress on male youth here because it is taken-for-granted by them that they buy drink for the girls they are with, as well as for themselves. The girls only bought drinks for themselves, or for other girls, when they were in all-girl company. In a mixed scene there was no thought of going 'dutch'. This form of sharing could never take root in a culture where a male's relationship with a girl was primarily seen in terms of ownership and extending or offering physical protection. There being a literal (buying drinks) and a metaphorical (showing 'consideration') tithe linked with this sort of possession.

When 'trouble' does occur the attendants come into their own. They are not supposed to terrorize the offender(s) but just, in the words of one manager I spoke to, 'show them who's boss without setting off a bloody riot'. Normally, this could be achieved without much difficulty. Many of the fights were sham affairs, characterized by a lot of posturing, arm-waving and shouting and not much else; each protagonist being easily restrained from hitting another. If it was more serious, it was difficult for the 'attendants' to intervene without compounding the violence. There were several reasons for this, not the least being their own partiality for fighting. Although the dance-hall managers officially deplored attacks on their own recalcitrant customers, it was difficult to imagine bouncers behaving in any other way. They are chosen for their size and their kind of bravado; they know this and on occasions are inclined to act up to it. Again, many of the attendants I talked to, looked forward to 'trouble'; a good punch-up was a way of livening up an otherwise dreary evening for them. For a bouncer at the mass-dance, fighting was a form of 'easing time', (5) a welcome break from the dull routine of checking and watching. Moreover, the fight was not only excitement, it was also - provided they were only taking on youths - mostly danger-free as well. Because they were usually much bigger than their 'adversaries', the flow of fists was invariably one way.

The problem of control and regulation was brought into focus through the way in which the creation of the mass-dance resulted in a concentration, for a few hours every Friday and Saturday night, of previously disparate territorial groups of youths. The halls, especially in their early days in the late 1950s and the early 1960s served a youth clientele that was largely non-mobile. Mobility, in this context, has two aspects to it; first, geographical, meaning that youth tended to live in the same area or community that their parents had lived in for years and possibly for their entire lives. Second, few of the male youth, and almost none of the girls, had cars, which severely limited the range of evening leisure activities open to them. With the exception, then, of the centre-of-town forum provided by the mass-dance hall, it was typical for working class youth not to venture far away from their own patch. Such enforced parochialness had a multitude of consequences for the youth concerned. On the one hand, this effective 'ghettoization' both reflected and reinforced the tightness and solidarity of working class community. Yet here, as elsewhere, that line of thinking which leads to the romanticization of the notion of 'community', the resurrection of the comforting imagery of the micro-universe of 'gemeinschaft', should be resisted. Youth, in this instance, are not the product of some society of levellers, but members of a class community. One result of this convergence is that youth comes to share many experiences and problems with the generation of their parents, in the way that Cohen (1972) has described so well; it also means that youth becomes a carrier of their prejudices and insularity as well. This particular continuity is especially marked in those cities where - like the ones in which I studied the mass-dance - the range of jobs open to working class youth is limited, so that male youth tends to take the occupation of the father, and the girls to follow their mothers into an early marriage.

To return to my main theme again, the arrival of the mass-dance had to contend with this strong sense of 'territory', territorial aggression manifesting itself largely in fights between groups of male youths, the objects of the struggle usually being girls. A typical scenario here would comprise a group of youths waiting outside of the dance-hall for 'their birds' (in the sense that the girls came from the same neighbourhood) to come out and be 'escorted' home. Their ideas about the importance of territorial possession and defence were so highly developed that the ethnography of youth, in this setting, needed for its description the language of Desmond rather than Terence Morris. The opening of the dance-halls that I looked at pre-dated the introduction of comprehensive secondary schooling in the cities. Whatever else these schools might have done, they went some way toward eroding traditional barriers between different segments of working class youth, particularly since the creation of these schools was often associated with the displacement and resettlement of the adult population (i.e. through slum clearance or urban 'development' programmes).

I said something earlier about the regulation of the dance and the management's insistence upon a 'decent' or 'respectable' standard of dress from the followers of the mass-dance. Putting the ballroom attendants ('bouncers') into dress suits helped emphasize the managerial obsession with 'standards'; 'setting the tone' being the justification for pouring large bouncers into suits that rarely caught up with the size and shape of the wearer. Dress regulations were happily accepted by youth. There was no sense of being imposed upon; dressing up was part of a good night out and no one was able to comprehend the 'mentality of those who come all scruffy'. A night out 'in the scruff' was taken to be the hallmark of the yobboe, hippie or student - and was despised. There was nothing outrageous or unconventional about the dress and appearance of working class youth at the mass-dance. And if a deviant had ever managed to slide in, the kind of reaction he or she would almost certainly have provoked from the youth present, would be of the order neatly captured by Wolfe (1969) in his notes on 'The Noonday Underground':

> down into Tiles comes a 17 year-old kid wearing a non-mod outfit, a hobo outfit, actually, a pair of faded Levi's and a jacket cut like a short denim jacket, only made of suede, and with his hair long all around after the mode of the Rolling Stones, and he talks to a couple of girls on the edge of the dance floor and he comes away laughing and talking to some American who is down there.
> 'Do you know what she said to me?' he says. 'She said, "Sod off, Scruffy 'erbert." They all go for a guy in a purple mohair suit. That's what they call me, "Scruffy 'erbert"' (p. 82).

The refusal of some sections of working class youth to be incorporated into the order of the mass-dance is, then, condemned as much by their fellows as by management. The demand of the latter for neatness in the presentation of self ('long hair is fine provided it's not too long'; 'ties are important to me, very important: it's a sign that the person is making a bit of an effort - that he's got some pride in himself.' These comments, offered to me by supervisory staff at the dance-halls, reflect the dominant mentality) are eagerly endorsed by youth itself. The request for order gets not a raspberry from youth, but a demand for an encore.

For the management, the regulation of the dance has been made easier by what might be termed the differentiation of the dance, that is, the emergence of some alternative modes/form of dance, which cater for a rather more specialized dance audience. Differentiation has proceeded in two ways; one being the spread of clubs and discos that have developed quite separately from the mass-dance centre, and outside of the control of those corporate interests who finally administer these centres. In this category we can include the emergence of 'ethnic' clubs - usually black - which have in part been a response to the admission policy of the mass-dance controllers, and which attract a definite following from among college and university students (a group who could gain entrance to the mass-dance, but who reject the demands for conformity in dress and appearance). Also included would be the new wine bars/discos (which tend to cater largely for young middle class professionals, and is a response to the affluence of this class), and those more expensive discos which cater for the over 20s or the over 25s. The other type of differentiation has been initiated by the organizers of the mass-dance themselves, though their offerings - as purveyors of mass entertainment - are inevitably more eclectic. So their contemporary manifesto will list an over-25s night (known, irreverently among the working class youth patrons of the mass-dance, as 'grab-a-granny night'), folk dancing evenings, old-tyme dance nights as well as disco evenings where a particular kind of record (e.g. 'soul', 'rock') only will be played. But this diversification does not spill over to Friday and Saturday nights; on these nights the mass-dance is still easily supreme, with attendances of 2,000 not being uncommon.

Through all these changes the regulation of the mass-dance remains the same. While its music may change, while shifting fashions and tastes may chase after new stars and performers, social relationships inside the dance-hall stay unchanged. There is order and youth partakes of it gladly. Respectable working class youth, on its nights out, is largely quiescent and conforming. In the next section of this paper I look at the say in which relationships between youth at the dance, and particularly between men and women there, simply give a new dimension to order. The routine of the dance that I shall describe is a joyless affair; not that youth, on these occasions is unhappy, but that their social and emotional responses to their situations are routinely stereotypical. (6) The dance becomes a mechanical configuration; it represents, as it were, the Meccanization of the sexual impulse.

THE DANCE: STEP TWO - EXCHANGE AND MART

> I saw this girl at a dance the other night. I could tell she was lonely. She had her telephone number tattooed on her forehead.
>
> Can you do this dance?
>
> No - but I don't mind holding you while you do it.

This section is specifically about youth in pursuit of itself; it is about, in other words, the character, style, organization and ritual of social relationships between male and female youth at the mass-dance. The situations I shall be referring to involve 'unattached' youth, those who are at the dance to find a partner. Again, many of the encounters I describe are in no way specific to working class youth; anybody, for example, with even an elementary knowledge of social life in campus or university communities will recognize the universal character of some of the social exchanges I noted at the mass-dance.

Youth in pursuit of itself is also youth in fear of itself. Male youth is, as often as not, ill-at-ease when in or near the company of girls. Popular talk alleging 'permissiveness' or 'wantonness' appears quaintly defamatory if matched against actual attitudes and behaviour at the mass-dance. Why this awkwardness and embarrassment that is only usually overcome by the old resort to drink? ('When I'm half-cut I'll have a go at anythin'.') Part of the answer is to be found in the curious segregation of youth in our culture, by sex. Until recently - that is, before the widespread emergence of comprehensive schools - the majority of adolescents did their school time in single-sex secondary schools. Many of us, even now, will be familiar with situations where schools for boys and girls are built on adjacent sites, but kept apart by bare iron railings or by glass-topped high brick walls. Inside the school, of course, the curriculum and the institutional culture teaches that boys are boys and girls are girls, and that each has their pre-ordained place in the great scheme of things. Out of school, too, the streaming of youth continues, and in the work world the separation is most effective (i.e. total) and bears most heavily upon working class youth. Typically, their step from school is not one which takes them into white-collar work, the professions of higher education, all of them sectors where men/boys and women/girls enjoy a better chance of working together than that offered by the ordinary range of working class occupations. This segregation of youth also appears, in a different form, inside the family, where strict sex-typing becomes important in shaping the attitudes and beliefs of adolescents about one another. If we aggregate these factors then we should not really be surprised that youth, at the dance, often experiences the making of contact with the opposite sex a hazardous project. The result, or one of them, of the segregation of youth that I have tried to describe, is to make the pursuit after girls at the dance both relentless in character and gauche and clumsy in style. Consequently, a great deal of 'face' is invested in chatting up a girl. It becomes the centre-piece, the core drama of the evening's play. The tactics of the move are pored over, debated and discussed in obsessional detail. It is understood by the males involved that some fine calculations have to be made. When to move in on the girl, and how? Do you wait until the last few dances, when the tempo of the music begins to slow and you can feel more confident about taking her onto the dance floor without making a complete fool of yourself? (Few male youth dance well, even fewer seem to enjoy it and the majority settle uncomfortably for shuffling around the floor with a girl when the group is playing its slower numbers. 'Well - if nothin' else it gives you a chance for a bit of a grope don't it? Most birds love it - that's what they come for innit?') This strategy has the advantage that if 'you makes a duff choice' the end of the dance, which would not be far off, would offer a quick exit route, saving the embarrassment of attempts at disengagement while the dance is still in process. For that which is painfully put together is not easily turned asunder, at least not without the acute discomfort of one of the parties concerned. It is a device that also bestows the not unimportant advantage of economy for male youth; thus a late approach might well secure a 'nice' girl with time enough only for a couple of quick slopes around the dance floor which means no time to buy drinks. On the other side, however, this strategy is not very popular with the girls, who often regard these last-minute bids for them as the worst kind of pick-up. 'Too many of the blokes here just take you for granted. They watch you all evening along with their mates. There's no talking to you. They just expect you to jump at them when they finally bother to come over.'

These calculations of male youth generate their own sort of nervous tension. The will to act is slowly reinforced by more drinking. For those who want to make a move, there is no lack of encouragement; there is always a chorus of background advisers and yea-sayers. 'Go on yer silly sod - she's gasping for it.' 'What about her over there then? You'd be alright there mate.' If a move is made, and made successfully, this gives status to the male, at least in the eyes of his own peer group. 'You watch him pull the birds in. He's bloody fantastic at it.' Even failure, for males, is not too bad. A joke can always be made of it, or some other kind of rationalization dragged in. 'I didn't fancy it when I got up close.' It's always possible to be enveloped again in the warmth of the group with its seedy machismo, or to be propping up the bar and pulling out stories about the girls that were had, or nearly had, the previous week; or what they predicted they would do next week, when 'you might at least get some decent looking pieces in the place'.

There is no doubt that these endless encounters have their own humour and fascination, as well as providing the basic staple of conversation for both boys and girls at the dance. But at the same time the character of such exchanges are strangely deformed, and limited. The language of the exchange, when contact is finally made, is stilted and ponderous. The sexual tension latent in these situations cripples attempts to do anything better or different. Girls become objectified as 'it'; something that's just a kiss apart, that smells and looks good, something to act upon, to use. Typically the girl is seen as having no intrinsic merit or worth of her own. She is the object of the pursuit, but the rules of the hunt are not of her devising. It is her job to respond, not by challenging the conventions of dating itself (which is not really possible, for there are few precedents for this kind of rebellion in working class youth culture; and in any case any resistance would first imply more broadly based changes in male-female relationships in society), but by playing up to the rules of the game thereby partaking in their own domination.

Because the girls are responders rather than initiators in this context, they usually have the worst side of those encounters I earlier sketched in. Convention demands that the girl waits for an invitation to drink or dance. To try and reverse this relationship is only to provoke abuse from males ('bloody tart - always on the look-out'); the basis of this abuse is fear - it constitutes a serious threat to those who already feel threatened and uneasy in their relationships with girls. So for the girl then, trapped in a structure which only allows her to accept or reject, the problem is one of deciding whether or not the latest offer they get is going to be the best one. Is it worth holding out for a bit longer in the hope that 'well, you know, somebody really nice might come along - somebody you could really fancy'. The girls, in Seabrook's phrase, speculate endlessly about 'love', like characters from a romantic comedy. As a consequence, their weaving of images of what might be possible sometimes makes it difficult for them to settle for any offer they get from a male. The difficulty here concerns the facts that a refusal made once too often may result in getting no boy at all, even for a couple of dances at the end of the night. For girls, being alone in this way is not just simply a matter for small regret. Having to go home alone is a conspicuous setback for a girl, a highly visible sign of 'failure'. While it may well be that some girls themselves do not regard being without a boy as a failure on their part in any sense, there is no doubt that their contemporaries - of both sex - view it in these terms. It is easier for male youth to pretend that failure was no failure at all; he, at the end of a barren evening, is able to say either 'I didn't fancy anything here tonight', or 'I'm only here for the beer', and no-one thinks much more about it. This sort of rationalization, and its acceptance, only makes sense if we bear in mind that this is a culture where men can decide whether or not to make advances to women. Ending up alone at the end of the dance is merely a sign that the male has decided, on this occasion, not to bestow his favours; literally - 'I didn't fancy anything here tonight.' Such an account is not permitted from girls; if they go home alone it is implied that few males thought them sufficiently attractive to pursue them. While this may be well wide of the mark in real terms, youth will not entertain an alternative explanation. I shall say something more ahout this in the next section of the paper, but for the moment I want to return to the subject of actual social encounters at the dance.

The tension of so many of these contacts is compounded by the existence of certain 'body taboos' and by the sanctity of 'personal space' in our culture. The youth at the dance was remarkably undemonstrative, except when drifting towards heavy drinking or actual drunkenness. For example, by body taboos I am referring to their reluctance to touch friendly others, when together in a public place like a dance hall. The social kiss is rarely used by working class youth; few handshakes are ever exchanged. Displays of affection in public are discouraged, even in the relative anonymity of the mass-dance setting. the protection and defence of personal space is simply another dimension of this desire not to be noticed, to be private in public space. Among its manifestations are the extreme and convoluted attempts to avoid touching or brushing against others in the densely crowded forum of the dance. If physical contact is inadvertently made it is invariably followed by a profusion of apologies. On a more general scale this is the sort of behaviour we can observe on any Saturday morning in a crowded shopping street in any fair-sized town, where people will try hard, against all the odds, to walk an elaborate quadrille that will keep them physically apart from other shoppers. Peoples' behaviour in lifts, too, is another small but significant expression of the desire to be invisible. Step into a lift that is already occupied and you will find that those already there have crept into (taken) the corner positions. Thereafter, you hold as close to the wall as possible and when the lift fills up, the effort is still make to preserve space between its occupiers; the collapsing of space only being legitimate in moments of crisis - in any other situation its elimination causes acute discomfort. These examples suggest, of course, that this aspect of the behaviour of youth at the dance is borrowed or derived from prevailing cultural norms, and there are few signs that working class youth has transcended this particular part of its inheritance.

Such taboos co-exist, at the dance, with youth's strong interest in sex. By 'interest' here I mean not any particular obsession about having sexual intercourse (for reasons I'll explain in a moment), but a ceaseless speculation and fantasizing about what 'it' might actually be like. For male youth, there is also the additional interest in 'what sort of bird will do it'. But while opinion and comment is freely and liberally offered, in real terms youth at the dance was remarkably circumspect about its actual sexual experience - because few of them had ever had any. The determining factors in this situation are rather more complex than those usually thought to be dominant. Consider, for example, this passage from Coleman's study of American adolescence, which seems to summarize mainstream wisdom on the subject:

> The boy is the pursuer, the girl is the pursued. If she fails to withhold anything he seeks, the cause for the pursuit is gone. Thus it becomes crucial for her status personally and for the maintenance of the system itself for her to be selective and dispense favours with extreme care. If not, the culture is threatened by her philanthropy and punishes her by "ruining her reputation" and taking away her status.
>
> A boy's sexual behaviour, however, is not threatening to the culture, because he is the pursuer. His sexual exploits are conquests, and thus actions that gain him status rather than lose it (1961, p. 123).

Clearly there is much in what Coleman says when he talks about the double standard applied in the dating rules of each sex. Yet among working class youth at the dance the preservation of virginity, for example, rests often upon a lack of opportunity to lose it, rather than upon a surfeit of morality which seeks to protect it. The governing utilitarian calculus here centres upon the absence of facilities where intercourse can be done with dignity and in comfort. Most of the working class youth at the dance lived at home with their parents, so there were precious few chances there to indulge. Very few lived independently in flats, there being no tradition for this and in most cases not enough money either. Again, hotel rooms - always a useful retreat for the middle classes - never played any part in the sexual calculations of youth. Money, again, was largely the reason here, but equally important was the fact that the use of hotels for this purpose was completely outside of the range of their social experiences and imagination. Finally, only a tiny minority of the youth present owned a car. (7) This significance of car-ownership in this context has been spelt out in several studies of the car-heavy American middle class youth culture:

> the role of the automobile is found to be of basic importance.... The automobile gives anonymity, mobility, and complete privacy. It ... enables the carrying on of several concurrent affairs.... The free and unchaperoned use of cars is one of the most important elements in heterosexual deviances. Forty-one per cent of Kinsey's respondents noted the automobile as commonplace for premarital sex relations (Smith, 1962, p. 171).

There exist a further set of calculations which made the girls, in particular, extremely cautious about casual sexual intercourse, namely the fear of pregnancy. But here again, the primary considerations tended to be ones of expediency rather than a response to any moral promptings. Who would look after a young child? The addition of a baby might well be destructive of fragile personal and family economies, if it means someone having to give up work in order to look after it. In other words, there seemed to be no special significance attached to the virgin state or to the loss of it, merely a recognition, instead, that these various material constraints act effectively against it.

As the dance moves to its close, it constructs its own statuesque imagery as hundreds of couples shuffle slowly around the floor. For many of the girls, who include all the best dancers (a few male youth can dance well, but unless they come with a girl, they soon learn to hide their skill. Parading it is to pose a threat to other males and to invite threats. 'Who the fuck does 'e think 'e is - the bloody ponce'), this is the experience of being shackled to a corpse - such is the lack of animation of the average male dancer - or a potential (drunken) molester. So inert do the proceedings become that on occasions the turn of the stroboscope lighting is the only thing that gives the impression of any movement at all. In the next, and penultimate, section of the paper, I look at what happens in the final stages of the pursuit, when the dance has ended and youth prepares for the journey home.

THE DANCE: STEP THREE - DENOUEMENT AND DISENGAGEMENT

> 'Hello,' she says, 'I've brought my friend along. I hope you don't mind.'
>
> 'Oh, no ... no', I say, like a clot. But what else can I say, for Pete's sake? My heart's dropped down into my boots with a thud because I know straight off my number's up. This is one way of doing it, giving you the shove. They don't refuse the date but they bring a girl friend along to keep you at arm's length; and if you don't ask them again, well, that's okay, because that was the idea in the first place.
>
> I look at them standing arm-in-arm under the lamp: Ingrid all neat and clean and fresh-smelling as usual, and this plain Jane with a muddy complexion, a big nose, and a mouth like a crack in a pie. I often wonder what makes bints pair off like this, one lovely and one horrible. You see it all the time and it must have turned more lads against one another than nearly anything else because if you're hunting in pairs somebody's got to have the horror (Barstow, 1962, pp. 65-6).

Barstow's account, though fictional, is perceptive enough to characterize some of the parting exchanges between youth at the end of the mass-dance. Often the criteria used in sorting out who goes home with whom, and who goes home alone, are harsh. The world of the dance is for those like Barstow's Ingrid. Physical attractiveness is a crucial factor in selection. There is no time at the dance to develop or advance alternative criteria. The necking order, then, is constructed around the pretty; in one sense, the end-of-the-dance pick-up situation contains all of the elements of a fascist universe. First choice is given to the best stock; physical excellence counts for much more than anything else. In this scheme of things, the 'plain Janes' have to make their own way. It is also a regime, of course, which grants certain advantages to the attractive girl; not only does she get more offers, she can also use the 'unattractive' girl as a bargaining counter or as a protection. Either way, the latter suffers; if she is not wanted she has to make her own way home, or leave with another girl like her, the two of them forming part of the debris of the dance. Their failure is tangible and felt. There is no way of explaining it away, using the kinds of excuses and evasions that male youth can fall back upon (which I described in the previous section). If she is wanted, she knows the reason why and the journey home is a monologue from the pretty one about what was at the dance, broken only by the occasional question 'Do you think I should have let him take me home?'

Although the plain girl has no way of saving face in these situations they return to the dance again and again. There is always hope; and besides, there is nowhere else to go. Sooner or later the constant rejection produces tears, but these are welcomed by nobody. It is not that youth is hard, or without sentimentality, but rather 'Well, of course I feel sorry in a way for birds like that, but that's the way it is innit? There's nothin' I can do about it is there?' The girls themselves come finally to accept the situation. Their expectations are low, since they learn that there is very little to be hoped for.

Moreover, because marriage and having children is - has to be - the primary objective of working class girls, the best has, fatefully, to be made of a bad job. The commitment to the idea of marriage among the girls is something that those from other class backgrounds sometimes find difficult to understand. It is an ambition that has its roots in the structure of the family the girls come from and in the kind of work they do. The latter is usually a time-filler, a limbo state between school and 'real fulfilment' (i.e. marriage and motherhood). Work itself has no intrinsic merit; it requires little skill and no formal educational qualifications (which is how they came by it in the first place) and there is no career or 'prospects' associated with it. And one of the reasons why the girls are not bothered much by this is to be found in their primary orientation towards marriage. More than this, there is not much of a place for a single working class woman in society. This is not simply a question of economics - though it will mean a life lived on the low wages of women in working class jobs - but of being forced to live as a marginal person in working class society. The girls themselves knew full well what this meant. 'I've got this auntie - Auntie Elsie - she's ever so nice, but she never got married. So she misses out on a lot of things really. I mean, she goes around with me mum and all the family and them, but - well - she just sort of has to watch. Know what I mean? I don't want to be like her.'

This is why the dance is important as a 'meeting place'. This is why the girls define their future almost entirely of when and whom to marry. While they will talk for an age about 'choosing the right man', in truth the basic choice has already been made for them. The circumstances of their lives dictates that it must be marriage. As Orwell put it when writing about working class attitudes to marriage, it is implied all along 'that marriage is something profoundly exciting and important, the biggest event in the average human being's life' (1970 edn, p. 148). To be left on the outside, to miss out on the great 'fest' is unthinkable; it is to be left with nowhere else to go - to be reduced to a condition where, like Auntie Elsie, you are 'tolerated' on the fringes of your own society.

It is harsh realities of this kind which help to preserve, or which are perhaps reflected in the rigidly structured social encounters and exchanges of the dance. I said earlier that some of the things I would be writing about would not necessarily be specific to the youth of any particular class. One point of convergence between the culture of very different classes of youth that comes to mind concerns the rigid social conventions of the dance. I am thinking here of student dances and the occasional staging, in campus communities, of the so-called 'emancipation disco'. At these the social roles of male and female at the dance are reversed for the night; it is the girl who invites the man to dance and who takes the lead in chatting-up. But paradoxically, the very popularity of these events serves only to confirm the pervasiveness and deep-rootedness of the dominant institutional arrangements. In a truly emancipated culture there is no need for an 'emancipation disco'. The obvious analogy is with certain of the medieval mummers' plays where the fool or jester is made king for a day - but only for a day.

In the last section of the paper I want to try and draw together some of the themes and issues touched upon so far; and, as far as possible, to put these observations into some sort of theoretical order.

CONCLUSION

> We are in the presence ... of an entirely new phenomenon in human history: that youth is rich. Once, the 'jeunesse dorée' were a minute minority; now, all the young have gold.... Today, age is needy and, as its powers decline, so does its income; but full-blooded youth has wealth as well as vigour. In this decade, we witness the second Children's Crusade, armed with strength and booty, against all 'squares', all adult nay-sayers. An international movement, be it noted, that blithely penetrates the political curtains draped by senile seniors, as yet unconscious of the rising might of this new classless class (MacInnes, 1961, p. 47).

> Very few of the young understand any more than their elders the society they are living in. They are like the protagonists in a classical tragedy, who fulfil a role, the significance of which in the total drama is not revealed to them. Most of the young have no real alternatives. They reject the past, and proclaim exultantly that they want to live. But their freedom is a diminished and truncated thing. They are no less manipulated, no less in bondage, than the sad and dutiful mill-girls who filled the streets with the clatter of their clogs half a century ago (Seabrook writing of youth in a cotton town in northern England, cf. 1973, pp. 153-4).

Are we to take the above as two entirely subjective accounts of the contemporary condition of British youth? For most people the first quotation - which is a comment on metropolitan youth in the heady days of the late 1950s and early 1960s - will read as coming closest to the mark. The sentiments that MacInnes expresses reflects something of the unqualified optimism of social and political commentators during that particular period in post-war British history. Confidence was easy come by; the land seemed heavy with affluence. Tomorrow could not hope to be anything other than a bigger and better version of today. The political slogans of the time reflected this mood: 'you've never had it so good', and 'we are all middle class now'. Academics, too, put their shoulders to the golden wheel; hence out of this period came (or if not actually conceived there, was consolidated then) ideas about 'embourgeoisement', theses on the 'end of ideology', and some sightings of 'post-capitalist' society. Talk of British society in class terms was discouraged, unless it could somehow be shown that we were all becoming middle class, which was acceptable because this was seen as a sign of progress. There was a wide and receptive audience for this kind of rhetoric and these sorts of claims.

Seabrook, however, has a very different story to tell. His

account is ten years on and describes the condition of youth in a part of Britain where the writ of 'affluence' never really ran. From this view the young do not represent a new and radical threat to the order and well-being of society. They are, to borrow Seabrook's term 'fundamentally quiescent'. Moreover, the abandonment of the twin themes of affluence and the alleged classlessness of teenage youth culture, which have so dominated post-war writings on British youth is, in part, a response to the dissolution of optimism itself and of hard contemporary economic realities. In other words, these theories become difficult to sustain and defend when unemployment and economic uncertainty increases and with it the numbers of working class youth forced onto the dole. Indeed one of the dismal achievements of the present crisis in the British economy is to demonstrate to those who might have been persuaded to think otherwise, the fragility and impermanence of the post-war economic gains of large sections of the British working class and of working class youth in particular.

There have been other writers in this book and elsewhere (P. Cohen, 1972; S. Cohen, 1972) who have demolished the myth of youth as a 'new classless class'. I wish to reinforce their general arguments, while also seeking to develop them in a different way. We have available to us then, important empirical studies which have effectively denied the 'classlessness' of youth. This process of refutation, by showing some of the primary internal divisions of youth (e.g. by class, race, sex), attempted to integrate the study of youth into theories concerned with the structure of political society and of systems of social stratification.

However, these critiques of the conventional wisdom about the nature of British youth have, typically, concentrated on unconventional fractions of youth - especially working class youth. The fascination for the bizarre, the esoteric, the pathological, the marginal elements of youth behaviour and ideology has, in some respects, had effects other than those the researchers intended. Their interest in the 'unusual' aspects of youth culture has been returned in full. Though they would be dismayed by the proposition it is at least arguable that the particular orientation of their work (in terms of subject matter) has tended to underwrite popular notions about the uniqueness and separateness and abnormality of youth. By this route, youth comes to be regarded as strangely different; they gather in large cohort groups at seaside resorts, they fight to, from and at football matches, they loom large as regular delinquents. The unintended consequence of this corpus of work may actually be to underwrite those explanations of youthful behaviour and attitudes which have been framed in 'generational' terms, and those which have sought to celebrate the 'specialness' of youth, to the exclusion of all other interpretations.

The subject orientation of this paper has been quite different from those I refer to above. Through a study of episodes in the provision of a mass leisure facility for 'respectable' working class youth I have tried to illustrate the sheer ordinariness of this corner of 'youth culture'. They revealed themselves to me as conservative and quiescent; a group who, measured in terms of their work, leisure and minimal aspirations, demonstrated at every turn a continuity with the world of their parents' generation. These were not the 'marginal men' or the 'wild ones' whose exploits fill the pages of so many studies of youth cultures. Any marginality they exprienced was not due to any flirtations with deviant behaviour (their veneration of 'law and order' was manifest in frequent denunciations of 'yobbos', 'hooligans', 'scruffs', 'layabouts', 'addicts' and their support for punitive control measures. The demand was for the rest of the world to be like them, and they saw themselves as hard-working, decent and law-abiding), but was economically determined. This last point is important because the worry about work, the nagging fear of being without it, linked them firmly with their parents' generation and was the basis of a deep-rooted conservatism. They had learned, from their parents, from older working class relatives and from their own experience of the world not to expect very much. They saw the future not in terms of any possible prospects for advancement or change, but as a search for something secure. For the girls this could be achieved largely through marriage; for boys it was represented primarily by laying claim to a 'steady job'.

For some of them - a small minority - education offered an alternative route, based on the slow accumulation of qualifications at night school or in day release classes. It was clear that any ambitions here were not purely personal but were heavily underwritten by the parents. Sadly, their encouragement rested on a kind of self-hate and rejection of their own social situation that was sharply felt by the youth concerned. 'Get educated son - you don't want to become like me', or 'Get your qualifications - go out and better yourself', are cries which have rung in the ears of many socially mobile working class youth. It is always 'said for the best' but its effect is to define education as an escape route - the upward end of which leads to the good life, while its downward slope takes you to your own parents. There have been those like Hoggart (1958) and Jackson (1972) who have written - partly autobiographically - of what happens to some working class youths who won places at grammar schools. But their experiences were largely defined in terms of the ragging they received from their left-behind old junior school mates or rather vague talk about 'identity crises'. What we lack, however, are any detailed accounts of the kind of tensions created inside working class families when education is defined in the way I earlier described and when one of its children takes advantage of it.

But for the great majority of youth at the dance the defining character of the basic routines of their lives was permanence. The modal points of their universe centred upon marriage and job-security. Much of their talk on these topics would not have looked out of place in the pages of Orwell's observations on British working class culture, made in the 1930s. Then, for example, according to Orwell, 'youth and adventure [were seen to] end with marriage' (1970 edn, p. 149). The youth I met came up with similar ideas: 'of course, you have to settle down after getting married'; 'couple more years and I'll suppose I'll get married and that'll be the end of coming here [to the dance]'. Both groups regarded 'being free' as only a temporary release. No one expected it to last long, even if the licence for freedom has been granted a slightly longer run in the post-war period, because of the improved economic circumstances of youth. The inevitability of such attitudes is fed by the structure of the family and by the nature of (and rewards for) working class work in British society. As I have tried to suggest - and as the youth I talked to are aware - youth has few options open to it. Its cramped condition gives no cause for mystery or surprise, if we remember that working class youth are members of a society that has always borne down most heavily and oppressively upon its own working class.

NOTES

1 Roberts' book described life in Salford in the first quarter of the twentieth century. Another book of the time, though about very different people and places, revealed that the concern abou the shortage of 'eligible' men was, as a result of the war, shared by the gentry as well. Barbara Cartland, who was preparing to 'enter society' in the immediate post-war period wrote: 'I never thought for one moment that I wouldn't get married. Indeed, there was no other career open to women save that of being a governess or a companion.... But I and my contemporaries at school had realised that because of the war, finding a husband was not going to be as easy as it might have been had we emerged from our chrysalis five years earlier. A million men who should have been in the right age group to be potential husbands had been killed, and we learned with feelings of anxiety that in consequence there were two million surplus women' (1973, pp. 11-12).

2 As Oliver put it when talking about some of the blues music that Southern negroes in the United States danced to; 'Innocuous words are often giving secondary meanings which are closed to all but the initiated and by their use the Negro can be more outspoken in the blues than might otherwise be prudent' (1972, p. 319). In the same spirit two famous dances favoured by plantation negroes when they were called upon to entertain the slave-owner and his family, were 'the Gollywog Cake Walk' and the 'Chalk Line Dance'. Both dances cleverly parodied the manners and conventions of white plantation society - which never saw the satire in them.

3 Goffman (1971) has dealt at length with non-verbal communication, see especially pp. 13-27 and chapters 1 and 2. One of the examples Goffman cites is a novelistic incident in which Preedy, an Englishman on holiday in Spain, makes his first appearance on the beach of his summer hotel; 'But in any case he took care to avoid catching anyone's eye. First of all, he had to make it clear to those potential companions of his holiday that they were of no concern to him whatsoever. He stared through them, round them, over them - eyes lost in space. The beach might have been empty. If by chance a ball was thrown his way, he looked surprised; then let a smile of amusement lighten his face (Kindly Preedy), looked round dazed to see

that there were people on the beach, tossed it back with a smile to himself and not a smile at the people, and then resumed carelessly his nonchalent survey of space' (p. 17). Quoted from W. Sansom, 'A Contest of Ladies', Hogarth, London, 1956, p. 230. Preedy would know his way about the dance-hall well enough.

4 From a report in the 'Daily Telegraph'; quoted in the 'New Statesman' 25 October 1974.

5 For an interesting discussion of the notions of 'easing time' see Cain (1973).

6 In their study of 'Ashton', a Yorkshire mining village, Dennis et al. (1956) give an account of a typical Saturday evening dance at the Miners' Welfare Institute. Four or five hundred youth (i.e. 75 per cent of the town's population in the 15-22 age group) would normally be there. It was a 'community dance', filled mainly by people who had some acquaintance with one another. It was sometimes advertised as 'Saturday Night is Riot Night' (p. 126), and the communality of 'Ashton' made a night at 'the Welfare' a less inhibited affair than that of the mass-dance. As one of their respondents put it: 'I spent the happiest two years of my life at Ashton Miners' Welfare, you could let yourself go there' (p. 127). The spirit of Ashton contrasted with the effect produced by the conglomeration of stranger relationships at the mass-dance, given the particular purpose of the dance.

7 Occasionally, in the dance-halls I observed a small group of students from the local university would turn up. These were almost invariably male, and car owners as well. For them, as middle class youth, going to the mass-dance was 'a bit of a laugh', something to do 'that's a little bit out of the ordinary'. They went both as voyeurs and predators. On the first count, they came because 'We've never been to anything like this before. Isn't it bloody awful?' On the second count they were foraging for girls. While this was acknowledged by them to be a risky enterprise - since students were almost always disliked by the male working class youth present (who saw students as 'parasites', 'scroungers', 'troublemakers', 'useless') - it was thought worth the effort because they defined working class girls as more sexually 'permissive' than other girls. The fact they were wrong about this is of less importance th n the insight this little episode provides into an aspect of the relationship between sexual deviance and social class in British culture. Thus it is not stretching a comparison too far to see the behaviour and attitudes of these students as akin to that of the younger sons of the aristocracy laying domestic servants, during that epoch when there was large servant class in Britain. In each instance the male defines the encounter as 'fun', or as a vindication of their belief in the greater 'permissiveness' of lower class girls, never seeing their acts for what they really were - as exploitation. But in this, as in other things, the aristocracy had more success than the middle classes.

Chapter 5

BEYOND THE SKINHEADS: Comments on the emergence and significance of the Glamrock Cult

Ian Taylor and Dave Wall

Students of youth culture in Britain are agreed that the skinheads are dead. But it is some indication of the inadequacy of youth cultural analysis that no analytically or politically useful post-mortem has been effected. Most sociological explanations are derivations of so-called 'deviancy amplification' theory. Here, the suggestion is basically that the initial and continuing behaviour of the skinheads was responded to by a powerful audience (teachers, social workers, police and the courtroom); that it was spuriously dramatized (such that the wearing of skinhead garb was sufficient to excite ostracism or punitiveness), and that a cybernetic system of stimulus and response was initiated, resulting in the further polarization of the original skinhead (now 'cast' emphatically as a social outcast) and his audience. Ultimately, the argument goes, the 'societal reaction' to skinheads was so strong and all-pervasive that it effectively deterred or defused the preference for a skinhead life-style. Much the same kind of model has been used to explain the societal reaction to teddy boys in the 1950s, mods and rockers, greasers and Hell's Angels in the 1960s. But the model nevertheless says little about the rationality or purposes informing the original youthful adaptation, and, in its account of the decline and fall of each youthful culture, goes perilously close to being an elaborate but mechanical sociologizing of judicial deterrence theory.

A slightly different account (which is used by Stan Cohen in his explanation of the creation and the demise of the mods and rockers) is what might be called the 'recasting theory' of youth culture. Here, the argument is that 'society' continuously creates new 'folk devils' over time, relegating earlier devils to 'relatively benign roles in the gallery of social types' (S. Cohen, 1972, p. 200). This recasting depends on the (unexplained) emergence and availability of alternative folk devils who can effectively act as the focus of moral indignation - indeed, who can act (in true Durkheimian a fashion) to unite 'upright consciences' in defence of adult values.

Now both the deterrence-deviancy amplification and recasting theories seem to imply that the embrace of a particular youth cultural style may, literally, be a fad, (1) or, slightly more crucially, essentially temporary (and hence tentative) a solution to essentially temporary a problem. Hence, there is a suggestion here that the skinheads were simply a reaction against the mushrooming middle class youth culture of the 1960s, a one-off assertion of identity by working class youth excluded from the action. The emergence of a hard 'Glamrock' culture in the early 1970s - in the shape of Slade, the Sweet and Gary Glitter - resolved the problem of exclusion, defused the 'aggro' of skinhead culture and allowed the expression of working class identity a prominence it had previously been denied. But there is a severe problem in such an account. One irreducible theme in youth cultural analysis is that entry into a subculture represents the individual's solution to a collectively (i.e. structurally) experienced problem. The emphasis in deviancy amplification theory and in recasting theory on the tentative and transitory nature of working class subcultural identification (here, the skinhead identification) underplays the ongoing reality of the repression of working class youth. It ignores the continuous need for working class youth to resolve the problem of repression and exclusion (expressively - in leisure time - or, instrumentally, at work); and neither does it tell us how the replacement of one cultural preference by another relates to, or reflects, changes or continuities in the situation of working class youth.

Our intention in this paper is to identify two problems in descriptions and explanations of the demise of the skinheads, and the subsequent replacement of skinheads by the Glamrock adaptation as the 'focal cult' in working class youth culture. These are:

1 The inability of existing theories to account for the decline of a youth culture that almost without exception is characterized as a 'rough working class' adaptation - in a period when one might have expected an increase in recruitment to that culture. In a period of high youthful unemployment, reported increases in juvenile delinquency in general and class-based hooliganism in particular (i.e. around football), and polarization of the classes in industry, why did the skinhead adaptation prove to be untenable?

2 The inability of those theories to account for the replacement of a rough masculine, sexist and racist adaptation (skinhead culture) by a youth culture which quite specifically accepts - if does not actually celebrate - a hard-rock culture, acceptable to girls as well as to boys, led by the bi-sexual David Bowie. Whatever else, this culture is not simply a resuscitation of exclusively working class values, and neither is it (as Phil Cohen would have us believe) 'a movement (from the Skinheads) back towards the original Mod position' (P. Cohen, 1972, p. 25). A consequential youth cultural analysis has to be able to explain the acceptability of the culture to its audience as well as the form it apparently assumes.

This paper will be concerned, therefore, to locate the problem of skinhead and Glamrock cultures within the context of identifiable changes in the general economic and leisure situation of youth, and in the context of the cultural preferences of youth as expressed by a sample of working class youth themselves.

THE RISE AND FALL OF THE SKINHEADS

According to John Clarke (1973) and to the editors of 'The Painthouse' (1972), the skinheads emerged in the East End of London sometime during 1968. It is not our intention to dispute this here, since little clear documentation exists. It could, however, be crucial to investigate this further - if the decline of the skinheads, and the significance of their replacement, is to be understood. Certainly, the 'Daily Telegraph' of 11 August 1969 was unaware of the skinhead when it reported that 'a gang of 100 Portsmouth (football) supporters in Blackpool ... had cropped hair, thin braces supporting jeans worn at half-mast and brown boots.' Chief Inspector Cheetham of the Blackpool force was quoted as commenting: 'I understand it is some skit on the Royal Navy who are, of course, very closely connected with Portsmouth, and who wear something like this when they are on fatigue duty.'

Later in the same month, in 'Black Dwarf', John Hoyland saw skinheads as a phenomenon emerging out of the 1968-9 football season, characterized their garb as 'a combination of (that of) an ordinary English workman and an American teenager of the fifties' and identified their attitudes as 'a crude expression of a lumpen working-class identity which has been untouched by psychedelia and (middle class) Swinging London' (30 August 1969). Similarly, Pete Fowler: '... the skinheads came out from the same areas that had witnessed the rise of the Mods - the East End of London and the outer ring of suburbs. But whereas the Mod had seen his "enemy" as the Rocker, and had rationalised his style accordingly (Cleanliness vs. Grease; Scooter vs. Motor Bike; Pills vs. Booze), the new Skinheads reacted against the Hippies. Their hair was short to the point of absurdity, they were tough and they went round in "bovver boots" for the express purpose of beating hell out of deviants, and they wore braces. Braces! For God's sake, some sort of weird throwback to the Thirties' (Fowler, 1972, p. 19).

Whether the skinhead garb and presentation of self was essentially an extension of naval uniform, the casual denim of 1950s middle America, or, as seems more likely, an assertion of an orthodox proletarian identity, the content of that adaptation was widely agreed, though not so widely proclaimed. It was reactionary, racist and sexist: an authentic but totally limited response to the closure of opportunities for working class youth under a declining British capitalism. 'There's nothing nice about the Skins. And likewise there's nothing nice about their taste in music. They completely reject the music of the counter-culture.... Music is for dancing to. Music is for getting off with birds to' (Fowler, 1972, p. 19). The only trace of oppositional activity in skinhead behaviour was to be found in their preference for the expressive role of football supporter over a passive acceptance of the role of spectator. Here, traditional working class concerns of neighbourhood, local and kin identity, desire for participation and a populist egalitarianism (a resentment of 'stars') informed their necessary participation in reactive acts of violence around soccer. Even here, however, the concern of soccer supporters in general (and skinheads were in no way the vanguard of what was initially a much more general movement) was adaptive rather than directly oppositional - in that the violence around soccer represented an attempt to conserve traditional conceptions of soccer from emasculation by an alien, and bourgeois, conception of soccer as business. (2)

Populist eulogies aside, (3) the skinhead was a juvenile redneck. As Fowler rather uncritically notes, he was about style (i.e. form) rather than about content. His relationship to music, to others, and to blacks was essentially impersonal - the skinhead liked Motown music, not the Four Tops (and music was always peripheral and instrumental, in any case, to other activities), they hated others (in the same class, on the same street, on the same shopfloor); they 'made' 'birds' and, not so infrequently, with West Indian 'skins' in tow, they bashed the pakies.

Once this is said - and it is said out of analytical as well as moral conviction (4) - it becomes clear that the skinhead adaptation was dysfunctional in its own terms. The intensification of skinhead aggro in the late 1960s was bound to meet up not only with 'societal reaction' (i.e. repression by teachers, police and court, if not by parents), but also with contradictions and failures in its relationship with other youth. Interviews we have carried out in Sheffield with greasers, ex-greasers and unaffiliated working class youth emphasize the lack of support and sympathy for the skinhead aggro of the late 1960s.

> 19 year-old ex-greaser: 'I asked a copper once: who gives you the most trouble? He said: It's about the same. Skinheads, he said, they came down the station mainly for fighting and that. Greasers, they come down for causing damage, stealing motor bikes and stuff. Not really for fighting. Not like Skinheads. Greasers were a decent lot, actually. Mind you, when Greasers got together, they'd get their own back on Skinheads. That were OK.' (5)

Intensification of the attack on working class power during the late 1960s and early 1970s resulted, amongst other things, in an increase in juvenile unemployment, and a consequent tightening-up in the class in the search for apprenticeships and job security. The percentage of the working population unemployed throughout Britain rose from 2.2 per cent in 1967 to 2.6 per cent in July 1974 (periodically approaching 4 per cent, as in 1973). The proportion of these totals contributed by school-leavers rose disproportionately from 9.1 per cent to 13.4 per cent (with a high of 19.1 per cent in 1973) over the same period. (6)

In addition, the competitiveness that resulted fuelled a racism that was deeply embedded, and largely unchallenged, in the British Labour movement and working class. The alliance of skinhead and West Indian, and the domination of Reggae as a music and a style for a multi-racial youth culture for the rough working class, was to be short-lived. A crucial date in the 'natural history' of the skinheads was the summer of 1972 and the attack with white Liverpudlians on second-generation blacks in the Toxteth area of Liverpool 8. The death of 'inter-racial Reggae' and the segregatinn of black culture in general, was symbolized in the publication, in November 1973, of a new 'Black Music' paper, directed at the

West Indian population in Britain.

Associated with the decline in the material situation of the working class, moreover, was an accelerated collapse of the traditional institutions of working class leisure - the arenas in which the class derived some compensation for its weekly subordination to labour and regimentation. The centrality of the local professional football club in proletarian weekend culture has been eroded, the gradual incorporation of 'the club' into a national middle class culture translating the supporter into a spectator and widening the distance between player and fan. The local pub has been increasingly transformed from a neighbourhood bar into an impersonal retail outlet for consumer capitalism. And, finally, the local working men's clubs have been very extensively updated (or else outmoded) by the mass night-club chains (owned by Bailey's, Fiesta, Mecca and Top Rank). The collapse of the working class weekend, signalling the demise of collective class leisure has left a void in working class culture, a void which has been successfully closed by an institutionalized form of individual or family leisure, dominated by the cash nexus (the ability to pay).

It is not that this incorporation has been accomplished without resistance. The significance of the soccer hooliganism in this respect has been underlined (cf. Taylor, 1971a, b) but it is also possible to see the everyday interactions in night-clubs or in bistro-type pubs (or, for that matter, in restaurants or dances) phenomenologically as an assertion or continuity of traditional class activity. 'Pub brawls' (a commonly held expectation in the 'local') are in night-clubs a matter for bouncers, and are sanctioned by the exclusion of the individuals in question. Some index of the ongoing 'bourgeoisification' of leisure in Britain can indeed be derived from the numbers of banned individuals on the roll of any of the new night spots, and the number of arrests over the last ten years on the soccer grounds of the nation.

The skinheads were, of course, heavily involved in the resistance to such changes. Their significance lies in the violence of their attempt to express the reality of exclusion, but it remained an attempt that was doomed to failure, not as we have said, primarily because of the severity of societal reaction nor even because of the emergence of alternative cultures which proved to them to be more attractive. It was doomed out of the impotence of the skinhead's general social situation. Importantly, for example, the collapse of the working class weekend was a crucial factor in the isolation of the skinhead (the mass of youth being inceeasingly alienated from football and from pubs). And the advent of a 'classless' but class-oriented night-life provided working class youth in general, and working class girls in particular, with a way of participating in leisure consumption that had not been built into the traditional institutions of the class.

One of our interviewees, a 19 year-old girl, confirmed that girls have been able to have greater influence, over the last few years, in deciding on weekend activity; and that they have had final say, in particular, over which concerts to attend and which clubs to frequent. The collapse of traditional class leisure has been accompanied, that is, by a weakening of class chauvinism. The paradox, of course, is that this process has been accelerated, if not actually precipitated, by the new capitalism that has grown up around the marketing of leisure. Consumer capitalism well realizes the importance of girls as a market for its products, and as trend-leaders in the marketing of clothes, records and night-club entertainment. It is no accident that most provincial night-clubs have special 'Nurses' Nights' and other incentives to encourage attendance (at reduced cost) by girls. At a time when traditional markets (like football, and pubs) are on the wane, the significance of using girls as a way of encouraging the boys (and their pay packets) to attend dances, to buy clothes and consume a new class culture, moving away from ritualistic attachments to pastures new, is clear. Consumer capitalism has aided a process of dissociation of the class from its declining institutions by endowing the translation with style.

Indeed, consumer capitalism has paid the skinhead the compliment of recognizing both their style and their class. But is so doing it has provided other working class youth (and, for the first time, working class girls) with a universal style - where, previously, the styles, like the youth themselves, had been sectarian. That style was most noticeably expressed in a class-based hard-rock music, in the ad-man's language a 'commercial sound' (Marc Bolan, Gary Glitter, the Sweet and Slade), and in a concern for clothing and presentation of self that would appeal to skinheads, to West Indians, Reggae fans, to the new mod and to working class girls alike. Chaz Chandler, the manager of Slade: 'For a period, there were no groups around that knew the same wage-packet type of background as the football fans: it was very much a students' thing. Now it is back to the people.'

The skinhead movement, therefore, was instrumental in alerting consumer capitalism to a market available for a class-based product - though, paradoxically, in a culture that had broken with the traditional institutions of the class. The significance of the records of Slade, Gary Glitter and others lies partly in their marketability as single 45s (especially in an industry that was unhappy about relying on the LP market for profitable returns); and partly in their more general role as a focus for a youth culture manufactured by consumer capitalism to fill the gap in the working class weekend.

The emergence of this culture is also to be explained as being enabled by the collapse of the underground, both in this country and in North America. The tranquillization of that culture, colonized on the one hand by mysticism and the other by commercialism in the shape of 'bohemian business' (Berger, 1963), is paralleled by the demise of the Beatles and the self-imposed exiles of the Rolling Stones, The Who and Bob Dylan - and their replacement, for a long time, in the LP market by what 'Ramparts' has called the 'limp-prick' music of Carole King and James Taylor. Whether the next phase is indeed to be a nostalgic return to country music or whether the hard Glamrock will indeed be institutionalized, the underground certainly can no longer claim to be producing music (or a culture) with universal appeal; and little is heard, in 1974, from those who would argue for the revolutionary appeal of 'youth as a class'. A materialist might argue, in fact, that the music of 'reflectivity' (Carole King and James Taylor) did indeed reflect the turning-in-on-itself of a class, in a period of increasing class polarization: in this case, the class-in-itself being the younger bourgeoisie.

Our argument here, however, is that the polarization of class culture and class music has been disguised and popularly unseen, and specifically that there has been manufactured a music culture that appears to be classless and universal (taking up both underground and commercial themes), marketed by and large to the mass of working class youth. David Bowie, after an imitative period as a second-string Anthony Newley and a short presentation (particularly in North America) as an individual exponent of the soft 'head' music of the Moody Blues, has been very strategically marketed as a new kind of media product - a bisexual short-haired mod who preaches a spiritual nihilism (in counter-cultural form) to an audience across the class and age groups, but to the backing of a working class rock beat.

DAVID BOWIE AND THE YOUTH CULTURE

Both within the skinhead and underground cultures there were severe internal contradictions. Jock Young has documented the contradictions in life-style preference and opportunity for the different members of an apparently monolithic underground culture in Britain (Young, 1973), and we do not have the space here to expand on this analysis. We have already indicated ourselves that the skinhead adaptation, likewise, proved untenable over time, in setting up conflicts within working class culture. In both the underground and the skinhead case, there is the need to place these descriptions of internal changes within class culture, in the context of the more general economic and structural changes occurring around these classes.

Neither the skinheads nor the underground, in the period under discussion, were 'beyond scarcity'; and the failure of the latter, in particular, can be attributed, in part, to the decline in the graduate and middle class job market in the later 1960s and early 1970s. Increasing difficulties in assuring oneself of employment induced a competitiveness and a privatization that was alien to the counter-cultural tradition, and which therefore could not continue as counter-cultural sustenance. In 1967, some 11.2 per cent of the total unemployed population (2.2 per cent of the overall population) were school-leavers and 'adult students', and by 1972 the proportion had increased to 28.1 per cent). (8) There was little in counter-cultural ideology or in its institutions (at least in Britain) to prepare its adherent for 'scarcity' or to provide a clear understanding of it. Writing of America, where the 'counterculture' response to the beginnings of scarcity appears to have been to return to the basic American institutions of homestead and farming country, Paul Piccone has this to say:

> The self-liberation realisable within the counter culture, to the extent that it does not alter the concrete social context

> within which the liberated individual will have to operate, can only be temporary, for the real causes of alienation and isolation that presently reduce the human subject to the level of a mere repressed and abstract consumer remain operative. Thus the counter culture can become just another political dead-end that in the ultimate analysis simply duplicates the cultural avenues of social integration that the establishment so desperately needs in a period of deep social crisis (Piccone, 1969, p. 17).

The recent history of working class youth culture, and the associated patterns of consumption and leisure, provides clear evidence of this duplication convention. The creators of the new 'classless' product for consumption by a class appear to have successfully neutralized any liberatory potential there might have been in the condition of youth in the 1960s, and have achieved this in no small measure by marketing a product that is economically obtainable by the masses (cheap clothes, clubs and records). The inequality of access to the middle class culture of liberation has been resolved at the expense of the content of that culture. Instead the system markets the form and the style of that culture - providing a mass of goods (magazines, clothes, records and 'stars') that celebrate and play back onto the consumer his own perception of the emptiness and decadence of bourgeois society. Thus, the youth culture of consumer capitalism is one which celebrates existing forms as universal and inevitable, rather than particular and open to change, instrumentality (music for relaxation, dancing, and sexual conquest) rather than expressivity (music of an alternative life-style, imaginativeness or protest) and, most crucially, financial consumption rather than human participation.

A content analysis of the Top Twenty records and an inspection of the changes in the sales figures of periodicals bought by the youth population gives some indication of the major trends in youth culture in the late 1960s and early 1970s.

The importance of the skinheads, and their influence over broader cultural phenomena, is illustrated in the chart entries of 1969. The singles' chart entries were dominated, on the one hand, by the 'ageless' artists (Cliff Richard, Elvis Presley) and, on the other, by Motown music (Marvin Gaye, the Isley brothers, Diana Ross and the Supremes, and Stevie Wonder). But earlier, during 1967, the most consistent sellers were from three tendencies; the 'ageless' again, the groups who had survived from the mod era (the Small Faces and The Who), and some underground artists who had produced singles (Hendrix, Pink Floyd, The Cream and Donovan).

Today, whilst Motown music retains popularity, the major group of artists to be found in the Top Twenty are the white Glamrock bands and artists (Gary Glitter, Slade, T. Rex, and Bowie). Not surprisingly, most of these records are custom-made for discotheques. The only significant innovation in manufactured style is, of course, the development of 'Weenybopper' music (David Cassidy and the Osmonds).

In these later developments within consumer capitalism, one can detect the clever selection and combination of themes that were stressed in both skinhead and underground culture, along with the exploitation of traditional working class youth culture as a whole (from the weenyboppers to the pubgoer). A comparison of the sales of football papers, teen papers and music papers over the last three years reveals some of the resulting changes in consumption patterns of youth. The three major football papers - 'Goal', 'Football Monthly' and 'Shoot' - lost 213,573 in circulation per issue between July 1970 and December 1972, whilst many of the others went out of circulation (Tables 5.1, 5.5). The more established music papers - 'New Musical Express', 'Melody Maker', and 'Disc' - on the other hand have increased their sales by over 60,000 per issue (Table 5.2). More recently established music papers like 'Sounds' (150,000) and 'Music Scene', have already established substantial circulations, and there are many more music papers appearing on the market every year. However, the most significant development of all is in magazines directed at the younger age groups. 'Fabulous 208', aimed at the younger teenager and below, doubled its sales to 300,000 between 1970-2, while 'Jackie', also aimed at the younger teenager, had established the enormous circulation of 700,000 in 1974 (Table 5.3). In 1974 other magazines appeared in this table, the most notable example being the 32-page magazine 'Fan', a weekly selling at 12p per issue. The central content of these magazines is the endless reproduction of stories and pictures of the main stars in teenage Glamrock. In contrast, the less musically oriented, and more conventionally 'romantic' magazines are more or less stationary in circulation (like 'Mirabelle') or else sharply declining in sales, as with 'Valentine' (Table 5.4).

TABLE 5.1 Football papers (average sale per issue) (9)

	Feb. 1972	Jan.-June 1973	1974
'Goal'	300,000	247,603	no return
'Shoot'	225,000	137,447	242,478 (10)
'Football Monthly'	164,451	90,828	no return
Total	689,451	475,878	

TABLE 5.2 Papers with exclusively music content (average sale per issue)

	July-Dec. 1970	Jan.-June 1974
'Disc'	80,654	92,039
'Melody Maker'	145,644	209,782
'New Musical Express'	173,175	198,615
Total	398,873	500,436

TABLE 5.3 Music content teen magazines (average sale per issue)

	July-Dec. 1970	Jan.-June 1974
'Jackie'	613,985	700,000 (11)
'Fabulous 208'	151,344	227,870
Total	765,329	927,870

TABLE 5.4 Romance teen magazines (average sale per issue)

	July-Dec. 1970	Jan.-June 1974
'Mirabelle'	189,615	135,185
'Romeo'	202,358	no return (1972, 151,204)
'Valentine'	188,708	100,517
Total	580,681	-

TABLE 5.5 Some comparative figures on teenage magazine circulations

	Football papers	Exclusively music papers
Net increase/ decrease	- 213,573 (1972-3)	+ 102,653 (1970-4)
Percentage increase/ decrease	- 33.2	+ 49.4
	Music content teen papers	Romance magazines
Net increase/ decrease	+ 162,541 (1970-4)	- 193,960 (1970-2)
Percentage	+ 57.2	- 30.0

Two observations are in order about what are, quite clearly, very general figures. Using the Registrar-General's Estimate for the size of the 1972 population aged between 10 and 25 (that is, 5,452,100 males and 5,242,500 females), one can be sure that the percentage of that population reading papers with any music content (either in the teen category or in the exclusively music category) must in 1972 have been at least 21.2 per cent (assuming that each person read only one). The percentage of the females in this age category reading 'music content' papers must almost certainly have been in excess of 30 per cent, and probably was as high as 40 per cent; whilst the proportion of the same age group (male and female) reading any football paper was no higher than 4.5 per cent. If ever it was the case that youth culture in Britain was a matter of football and little else, it certainly was not the case in 1972. The prime market for consumer capitalism was, and remains, popular music aimed at a mass base.

It is also worth comparing these impressions with the decline of the papers of the counter-culture. Even though these papers rarely made formal returns to advertising and circulation agents, some indication of the decline can be arrived at from popular memory and contemporary personal contact. 'International Times', which was the organizing paper of the 'head' scene in the late 1960s and had a circulation of around 100,000 at that time, is running at about 10,000 an issue in 1974 and declining. Richard Neville's 'Oz' also sold 100,000 of the issue it produced after the 'School Kids' Issue' had been on trial, but is now operating on about 40,000 circulation. 'Ink', possibly the most promising paper of the underground in its mix of politics and culture, reached 28,000 circulation before collapse, and no information is available for '7 Days', the photo-dominated left-underground journal of 1971-2, except that it is defunct. The only 'underground' paper that is on a secure financial basis is 'Rolling Stone', selling 40,000 plus in Britain, but that is only marginally an underground paper, being professionally produced largely in the USA.

The demise of the underground and the demise of the football culture is well illustrated in figures and impressions of this kind, and there is no doubt that the internal failings of both cultures are a large explanation for their replacement. But the activities of consumer capitalism in speeding that process of replacement, and in providing a 'classless' product that would effectively fill the void, is crucial in explaining the content of the youth culture that has been built on the ashes of the underground and the soccer culture. The launching and continuation of pop-oriented music and teen magazines directed quite specifically at the younger age-groups has been accompanied by the development of techniques for 'star' creation that were largely unnecessary in the underground, in particular, where appearances on campus and in night-clubs was the key to the underground network. (13) Underground artists typically stressed an intellectual commitment to their music and frequently rejected direct influence from commercialism. (14) This state of intolerant coexistence did not last long, and at all levels of the music and pop world the domination of consumer capitalism and its interests is unchallenged. One needs only note the change in atmosphere, and price, in places like Kensington Market, the general expansion and oligopolization of alternative boutiques and bistros, and with it the rapid commercialization of any underground artist who presents himself as outside and beyond any such incorporation. The collapse of the alternative political economy of rock has created an area of untramelled manoeuvre in which has occurred the rapid development of new marketing techniques for the creation (the imposition) of Glamrock stars.

In a publication about David Bowie, Tim Ferris (1973) comments on the new techniques for promoting an artist:

> The trick was to treat Bowie as a star even if nobody knew that he was yet. Defries (Bowie's manager) who refers to both an artist and his music as 'the product' puts it this way: 'I think making America listen to Bowie, in terms of listening to the product and making them aware of the product before he came here, is one way of doing it. The other way is to bring him here without knowing anything about him, and putting him on a second bill, and letting them learn first-hand in sleazy, dingy little places for two or three years. I don't think that that necessarily is the right way.

Andrew Weiner describes a similar policy (which failed) in the American promotion of Brinsley Schwartz:

> In 1969 a management company known as the 'Famepushers' chartered a jet and flew some 100 bemused journalists out to New York to witness the debut of Brinsley Schwartz, bottom of the bill at the famous Fillmore auditorium. Objective: to establish the band as instant superstars of the 'progressive' variety. Result: Brinsley Schwartz impressed neither the New York audience nor the illustrious representatives of the English press. They received fairly grim notices, failed to become superstars, parted with 'Famepushers' and disappeared from sight (Weiner, 1973 p. 579).

The creation of a product in this way, however, is most stunningly illustrated in the mass promotion, through television, the teen papers and commercial radio, of the Glamrock stars - the most remarkable being Gary Glitter, who used to be Paul Raven on the early television pop programmes in the 1950s, and has been revamped, in his early 30s, as a teenage idol of Glamrock. Something of the same promotional ardour has also gone into the promotion of the younger Osmonds and David Cassidy through the junior pop press and children's television.

But David Bowie, more than any other artist, shows most clearly an understanding of his own both of the needs of the market and of the ways in which these market needs can be channelled for superstar success. His style is a combination of various themes in the style of the working class (and skinhead) culture and the content of the underground. The underground has stressed an individual and often exotic approach to fashion, which had started off in the junk shops but quickly was taken over by Biba's. Even then, the exoticism demanded a certain scruffy casualness or cool, where the skinhead style caricatured the clean and tidy presentation of their working class fathers, with a stylized uniformity of dress. The latest clothing styles promoted, most importantly, by Bowie, and imitated by other Glamrock artists, combine both these themes. Thus Bowie has successfully fused the form of commercial Glamrock (tied in, as it is, to marketing needs in clothing, and associated leisure consumption) with the content of underground music - but in the process has left the content imperceptible, emasculated and effectively irrelevant. He is the perfect representative for consumer capitalism with its concern to tranquillize the underground and its alternative market-place in order to create the appearance of itself as the universal source and market for goods and products for all needs. Bowie's exotic dress and presentation of self is combined with a meticulous concern for detail, a detail which has been extended to the uniform of unisex clothing. Thus, the latter-day 'underground' figure wears make-up, block heels and glitter in the hair; the skins' style has been softened to that of the smoothies, and the girls from both groups can use the bisexual styles as a basis for their own dress. In hastening this progress, Bowie has in effect colluded in consumer capitalism's attempt to re-create a dependent adolescent class, involved as passive teenage consumers in the purchase of leisure prior to the assumption of 'adulthood', rather than being a youth culture of persons who question (from whatever class or cultural perspective) the value and meaning of adolescence and the transition to the adult world of work.

The force of Bowie's contribution is illustrated by the fact that be is one of few contemporary artists who transcend different age groups. In the interviews we carried out in Sheffield with schoolchildren aged 12-18, we confirmed that Bowie was definitely the most popular figure amongst the older age groups, but we also discovered that his name was mentioned as important by all the other groups. The older children who identified with Bowie tended to interpret his music as an extension of the underground music of the 1960s, a music to be listened to for its intellectual content, but amongst the younger groups, Bowie's name was mentioned alongside those of Glamrock artists like Gary Glitter, the Sweet, Slade and others; and he was described in terms of his visual impact and only very loosely in terms of his material. Very few of the younger children thought the words were important in his songs. But, most interestingly, most of those interviewed recognized the commercialization of artists like Bowie:

> 14 year-old male: 'Well, he earns his living. He must be good to get the money he gets. It's not a case of what I think. It's a case of what all these top men think in the bowler hats. They like him because he brings in the money.'
> 16 year-old male: 'Today is mainly ruled by commercialism; it's all geared to getting as much money from one artist. Thousands of pounds are invested in one artist and all his potential exploited - and the agents get a big fat fee for the one artist.'

Many of the older children did draw distinctions between underground and commercial Glamrock (Emerson, Lake and Palmer being frequently mentioned as examples of the former, Gary Glitter and David Bowie, depending largely on whether the respondent liked him, as examples of the latter). Other young people who had identifiably become members of youth groups (like the smoothies or the Glamrock cult) were described as 'following the fashion' or 'following the here', etc., but generally the respondent never described his own behaviour or preferences in these terms. The 'sheep' syndrome was explained in terms either of a reaction to boredom, an attempt to hype up one's life-style or to seek kicks, or in terms of commercial interests being successful in creating heroes accepted in a passive way by their followers.

> 13 year-old male: 'There were skinheads and something else has started now. They'll start with Bowie and then in a year

> or two something else will start and they'll follow them.'
> 16 year-old male: 'It's just caught on. (Bowie) A few people thought it would be daring to dress up like that and it caught on (like the skinheads caught on. You can make anything catch on). If I wore a top hat for long enough probably everybody would be wearing top hats. If you did it in London, it would be a cert.'
> 16 year-old male: 'I used to be a skinhead but I was just following a trend and it made me sick. So I suddenly grew my hair long. I've taken part in wrecking a train. It's a trend. Everybody does it. A bit like sheep. I suppose I didn't want to be left out.'

To some extent, Bowie's acceptability seems to lie precisely in his ability to play back the youth culture's own awareness of exploitation and emptiness.

> 'At least part of me is into saying what a load of rubbish the whole rock business is and what a load is written about it. And if I can tart it up enough maybe people will see that it has a lot to do with them. We're not the great thinkers of our time, as you might believe from all the interviews we have to do. We're as close to real thinking as Mary Whitehouse, just as naive and bigoted' (Bowie).

Ben Gerson, in a 'Rolling Stone' review of the Bowie LP 'Aladdin Sane', writes:

> A lightning bolt streaks across David's face. On the inside cover, the lad is airbrushed into androgyny, a no less imposing figure for it. Though he has been anointed to go out amongst us and spread the word, we find stuffed into the sleeve, like dirty underwear, a form requesting our name, address, favourite film and TV stars plus $3.50 (50p in England) for membership of the David Bowie fan club.
>
> Such discrepancies have made Bowie the most recently controversial of all significant pop artists - all of it owing to the confusion of levels on which he operates. His flamboyant drive for pop-star status has stamped him in many people's eyes as a naked opportunist and poseur. But once it is recognised that stardom represents a metaphysical quest for Bowie, one has to grant at least that the question of self inflation is in his case unconventional (Gerson, 1969).

This confusion of levels is unconventional only if one extracts Bowie from the strategies used in his commercial promotion. The youth we interviewed had little difficulty in coping with these different levels, and the commercialism of his presentation was conventional to the point of unremarkability. The attraction of Bowie for the older youth lay in the form and content of his music, but, if asked, they rejected his bisexuality. Younger children tended to admire his dress and the style of his music, ignoring the content of his songs, and often being unaware of his profession of bisexuality. (15)

> 14 year-old girl: 'I know he is (bisexual) - at least I've heard rumours that way but I only think of him as a singer. I think his clothes are great. I like him altogether, the music and the words ... he's in a world of his own. A lot of

> them say he's rubbish and queer but I don't think he is. He's not rubbish but I know he's queer.'
>
> 12 year-old girl: 'I think his dress is a bit ladylike. I think he'd look better in a plain suit.... I think he'd look better with trousers on. He'd still be popular.'

The younger girls generally found Bowie's exotic dress and heavy make-up very attractive, and considered it a potential model for themselves. Bowie's bisexuality is far from being celebrated, but the spin-off from bisexual style is viewed favourably - a source of style for consumer capitalism in search for a class-based, commercially marketable, clothing style.

The provision of a cheap and 'universal' market of goods, therefore, has been aided by the emergence of a focal figure, an artist who is willing and able to offer the bridge between underground and skinhead cultures and a thoroughly commercial style that fuses the two. The demise of the underground is such that it can provide no alternative; and the collapse of the skinheads is in turn to be explained in terms of the appeal of a class-based Glamrock version of exotic but passive entertainment.

In the article quoted earlier, Piccone argued that the counter-culture, however much it realized the irrelevance and emptiness of official culture, could do no more than attempt to provide an alternative culture. It could not penetrate what Piccone called the 'precategorical realities' on which official culture was based - and hence, in the end, it was doomed to become merely another 'alternative' expression of those same realities (of inequality, powerlessness and alienation). The counter-culture appears now to have been absorbed almost entirely into official culture, however, and Piccone's pessimism is all the more underlined. The fact remains, however, as Piccone says, that the pre-categorical realities of capitalist society have changed:

> The precategorical foundation is nowadays to be found beyond the life-style of bourgeois society, where the foundation is no longer an empty stomach, but an empty spirit ... and therefore an empty life, notwithstanding its chrome and its plastic. Here is where the new theories of revolution begin to gather momentum: bourgeois life, even by bourgeois standards, is becoming unbearable. In the world, the objective conditions between labour and capital have been transposed to reappear on the international level between advanced capitalist societies and the third world, and, internally, between producers and consumers; culture becomes the mediator between the two. Within such a context the rise of the youth culture can be a crucial moment in the development of a new revolutionary consciousness. But its catalytic function is misconstrued and seen as the revolution itself. It simply becomes another mystification of the real revolutionary possibilities that it carries (Piccone, 1969, p. 17).

By an expression of the impermanence of himself, David Bowie, above all other recent and contemporary song writers and performers, describes and celebrates (because he does not challenge) the empty spirit and unbearable standards of bourgeois society. He says, in a verse from 'Changes', written in 1971:

> I still don't know what I was waiting for

And my time was running wild
A million dead end streets
Every time I thought I'd got it made
It seemed the taste was not so sweet
So I turned myself to face me
But I've never caught a glimpse
Of how the others must see the faker
I'm much too fast to take that test.

Consumer capitalism, and the class cultures that it has spawned, are the institutional expression of just such a spirit, and the frameworks through which a dying bourgeois society attempts to celebrate its defaults amongst the young. David Bowie has colluded in such a process, and has provided for the development of a consumer capitalism which, more than ever, plays back the alienation of youth onto itself, turning again and again the screws of a spiral of nihilism and meaninglessness onto a youth culture that could have been offered an alternative.

CONCLUSION

We have attempted in this paper to place the development of working class youth cultural style into the context of economic and political changes in the wider society, but specifically to understand these changes as being apprehended and used by the consumer-oriented branches of capitalist production for marketing purposes and regeneration of a viable culture for sales. It is our contention, therefore, that changes in working class youth culture are, in an important sense, manufactured changes, imposed on the mass via the media, and determined primarily by sales potential. Clearly, in saying this, we are rejecting attempts to explain the demise of the skinheads and the rise of Glamrock in terms of the deterrence-amplification and forecasting (or fad) theories we identified earlier. In any new cultural phenomenon, there will be found a dialectic between the form and content of previous traditions (in this case, the skinhead and underground cultures) and the range of choices made available for youth by the broader social conditions. These broader social conditions will include very centrally the economic and employment conditions within which such a cultural innovation will be developed, and we have argued here that the collapse of the underground, and the loss of underground ideology in the content of popular music, is in part explicable in terms of the recent political economy of youth.

In circumstances where the cultural domination is economically determined by a consumer industry, the cultural innovations will be both circumscribed and distorted by the marketing initiatives and strategies necessarily engaged in by the agents of consumerism. So that the 'liberation' of females anticipated in underground culture has been accomplished but in the highly distorted sense that the girls and women have become trend-leaders for advertising and equal targets in consumption outlets. This may be mirrored in a reduction in the more overt use of sexism in the media or in popular culture, but it is not equivalent to the structural reformation demanded by underground ideology and earlier pop cultural forms. In the same way, the sense of classlessness conveyed by much contemporary pop music and youth cultural style is merely a reflection of the creation in a consumer capitalist society of a one-dimensional economic product for universal consumption; the subjugation of all classes in youth to a repressive culture of style and no content. Glamrock culture is the culture of political nihilism, and the vehicle of a capitalist ideology can understand youth only in terms of changing patterns of consumption.

NOTES

1 As some of our quotations reveal, the 'fad' theory is very popular as an explanation of cultural changes amongst the participants themselves - but (given that the actors mainly refer to others as following a fad, and rarely see themselves in this way) our argument would be that this says more about the power of the media and the explanations it offers (for cultural change) than it says about the authenticity of the accounts of the participants.

2 This process of resentment and reaction has been in progress at least since 1961, and was only translated, by the media and the football establishment, into a 'moral panic' about skinheads as such in the first few months of the 1969-70 soccer season. Cf. Clarke 1973; Taylor, 1971a and b.

3 The most telling example of the Left fawning on the skinheads is the (in)famous 'Agro' pilot issue - 'Up Theirs' - published in December 1969. 'AGRO is going to be about hate - the agro we feel towards each other, and the agro we feel towards THEM. It's going to be about the institutions, family, school, borstal, etc. that are trying to manipulate that hate.' The second promised issue never appeared.

4 It is our conviction that some of the work carried out by sociologists of deviance in the late 1960s was itself informed by a rather uncritical ascription of authenticity and approval to nearly all deviant groups studied; and, since this approving stance was in part a function of the sociologist's own urban populism (to translate C. Wright Mills on the rural populism of early American sociology) (Mills, 1943), so the assertion of authenticity was all the more marked the more proletarian the phenomenon studied. Hence, in much of that work (cf. Taylor, 1971a and b), there is an apologetic tendency to wrench youth movements out of their broader social and economic contexts with a view to simplistic analysis of their activities as significant in terms of the 'attempt to assert control'. No real attention is given to more functional, and less reactionary, possibilities, e.g. for control over work and life, and over self and machines, that were attempted by others. For a confessional on this question, see Taylor, Walton and Young (1975).

5 Our purposes in this paper prevent extended discussion of a persistent theme in these taped conversations - the attempt

to justify certain forms of (essentially) property crime, and to distinguish this from fighting. The stereotyping of skinheads by other youth as 'ignorant' seems to be a code for decrying their choice of method (violence) and victim (other youth).

6 'Department of Employment Gazette', vol. 9, no. 9 (September 1974).

7 Quoted in Lightbrown (1973).

8 Extrapolated from 'Department of Employment Gazette', op. cit.

9 Source of these figures (variously): 'British Rate and Data (National Guide to Media Selection), vol. 18, no. 6 (June 1971), vol. 20, no. 7 (June 1973), vol. 20, no. 10 (October 1973) and vol. 21, no. 9 (September 1974); also Billy Hack, The Riches in Soccer Rags, '7 Days' 15 (9-15 February 1972).

10 The increase between 1973 and 1974 in the sale of the relatively cheap weekly 'Shoot' is probably explicable in terms of the absence in choice in the weekly market of football magazines, after the collapse of 'Striker' (selling 120,000 a week in 1971) and 'Inside Football' (110,000). No information is available on these journals now, nor on the monthlies 'Football Pictorial' (60,000 in 1971), 'Football Fan' (40,000) and 'Football Academy'. It has recently been reported (September 1974) that the future of both the 'Football Association News' (owned by Pearl & Dean) and 'World Soccer' is very uncertain. Certainly, it would be difficult to imagine any publisher attempting again to market a publication like the 72-part egghead weekly encyclopaedia, 'The Book of Football', which was marketed by Marshall Cavendish late in 1971 at 23p a week.

11 This figure of 700,000 plus for 'Jackie' is actually a decrease on 1973 (when a return of 800,000 was made), and it may be that the mushrooming of alternative and similar magazines, especially marked during 1973 and 1974 contributed to 'Jackie's' relative loss of popularity within the category of music content teen papers. No figures are available for 'Melanie', for example, an extremely popular and slightly more glossy weekly, produced by IPC Magazines, and marketed through the well organized IPC outlets. 'Jackie' is produced by D.C. Thomson & Co.

12 Table 5.5 should be read very roughly as indicating general changes, rather than measuring the magnitude of such changes. The appearance of returns in British Rate and Data is unreliable, for reasons that are interesting in themselves, and very few figures are available for the ever increasing number of music content teen papers. There is no doubt that this category, in particular, could boast a much greater sale than that represented here.

13 It is not our intention here to enter into detailed discussion of promotional techniques at different periods in the evolution of the rock music industry. Our point is that the marketing of David Bowie was intended as universal marketing (across culture, class and age groups) whilst earlier hard-sell creations (e.g. the Monkees) had been intended mainly for sectional consumption. For a fuller discussion of the marketing of rock music, see Dave Laing (1969), chapter 3.

14 This point can be taken too far, but some indication of the ambiguous relationship of underground groups and consumer capitalism can be found in the number of charity concerts engaged in, during 1969-71, by underground groups (especially Edgar Broughton, the later Lennon and, of course, all those who played at the famous Bangla Desh concert). The illegitimacy of such concerts was apparent then, in commercial terms, and was again illustrated in 1974 when the police broke up the Windsor Free Festival.

15 The way in which Glamrock is received by the audience probably varies over class groups, ethnic groups and across regions. Glamrock is known, in certain parts of the country, as 'faggot-rock' - as music for gays, and some gays also define it in this way. The sexual imagery in Glamrock has not really been investigated as it is interpreted by the audience - and neither has the receipt of the nihilistic messages in the songs themselves. Our own research in Sheffield indicated that the older youth definitely understood Bowie to be bisexual and nihilistic, but we concede that this requires further empirical investigation elsewhere.

Chapter 6

WHEN PUPILS AND TEACHERS REFUSE A TRUCE: The secondary school and the creation of delinquency

David Reynolds

And now the time has come for his lesson
But all the kids would rather be 'messin
We dance and shout and throw books around
And some hit him as he has found
He shouts and screams till the lessons gone
But all the kids would rather sing a song
And now the time has come at last
To end the lesson and get out fast.
(15 year-old secondary modern schoolboy)

In 1967 Michael Power of the Medical Research Council's Social Medicine Unit published work derived from a study of secondary schoolboys in Tower Hamlets which showed large differences between outwardly similar secondary modern schools in their delinquency rates, differences which he could not explain by differences in the delinquency rates of the areas from which the schools drew their pupils (Power et al., 1967; Phillipson, 1971). His suggestion was that some schools may have been preventing the development of delinquency amongst their children whilst others - perhaps like the school described above - may have provided an environment within the school that led to delinquent behaviour outside it.

In spite of the importance of the work - one reviewer wrote that 'The work of Power et al. in East London seems likely to provide us with one of the most important new facts about delinquency for decades' (Downes, 1968) - and in spite of its obvious relevance to those teaching in similar inner city areas, permission to conduct further research inside the schools was refused by the Inner London Education Authority. Although the work has subsequently been criticized on methodological grounds (Baldwin, 1972) and although work in other London schools by the Cambridge Institute of Criminology has suggested that the schools that had a high delinquency rate were those which were receiving a more 'delinquency prone' intake at age 11 (Farrington, 1972; West and Farrington, 1973), other research has, in the past few years, also suggested that there is something about certain schools that makes a difference to the amount of deviance and delinquency exhibited by their pupils (Rutter, 1973). Exactly what that something is we do not know.

This chapter, based on a continuing long-term study of an homogeneous working class former mining community, is a preliminary account of work that is attempting to find out what it is about their schools that makes the difference for their children and what it is about some schools that may make their children different. (1)

THE MISSING SCHOOL

Sociologists and criminologists have for decades been attempting to discover why some people - delinquents or criminals - break more social rules more often than other supposedly 'normal' people. In this attempt to discover the causes of delinquent behaviour, researchers have invariably focused on differences between individuals in their personality, family background, intelligence and even their body physique as their explanatory variables; they have concentrated on explaining deviance as the result of individual pathology.

Although these individualized explanations of the generation of social problems, recently re-expressed in theories about the inter-generational transmission of deprivation, may enable the governments who have funded much of the research to continue blaming individuals and their families for not taking advantage of what the social system has to offer them, such approaches as these, which in turn reflect and then reinforce the initial ideology that created them, may only serve to prevent us asking more searching questions about the nature of the constraints imposed on people by the inequalities of our social system in general and by the operation of certain social institutions in particular. One such institution which appears to have escaped much of the attention that researchers have lavished on children and their families is the educational system. To say this is not, of course, to argue that criminologists have not given some attention to the way in which the educational system may impose strains on large numbers of its working class children. Cohen (1955, p. 112) notes that 'One of the situations in which children of all social levels come together and compete in terms of the same set of middle class criteria and in which working class children are most likely to be found wanting is the school.' Cohen argued that the educational system and the teachers that staff it may, because of their middle class values and assumptions as to what constitutes good behaviour and good pupils, deny working class children status within the schools because they have not been socialized to fulfil the status requirements of middle class society and are therefore unable to compete with middle class children. Delinquency may then be a form of solution to the working class child's problems of status frustration.

It is unfortunate though that the interest which sub-cultural theorists like Cohen have shown in the educational system as a 'generator' of delinquency has not, apart from valuable work by Hargreaves (1967), been matched by any substantial analysis of how the educational process actually produces the problems that it is said to produce. Phillipson, writing on the same theme, argues that 'Throughout the literature the reference is to the school rather than to particular schools; sociologists seem to be operating with highly abstract models of the school which rest on their intuitive hunches about what schools are really like' (Phillipson, 1971, p. 239).

Even recent developments within the sociology of deviance, which emphasize the importance of studying the interaction between rule-breakers and rule-makers and of studying the moral career of the delinquent, have - with the exception of Werthman (1967) and Cicourel and Kitsuse (1963) - neglected to study the key defining agency of the school and to ask whether different schools may, by labelling and processing their students differently, generate different delinquency rates. The result of our general ignorance as to exactly how the process of teacher/pupil interaction is producing the problems which it is said to be producing is that we are still operating with the implicit assumption that all schools of a particular type are the same in the type and quality of this interaction and therefore in their effects - as Phillipson notes, 'The implicit suggestion is that all schools are sufficiently alike to produce a standardised response from their pupils. The idea that there may be considerable differences between overtly similar schools, that some schools may facilitate and others hinder the drift into delinquency does not seem to have occurred to writers on delinquency' (Phillipson, 1971, p. 239).

Since children spend much of their time in schools, since the school is the first significant area of authority relationships that the child enters outside the home and since few criminologists would talk of 'the family' as if all families were the same yet regularly talk of 'the school' as if all schools were the same, it is worth while to begin by trying to discover exactly why there has been so little examination by criminologists as to whether different schools may have the effect of producing different pupils with differing rates of deviance.

The principal reason for the absence of such research is that educational research, to which one looks for a sociology of school differences, has tended to take the educational system for granted and to concentrate not on differences within the system but on the differences between pupils and their parents that can explain why some social groups get more out of the system than others. Education, almost by definition, is held to be good for children and more education is held to be even better for them - if they fail to take advantage of what the system offers them, then the explanation must lie not in the nature and operation of the system, but in the deficiencies of the children, their parents and their joint value systems. In fact governments, and those defining educational problems in similar ways to governments, have seen the educational system not as a generator of problems but as an effective antidote to their generation - the Crowther Committee, which reviewed the evidence that the peak age for delinquency moved up from 14 to 15 when the school leaving age was raised to 15, concluded that there was nothing in this state of affairs to make anyone doubt the value of the sort of education our schools were providing. In fact, the Committee argued, the delinquency may arise 'not because boys are at school, but because they are not at school enough' (Report of the Central Advisory Council for Education, 1969, para. 63).

The great majority of educational research has therefore simply individualized the explanation of educational problems by concentrating on the family background, ability, personality and character of the individual child that may lead to his deviance, maladjustment or educational failure without looking at the operation of the regimes from which he is held to deviate. A good example of this 'individualizing' of what may well be institutional problems is provided by much research into the phenomenon of truancy. One study (Tyerman, 1958) compared a group of truants and so-called 'normal' children and concluded that 'Few of the truants had a happy and secure home influence. Most of them came from broken homes or homes where there was open disharmony. In general, the parents set poor examples, and were unsatisfactory characters. They neglected their children, were ineffective in their supervision and took little interest in their welfare. The view of many writers that the truant is born in an inferior environment seemed to be confirmed.' Even where some of the truants gave reasons connected with school - such as fear of the teachers - as the explanation for their behaviour, the author comments that 'These reasons may to some extent be valid but it is unwise to accept truants' excuses at their face value. The limits of self deception are wide and it is easier to blame other people than oneself. Parents and children look for scapegoats and teachers are often chosen' (Tyerman, 1958, p. 220).

An alternative view of truancy - a view rarely adopted - is to see it as a form of rebellion against a system which the children feel has little to offer them. Working class children may thus see the school as an alien institution, whose middle class teachers deny them status, and may therefore rebel against it by truanting. Rather than discounting the reasons and motivations given by the truants for their own actions as the products of 'abnormal' personalities, it may be worth while to pay some regard to these accounts of 'deviant' behaviour, since in just the same way as truancy may result from an abnormal or disturbed personality, it can also be seen as a reaction to what the children see as an unsatisfying environment within some of their schools.

It is possible for educational researchers to defend the absence of any body of knowledge on the sociology of school learning and so on within school interaction by arguing that individual schools exert only a minor influence in determining the sort of people that their children grow up to be, when compared to the influence of the family, the peer group, the mass media and the pervasive influence of large and continuing inequalities in the distribution of power and resources within society. They could use as evidence the failure of specific programmes of educational reform to have much long term effect on their pupils and the general failure of the overall expansion of educational opportunities to benefit those social groups who have historically underachieved - as one author noted 'In summary, it may be said that liberal policies failed basically on an inadequate theory of learning. They failed to notice that the major determinants of educational attainment were not schoolmasters but social situations, not curriculum but motivation, not formal access to the school but support in the family and the community' (Halsey, 1972, p. 8).

Belief in the relative unimportance of schooling as a determinant of anything has been reinforced by the Coleman Report in the USA, the Plowden Report in this country and the recent work by Jencks, which agrees that differences between schools in their human and physical resources, in their curriculum and in their methods exert very little influence in producing differences in the attainments of their students. Yet these studies included very few school variables in their analysis and the variables that were included were resource based indicators such as class sizes, age of school buildings and number of books in the school library. Research into whether the school makes a difference because of its pupil/teacher ratios has been undertaken - that which studies the effects of different types of pupil/teacher relations has not.

Criminological research has therefore individualized the explanation of delinquency by concentrating on individual pathologies. It has not examined whether schools may differ in their ability to generate or prevent deviance in general and delinquency in particular because of the influence of educational research, which has concentrated on family, personality, intelligence and value differences as the explanation of individual success and failure. No systematic sociology of the school is available for use and development, since educational research has not - until comparatively recently (Young, 1972) - focused on how pupil/teacher interaction and teachers' definitions may affect the success and failure of individual pupils and perhaps of whole schools. The school is therefore assumed to have a constant influence simply because few people have attempted to study it in depth.

THE SCHOOL CAN MAKE THE DIFFERENCE

Work in our community, which has so far concentrated on a group of nine secondary modern schools that take what is regarded as the bottom two-thirds of the ability range at age 11 and on boys only within these schools, suggests that these assumptions of the constancy of school influence are mistaken. Table 6.1 shows very large differences in the sort of pupils that each of the nine schools have been producing over the academic years 1966/7 to 1972/3 on three measures of 'output' - average attendance, academic success (defined as going on to the local technical college after leaving school) and delinquency (defined as being found guilty before a court or officially cautioned by age 15). On attendance, the school with the top rate gets 89.1 per cent attendance and the bottom school 77.2 per cent. One school gets over half of its pupils into the local tech - which is regarded locally as the key to obtaining an apprenticeship or craft - and another gets 8.6 per cent. The school with the highest delinquency rate has 10.5 per cent of its boys recorded as officially delinquent each school year - the bottom rate school averages 3.8 per cent.

TABLE 6.1 Secondary modern school performance: academic years 1966/7 to 1972/3

School	Delinquency (first offenders per annum)	Attendance	Academic attainment
A	10.5%	79.9%	34.8%
B	8.6%	78.3%	26.5%
C	8.3%	84.3%	21.5%
D	8.1%	77.2%	8.4%
E	7.4%	89.1%	30.4%
F	7.2%	81.3%	18.5%
G	5.2%	87.0%	37.9%
H	4.5%	88.5%	52.7%
I	3.8%	83.6%	36.5%

The nine schools also exhibit a remarkable consistency in their relative performance over the years - the Kendall Coefficient of Concordance for the nine schools attendance rates over seven academic years is 0.85 and that for academic attainment is 0.563. Even with national social change, local population movements and with seven different intakes of pupils, the relative performance of the schools remains substantially unchanged over time. As Table 6.2 shows for the attendance figures, year after year the 'effective' schools retain their effectiveness.

The school differences are furthermore remarkably consistent with each other - schools high on delinquency are low on academic attainment ($r = - 0.526$) and low on attendance ($r = - 0.579$). The nine schools are therefore producing children who appear to be very different, to be consistently different over time and to be consistently different on three separate indicators.

It is possible that these officially generated statistics may reflect not just differences in behaviour between groups of pupils at the different schools but also variations in the administrative methods and definitions which are used to produce the statistics (Kitsuse and Cicourel, 1963), yet it is difficult to explain the differences in this way. The attendance rates were collected in the same way in the different schools and all the schools used an identical system of 'processing' the non-attenders by the use of education welfare officers, or 'mitch men' as they are called locally. The academic attainment figures of numbers carrying on with their education at the local technical college, the entry to which is dependent on four passes in the local school leaving certificate, are of course dependent on the numbers of children that the individual schools enter for the various exams. Although it is possible that differences between schools may reflect not real differences in the academic performance of their pupils but simply the fact that some schools enter a higher proportion of their pupils for the exams than other schools, who enter only their most able children, this does not explain these findings. If the entry policy of the school were the determinant of its results, we would expect schools entering only the most able of their children to have higher pass rates than those entering

TABLE 6.2 Attendance rates for boys at secondary modern schools by year and school: academic years 1966/7 to 1972/3

School	1966/7	1967/8	1968/9	1969/70	1970/1	1971/2	1972/3
E	88.5% 1	89.7% 1	90.9% 2	90.6% 1	90.0% 2	87.5% 2	87.2% 2
H	88.0% 2	87.3% 3	91.6% 1	88.9% 2	90.1% 1	88.2% 1	85.7% 3
G	87.1% 3	84.4% 5	86.5% 3	88.4% 3	87.6% 3	86.2% 3	88.2% 1
I	86.3% 4	87.9% 2	84.2% 5	84.6% 4	83.0% 5	80.0% 5	80.0% 5
C	85.0% 5	85.9% 4	84.5% 4	82.0% 7	83.2% 4	83.5% 4	85.2% 4
F	83.9% 6	82.8% 7	83.5% 7	82.5% 6	80.6% 6	77.3% 8	79.0% 7
A	83.2% 7	83.3% 6	84.0% 6	82.6% 5	77.6% 8	75.4% 9	75.1% 9
B	82.7% 8	75.4% 8	81.3% 8	77.5% 9	73.0% 9	79.0% 6	79.3% 6
D	74.9% 9	74.8% 9	77.7% 9	79.7% 8	78.2% 7	78.5% 7	76.5% 8
Annual average attendance for all 9 schools	83.8%	82.3%	84.1%	83.1%	81.1%	80.7%	80.9%

Kendall Coefficient of Concordance = 0.85 $P < 0.001$ significant

a greater proportion of their ability range. This does not happen - school D, whose total fourth year of 65 pupils were entered only for 60 different exams in the 1972 school leaving certificate, achieved an overall pass rate of 47 per cent, whereas school H, whose fourth year of only 27 pupils were entered for no less than 130 exams, achieved an 85 per cent pass rate. Since schools entering a small proportion of their pupils achieve the greatest failure rates of all, it is unlikely that the differences between the schools represent anything other than the fact that some schools are producing pupils who cannot - or more likely will not - show much academic ability.

The statistics of delinquency are perhaps those most open to doubt, since these rates may reflect variations in the processing of offenders by the local police force (Cicourel, 1968). It is easy to see how a school with a high delinquency rate may get a bad name with the local police, who may in turn patrol its catchment area more intensively and be more likely to 'book' offenders in that area rather than use their powers of discretion to warn them. Differences between schools may therefore be exaggerated by the results of differential police action. We know that area police based in the catchment areas of two of the schools have, in fact, been proceeding informally with offenders from those two schools - School A and School F - by taking them to their school for punishment, rather than by taking them through the formal legal processes, yet both these schools already have official delinquency rates that are above average. Since it is possible that other sources of bias might also be operating, we are currently studying the patterns of police patrolling to see if certain areas are 'over-patrolled' relative to other areas and are also giving self report studies of delinquent behaviour to samples of pupils in the schools as a check on the validity of the official records as indicators of the total amount of delinquency committed by their pupils.

The crucial factor is, of course, whether these differences between the delinquency rates of the nine secondary modern schools reflect the effects of different schools or simply reflect differences in the social background of the pupils attending the schools. Since the nine schools draw their pupils from geographically separate areas of the community and since there is no system of parental choice of school either, it has been possible to assess the social characteristics of the pupils at the schools by looking at census data on the individual wards from which the schools take their pupils. Table 6.3 shows the delinquency rates for the schools and the proportion of the population of the catchment area who are in social class 4 and 5 jointly and in social class 5 on its own. Although a high proportion of people in social classes 4 and 5 is often associated with the existence of educational and social problems in an area, since the correlations between school delinquency rates and the proportion of the population in social class 4 and 5 ($r = 0.229$) and social class 5 ($4 = 0.293$) are low, we can conclude that the school delinquency rates vary largely independently of the social class composition of the school catchment areas.

TABLE 6.3: Social class of school catchment areas and school delinquency rates

School	Delinquency (First offenders per annum)	Social class	
		4 and 5	5
A	10.5%	44.8%	10.4%
B	8.6%	38.1%	7.4%
C	8.3%	43.9%	16.3%
D	8.1%	38.9%	11.1%
E	7.4%	42.2%	12.0%
F	7.2%	43.4%	14.5%
G	5.2%	42.5%	8.9%
H	4.5%	37.5%	7.9%
I	3.8%	42.9%	10.0%

These nine schools therefore appear to be producing large differences in the rates of delinquency, truancy and academic attainment of their pupils, differences which do not appear to be significantly related to variations in the social background of the catchment areas from which the schools take their pupils. What is it about the schools that makes the difference? (2)

THE NATURE OF A TRUCE

A survey of the literature on secondary schooling for working class children would lead one to expect that social life in these schools should be characterized by a high degree of conflict between pupils and staff, high levels of coercion by the teachers and resulting high levels of pupil alienation from the goals of the school. Waller in his classic 'The Sociology of Teaching' first argued for a view of the school as a despotism in a perilous state of equilibrium. He thought that 'The teacher represents the established social order in the school, and his interest is in maintaining that order, whereas pupils have only a negative interest in that feudal superstructure.... Pupils are the material in which teachers are supposed to produce results. Pupils are human beings striving to realise themselves in their own spontaneous manner, striving to produce their own results in their own way. Each of these hostile parties stand in the way of the other, in so far as the aim of either are realised, it is at the sacrifice of the other' (Waller, 1932, pp. 195-6). This view of 'the school as fortress' is reflected in much of the writing on working class secondary schooling - Webb, writing about a secondary modern school in what might now be called a socially deprived area, argues that 'Hostility(between teachers and boys) is a key feature at Black School. It is present whenever a teacher deals with boys but varies in intensity' (Webb, 1962). Organizational analysis too would suggest that service institutions like the secondary school, the mental hospital and the prison will be faced with large numbers of clients who have no real wish to make use of the services provided or to be serviced in the way that the institution wishes, thus producing problems of control for that institution. Whereas grammar schools are able to offer a route to high status occupations as a reward for their pupils' acceptance of the schools' standards, secondary modern schools cannot expect such commitment because they have little to offer that their pupils want. Order within these schools will not be maintained simply by the normative or instrumental commitment obtained by the schools' unspoken promise of a successful future, and is only likely to be obtained by the increased use of coercion.

But this conflict that one might expect as a result of the secondary modern schools' position in the national educational system appears to be largely absent in most of our nine schools in the mining valley. At a time when de-schooling the educational system is held to be the answer to its problems and when journalists of the 'school as hell' variety are attracting increased attention, what is remarkable about social life and interpersonal relations in most of these schools is not that there is so much conflict but that there is so little. A preliminary analysis suggests that the crucial factor in determining a favourable overall response by the pupils to most of their schools lies in the degree to which both staff and pupils have reached an unofficial series of arrangements - or truces - which lay down the boundaries beyond which the participants in the schools will not carry their conflict. The truce is an arrangement for the mutual convenience of both sides in the conflict, made between working class pupils of low aspirations who seek a stress free time within their schools and teachers who realize that many of the rules and regulations which should, in theory, govern the interaction between them and their pupils would, if applied, only make their task as teachers more difficult.

A truce situation means, simply, that the teachers will go easy on the pupils and that the pupils will go easy with the teacher. On the teacher's side, they will no longer proceed against the pupils to any great extent to ensure compliance with expressive, non-pedagogic or character moulding goals since they know that to do so will only produce rebellion, a rebellion that by lowering pupils' overall level of commitment to the school will make it even more difficult for the school to maintain control. The acceptance of the truce offered by the children also means that the staff accept that their authority does not extend outside the school gates or outside school hours. Drinking in a pub under age, although technically an offence, will be ignored by the teachers, as will smoking going to and from school, and various petty misbehaviour such as fighting in the street.

Since the teacher has already agreed to much of his authority being eroded by the truce, school lessons are no longer the focus of conflict between teacher and taught. Lessons can be started with ten or fifteen minutes of light-hearted banter, jokes and discussions from the pupils dealt with and even repartee indulged in when someone is told to shut up, or stand up and answers back. Work in the lessons will now get done not by didactic command or by other authoritarian methods, but by appealing to the pupils, in a spirit of self-sacrifice, that 'it's time we got something done'.

For the pupils there is every advantage in making a truce with their school regimes and teachers. Secondary modern school to them is an irrelevance, a period of transition between the juniors and the real world of work, money and traditional valley life that they wish to pass to as soon as possible. Although many of them will later come to realize the advantages that school qualifications can bring, the possession of CSEs, GCEs, attendance prizes and good behaviour certificates is unlikely, as they see it, to make them a better plumber, bricklayer, miner or professional footballer. Their expectations of their future are low - the 'A' stream of one of the schools think that on leaving school they will be:

> apprentice carpenter, bricklayer, bricklayer, toolmaker, lorrydriver, painting, bricklayer, electrician, aero engineer, apprentice carpenter, outdoor labourer, roof tiler, factory fitter, fitter.

Even their aspirations are low - when asked 'Suppose you could do any job in the world and you had all the qualifications and experience required, what would you be?', they reply:

> draftsman, bricklayer cos it's good money, bricklayer,

draughtsman, painting and decorating, bricklayer, going on the dole, painting, pop singer, painting and decorating, anything that pays good, footballer, rooftiler, factory job, co-op job, geetarist.

To pupils of low expectations and low aspirations, the truce appears to be a sensible adjustment by an institution whose rewards they are not dependent upon - bargains can be struck with teachers to reduce the amount of written work that is set and to increase the amount of football that can be played instead of normal lessons. A certain amount of their limited rule-breaking will also be ignored - smoking in the toilets at break is no longer proceeded against, chewing of gum in class is permitted, and the wearing of supposedly forbidden 'Sta-prest' jeans instead of the approved trousers overlooked.

For the staff, too, calling a truce offers many advantages in promising an easier life. Few of them will have entered teaching with the 'character moulding' motives that may have influenced preceding generations of the profession. Many of the rules appear out of date and difficult to administer; and many of them realize that to proceed against the pupils in the 'non-academic' area of their life is to risk rebellion. Furthermore, agreements with the pupils that the teacher will go easy on written work, and replace much of it by discussion, on pop music, or football, is obviously easier for the teacher, since with 'easy lessons' he is usually guaranteed good order and relative silence from his classes. Other colleagues and the headmaster will will assume that 'Mr X' is a good teacher, because his classes are quiet, a claim that cannot be proved wrong by events since there is little external exam check to see how much has been learned.

A truce situation, then, means that stress will be reduced by both sides recognizing boundaries past which their conflict does not usually progress. Such boundaries are maintained on both sides by the use of informal social control and sanctions - among the staff, a new or overtly authoritarian teacher may be advised to 'ease up a bit - it's for your own good' or told to 'go easily - you'll find that with these children you'll get more done in the end'. Among the pupils, those making trouble in classes will often be shouted at by the others, hushed up and told to behave or 'it'll get the teacher mad'. Whilst occasional window smashing is unlikely to provoke much reaction from the other pupils and may even produce some admiration, smashing of twenty windows - since it is likely to disturb and break the truce - will be condemned by the majority of the pupils. In schools where a truce exists, social status within the informal pupil subculture will not necessarily be gained by a pupil's doing things which the school and its teachers believe to be wrong.

WHEN A SCHOOL GOES TO WAR

At some of the schools, though, no truce exists and the conflict between middle class teachers and working class pupils is played out with entirely predictable results. In the first two years of the secondary school, an anti-school sub-culture is usually absent;

forests of hands shoot up when a teacher asks for the answer to a question and the role of being the person who goes down to collect teacher's cigarettes from the sweet shop is usually accepted with pride. But by the beginning of the third year sections of that year will have given up the attempt to conform to school standards in the areas of dress, manners and morals and will have begun what one author noted as a process of dissociation from adult middle class standards (Downes, 1966). Their teachers may then either accept the situation, in which case the truce that they offer will be operative and respected by the pupils, or they can intensify their efforts to ensure compliance with their expressive, character moulding rules, in which case their problems will intensify.

Using School B as an example of an institution in which there is no truce, social relations between teachers and pupils are characterized by hostility and by the low regard in which pupils hold their teachers.

> 'I want teachers which associate with us pupils. The teachers like - can't take a joke or have a laugh.'
>
> 'Mr -, he's hard. He's more of an assassin than a teacher. I want teachers who can take a joke and understand you.'

Because of their lack of commitment to the teachers and their unwillingness to see them as 'significant others' in their lives, the teachers need to apply increased coercion to ensure their control.

> 'They hit you around like you were dirt here. Billy goes mad with you - he grabs your hair, pulls down your head and knees you in the stomach.'

The increased coercion is likely to produce lower commitment to the school on the part of the pupils and - as a consequence - lower expectations of the pupils on the part of the teachers.

> 'I don't like a few of our teachers. Some if you don't know what to do they don't help you and if you go out to ask them they just say why aren't you working why don't they help us? I think that's because we are in B that they haven't any time for us B Boys.'
>
> 'Some teachers just tell you what to do and if you ask a question says work it out yourselves and calls you a lout.'
>
> 'Only two or three teachers teach us our work properly. Others just write things on the board for us to copy. That way we don't learn anything for ourselves.'

The conflict between pupils and teachers is continually fuelled by the attempt of the staff to exercise control in areas of the pupils' lives where they expect autonomy, such as in their behaviour outside school.

> 'If they see you smoking in the night or in the pictures they get you when you come back to school. I remember one incident when me and my friends went to the pictures on a saturday night and we had all been drinking before we went, and as the ice-cream woman came around we all got up to buy ice-cream, and as we were buying it one of the teachers in our school came over and asked to smell my breath and he smelt my breath and he said he will see me monday morning. So I went home that night and told my mother what happenned she gave me a scolding for

drinking which the boys but she said it's nothing to do with the teachers. If we had more time I think I could go on for ages writing about the things about our school.'

In the schools - like this one - that have no truce, there are many pupils who wish for one.

'The rules that I don't agree with are no smoking and no talking in class. The rule of no smoking in the school is pathetic as if they stop us smoking in school we will only smoke outside or behind the teachers backs so is it worth punishing boys that do smoke as there are plenty more behind their backs.'

'And if they stop you talking in class - it's a load of rubbish. All boys will talk in class so is it worth bothering to keep this rule. Besides they can never stop you talking. You are punished for asking the boy you sit by what page is next in maths.'

Where there is this sort of conflict in a school such as School B, there will invariably be vandalism within it, truanting from it and delinquency outside it. Such a reaction from the pupils of these schools is likely to reflect a weakening of the 'moral bind' which ties the child to conventional adult life and institutions; and indicates that where the initiation of the child into the accepted ways of life of the adult community that the school undertakes is perverse, then so too will be the child's response. An initiation that the pupils are likely to regard as perverse is produced by the attempt of teachers to exercise control over the pupils in areas of their life where they feel they should have some autonomy, such as those concerned with the expressive areas of 'dress, manners and morals'. The attempt by the school to exercise control in this area is likely to set in motion a circular process of deviancy amplification - the pupils will regard the teachers as using illegitimate authority and will be less likely to defer to their wishes in other areas of school life. Teachers, perceiving increased opposition, may intensify their efforts to ensure compliance with their rules, which will invariably mean the increased use of coercion, as the teachers are less and less likely to receive the normative commitment of their pupils. Such coercion is unlikely to reduce the total amount of misbehaviour exhibited by the pupils, and may only increase it, since informal social status within an increasingly alienated student body will increasingly depend upon pupils doing things which are wrong in the eyes of the school.

Since the community in which this research is being done is very atypical in its social structure and history - indeed, it is difficult to know if the 'typical community' so beloved of researchers really exists anywhere - and since current work within the schools that is testing these ideas is still going on, it is unwise to say anything more than that with these pupils at these schools, what they most want is the power to determine the sort of people they want to be, a power which most of them obtain by a rational process of negotiating reality with their teachers to make the reality of school life more acceptable for both sides. But if their schools refuse the possibilities offered by a truce though, these pupils will regard their schools as maladjusted to their needs. Rebellion within and delinquency without will be the result when the teachers and then their pupils refuse to make a truce.

CONCLUSION

This analysis suggests that the school itself is - by the way in which its teachers treat the children in their charge - an important influence on the sort of young people that they turn out to be. In certain schools there exists a truce between teachers and taught, in which both sides bargain and reach a negotiated agreement to limit the intensity of their conflict. The teachers' part of the bargain is to reduce their stress on rules that attempt to control the pupils in the expressive areas of their lives. But where no such truce is offered in a school and where the teachers continue to enforce rules on such areas as school uniform, smoking and chewing gum, which specify alien middle class standards and values, then the pupils will rebel against that school and against those teachers. Any increased coercion that the teachers use to try to ensure conformity to these standards may only increase these rates of within school deviance and outside school delinquency even further.

NOTES

1 This study has only been possible with the generous help and co-operation of the Director of Education, Education Committee, teachers and pupils of the necessarily anonymous community. That educational authorities should grant a researcher virtually unrestricted freedom to visit and take lessons in their schools and also place no restrictions on the researcher's freedom to say what he wants about whoever and whatever he wants, speaks for itself.
2 This analysis is based only on informal participant observation within the schools that has included unstructured interviews with pupils and the taking of school lessons to generate hypotheses that could be systematically tested later. Work within the schools is still proceeding and is currently studying the operation of the school regimes, the staff and pupil sub-cultures and the process of within school and within classroom interaction.

Chapter 7

WORKING CLASS YOUTH CULTURES

John Clarke and Tony Jefferson

Graham Murdock and Robin McCron's earlier paper (Chapter 1) provides us with the starting point of our argument, and this essay takes for granted their critique of the idea of 'classless' youth culture; and it is from that position that we develop our analysis of distinctive styles in working class youth cultures. For the purposes of this paper, the examples we have used are the mods and skinheads. Though not wishing to deny the existence of some more general youth cultural developments during the post-war period, we feel that the analysis of styles, and the way they signify crucial themes, is of primary importance.

Some general comments are necessary by way of an introduction to this paper. First, it is essentially a 'work in progress report' on a collective project on post-war British youth cultures which is being undertaken at the Centre for Contemporary Cultural Studies. Consequently, we are indebted to all the other members involved in that project for the development of the ideas presented here. We owe special debts to those whose work has been specifically used in this paper: Brian Roberts, whose work on Phil Cohen's analysis of youth cultures in the East End of London is used in the argument; and Dick Hebdige, for his work on the mods which forms the basis for the discussion of the mod style. We would also like to thank Stuart Hall for his advice and suggestions. The paper represents an attempt, by us, to come to terms critically with some of the crucial theoretical formulations in this field, which at times necessitates extensive analysis of other authors.

For another reason also, the paper is rather dense and compressed in its presentation. This is because we have attempted to convey a full account of our analysis of youth cultures, rather than present one particular element of the work. This has meant that, instead of being able to present each aspect of the work with the full detail that it deserves, we have been forced to compress some difficult and complex arguments. We hope that the reader will follow this in the interests of having the overall approach established.

The structure of the paper is a movement through a number of levels of analysis, each necessary to a full understanding of the phenomena in question. We move from some necessarily brief introductory comments on the nature of post-war capitalist production and its relation to major post-war social changes. The effects of these on working class culture generally, and on the youth of the class, are next considered, to allow an understanding of how crucial aspects of those changes, and the responses of the young to them, become crystallized into distinctive styles of youth culture. Finally, we look briefly at some aspects of the social reaction to youth cultures.

I POST-WAR CAPITALISM AND THE PROBLEM OF HEGEMONY

Because we are not attempting to offer a detailed consideration of the forms of advanced capitalism, our comments here are necessarily schematic and brief. However, the consideration of this level is necessary for the further analysis of more general social change in post-war Britain. What we are concerned with here is the reorganization of capital, in response to its earlier crises, and the forms which this reorganization took. The shift to monopolistic and oligopolistic capitalism may be seen as an attempt to preserve capital from the threat of recurrent crises by increasing its stability, in the face of temporary economic fluctuations, through diversification and the rationalization of production.

Perhaps of more importance is the shift from product-oriented to market-oriented industry in an effort constantly to realize the surplus-value of the product by ensuring that it is constantly and fully consumed - an attempt to overcome the recurrent possibility of over-production. Thus the increased employment of sophisticated market research techniques and mass advertising are intimately connected to the need to ensure the matching of demand to production. Related to this is the continual effort to exploit existing markets more fully and to develop new needs, and new markets for new products, to maintain and increase profitability. (1)

Finally, we must note the increasing acceptance of the necessity of state intervention to minimize the worst effects of the economic crises on the mass of the population, to maintain what has more recently become known as 'the human face of capitalism'. These points direct us to one central factor which is crucial to the understanding of the social change of the 1950s and 1960s, which is the need for the bourgeoisie to rule by consent rather than by visible coercion. For example, consent is necessary to ensure the full consumption of products, including those which lie beyond necessary demands. To achieve this, the bourgeoisie must 'universalize itself', it must spread, to as much of the population as possible, its way of life and way of seeing the social world as being the natural and only possible patterns. In doing this, it must attempt to negotiate the sometimes conflicting demands of other classes, and to minimize the extent to which alternative patterns of life and ways of thinking about society have any force. This attempt to rule by consent, or as Gramsci (1973) terms it, hegemony, is at root an educational relationship in which other classes are made subject to the world view of the bourgeoisie. We trust that this general notion will become more explicit in looking at post-war social changes - the more visible forms of the reorganization of production.

Social change in the 1950s and 1960s

One of the most visible changes in the 1950s was the advent of 'affluence' - increased production and higher levels of income made the new patterns of consumption realistic ones for many families (albeit often underpinned by easier hire purchase arrangements). The shift in social emphasis away from work and production towards a focus on the home, leisure and consumption was one vital base for the 'consensus' politics of this period, offering visible proof that the problems of capitalism had been solved, and that politics was now about who could manage the new industrial society most efficiently. Consequently, the argument ran, as all could now share in this newly discovered affluence, class conflict was dead, trade unions and class based politics an unfortunate and redundant legacy from the 'bad old days'. One central commodity of this new era, the television set, was both a symbol of affluence and a channel which allowed the ideological designation of 'classlessness' to penetrate areas which might otherwise have remained impervious to it. Linked to this is the Conservative government's policy of creating a 'property-owning democracy' by focusing building resources on private rather than public development, again creating an image of a prosperous and open society (see Pinto-Duschinsky, 1970).

However, more direct repercussions were visible in public redevelopment (for the bulk of the population remained excluded from private ownership) which effectively destroyed many traditional working class communities. Whether such redevelopment took the form of moving families out of areas like the East End to new towns or estates, or the later form of rebuilding old estates, their consequence for the local community was the same.

The removal of families to new towns or estates fragmented the extended family links so central to the traditional community, and both this geographical movement, and the design of new houses and flats based on the needs of the ideal (i.e. bourgeois) nuclear family were instrumental in this destruction of the bases of the community. The further consequences for those who remained behind was either the 'downgrading' or, less frequently, 'upgrading' of the area. Downgrading was accompanied by the influx of numbers of coloured immigrants in search of inexpensive housing, whose presence was interpreted by the indigenous population as lowering the social standard of the neighbourhood. It also involved the presence of speculatory property owners whose minimal interest in the property furthered the appearance of decay and dilapidation of the area (see, inter alia, Rex and Moore, 1971). Upgrading involved the movement of young middle class and professional families in search of housing into areas possessing a certain local 'character'. Through either mechanism the end product was a further disintegration of the cultural homogeneity of the area. (2)

In the redevelopment of the areas themselves, the model of housing needs was again that of the nuclear family. And nor were whole communities (streets, families, etc.) necessarily rehoused in the same area. A further consequence was the destruction of what Phil Cohen terms 'communal space' and its major foci, the pub, the street and the corner shop. 'Instead there was only the privatised space of the family unit, stacked one on top of each other, in total isolation, juxtaposed with the totally public space which surrounded it' (Cohen, 1972, p. 16). As far as we are concerned, this destruction of the community is crucial, for we would follow Frank Parkin (1972) in seeing the working class community as being one of the central institutions of working class culture, a culture possessing its own partially independent sets of social relations and understandings of the world which differ from those of the bourgeoisie.

Another significant area of these changing social patterns is that of leisure, where previously clearly demarcated class boundaries became comparatively blurred. With the shift in emphasis from production to consumption, leisure came to assume increasing social importance, and leisure as a social problem has come to occupy the attention of applied social scientists, educational bodies, leisure consultants and so on. One major dimension of this change has been the decline of the neighbourhood as the focus of leisure and the concentration of major leisure facilities in city centres. The closing of local cinemas has been followed by the redevelopment of multi-cinema centre town sites, while city centre pubs have set the redesign standards and patterns for many one-time 'locals'. Many of the stylistic changes owe much to the image of the young as affluent and potential consumers.

This clustering of central facilities meant that local provisions have been forced into competing for trade on the terms set by these facilities - the result: the development of stylized interiors for pubs, the provision of evening discos and the restructuring of some surviving local cinemas. The changes in leisure provision are structured by a belief in the changing social composition of the users of such facilities, seeing them as all possessing the once clearly middle class characteristics of affluence, mobility, and the ability to make 'rational' selections among the leisure alternatives offered to them. This change is reflected in the emphasis upon 'competition' in the 'leisure industry', and is captured in the description of the image of the user as moving from that of 'member' to that of 'consumer', implying a more external and transient commitment to the object being consumed. (3)

The post-war changes in football illustrates these types of changes which we have just discussed in general terms, for football is important as a major focus of pre-war working class culture and relevant here in view of our later consideration of the skinheads. The main post-war changes in football may be summarized as those of professionalization, internationalization and commercialization. (4) These cover such changes as an increasing concentration on the physical, tactical and financial requirements for success, extra facilities to entertain the spectator and make him more comfortable, and the growing financial concerns of the game generally. Football clubs, anticipating the disappearance in the new social order of the traditional 'cloth-capped' fan, felt they would have to compete for audiences with alternative sources of entertainment, especially television. If the traditional fan no longer existed, then nor would traditional loyalties, and football clubs would have to compete for the favours of the new classless, rationally selective consumer of entertainment. Consequently, the game had to be made as exciting and dramatic as possible to appeal to the uncommitted, and the spectator had to be made comfortable and his every whim catered for, Furthermore, the uncommitted were unlikely to attend each Saturday to watch an unsuccessful team, and so greater attention had to be paid to avoiding failure. Ian Taylor describes the effects of these changes as 'bourgeoisification'. It is a process which 'legitimizes previously working class activities for the middle class, or more accurately, activities which were previously seen as legitimate only for the working class, such as watching doubtful films or congregating on the kop' (1971b, p. 364).

This process has carried with it a changed conception of the football supporter. The 'genuine' supporter is no longer the traditional cloth-capped figure, his own fortunes inextricably mixed with those of his team. The notion of the ideal supporter has become the man who is a passive, selective consumer (no longer a participant in the affairs of 'his' club). What he is meant to enjoy is not the physical experience of standing and cheering in a large partisan crowd, but the 'finer points of the game'. The game is transformed into a spectacle, and it is the role of the supporter to 'objectively' assess it, rather than cheering 'without reason' for his own end. Consequent upon this changed image of the supporter is the redefinition of certain previously normal aspects of crowd behaviour - notably those of physical violence and bad language - so that they are now defined as illegitimate. These changes are by no means total, either in the character of the crowd, or in the clubs' attitudes to their supporters, but the changes which have taken place have certainly had this 'new spectator' in mind.

One final area of these changes in post-war Britain was the growth of the welfare state, indicating the ability and will of the new social order to care for and protect all members of society 'from the cradle to the grave'. The welfare state performed a double function, giving a secure grounding to the establishment of consensus politics, and absorbing some parts of the produced industrial surplus. One central area for the young in this general provision of facilities (though not itself specifically part of the welfare state) was the change in education. The 1944 Education Act provided an ideological redefinition of the education system: it was no longer to be seen as a class-based closed shop, but as an open market. It signified a move towards an emphasis on the individual's ability and achievement - not his class position. Entrance into secondary education had been previously determined largely by income, thus making class barriers highly visible in the education sector. Now the only allowable and visible boundaries were those between the ability of individual children and youths.

Perhaps this only marginally affected the in-school experience of working class youths, who still experienced school largely as a situation where one was forced to take in irrelevant knowledge by external and alien figures of authority - the traditional THEM of working class culture. It nevertheless did have the effect of transforming the responsibility for educational failure from its previously class-based terms onto the individual himself through the mystifying quality of its very openness. This was especially true where parents invested their hopes in their children's performances in education as a means to success through the opportunities they never had.

To summarize this section of the paper, we would suggest that the major social changes of the 1950s should be seen as a move towards minimizing the economic crises of capitalism and to involving the working class in a major role in consumption. By mitigating the most visible forms of class inequality and subsequent conflict, at least at a symbolic level, the ground was laid for the consensual politics of a supposedly affluent and classless society. If this section has read as a somewhat 'conspiratorial' account of post-war social history, this is not our view, but emerges because we have collapsed the complex processes of class conflict and negotiation into what proved to be their hegemonic outcome. As Gramsci stresses, the maintenance of hegemony is always the outcome of a struggle against challenges to it. Thus we would suggest that what we have described is the result of the hegemonic incorporation by the ruling class of demands from the working class (e.g., for improvements in housing, education and for more state protection) into the terms of their dominant world view. (5)

Cracks in the veneer of classlessness

Nevertheless these moves have by no means been totally successful, and cracks in the veneer of classless ess became increasingly visible in the middle and late 1960s. In turn these challenges produced further attempts by the dominant order to come to terms with them, both in terms of social reorganization and at the ideological level of redefining problems. Thus, in the different areas we have noted above, stability and consensus became increasingly threatened. Industry and the state were confronted by worsening economic crises as the measures of the 1950s proved inadequate and even counterproductive, and new measures, usually involving more state intervention, were instigated, for example, the establishment of the tripartite National Economic Development Council, a variety of measures to control income and prices, and industrial relations legislation - all with the definition of the government in the neutral role of representative of the 'national interest'. One added feature was the effect of both economic crises and the increasing rationalization and mechanization in creating a growing 'reserve army of the unemployed'.

Local councils found themselves faced by mounting criticisms from the working class tenants of the new estates and redeveloped areas, and the general dissatisfaction of residents manifested itself in a variety of forms - rising request lists for transfers, tenants' organizations, rent strikes and increasing vandalism and delinquency. Some authorities responded by thinking their housing policies away from high-rise developments.

Deep discontents showed through in the educational sphere, especially in secondary education where teachers began to complain of having to face classes of hostile, disinterested and aggressive working class youths. Linked with this were academic criticisms of the poor performance of the meritocratic system in enabling working class children to take advantage of the supposed opportunities. Among the attempts to deal with these problems were to shift towards comprehensive education, the growth of Educational Priority Areas, the theories of 'cultural deprivation', and a variety of attempts at child-centred education and curricula redesign.

One must also note the emergence of a new 'social problem' - that of race. White racism, previously comparatively invisible, became increasingly overt and finally was given institutional definition and legitimation (beginning with Peter Griffiths' Smethwick campaign in 1964), shifting through a variety of measures such as conciliatory and assimilatory stages of Community Relations Councils and anti-discrimination acts, to more overtly anti-immigration policies. Finally, the politics of consensus were threatened from a variety of directions by groups who found themselves excluded from the legitimated parliamentary channels of democratic politics, or who found these increasingly irrelevant to deeper and more serious questions. Thus the late 1960s found growing trade union militancy, more overtly oppositional community-based politics, and the proliferation of direct action groups with both specific and wide ranging aims.

II THE WORKING CLASS RESPONSE

How did the working class respond to these changes? Before answering this question (and, more specifically, the question of how the working class young responded to these changes) we need some conception of how the working class responds generally, in its position of subordination, to the social formation it finds itself in: a social formation shaped largely by the bourgeoisie - the dominant class both in its actual and its legitimating power. In short, we are asking how does the social formation reproduce itself through its subordinate class?

We have amplified our discussion of this question with a diagram, Figure 7.1. We are all born into a social formation which is not of our own making or choosing (left hand side of diagram). Within this formation we believe it is possible and helpful to distinguish between 'structures', 'cultures' and 'biographies'. 'Structures' are all the elements of the productive system and the necessary forms of social relations and institutions that result from a given productive system: its necessary objectivations. By 'cultures' we mean attempts to come to terms with structures - attempts to impose meaning. As such they are internalized maps of meaning; ways of understanding the productive system; ideologies.

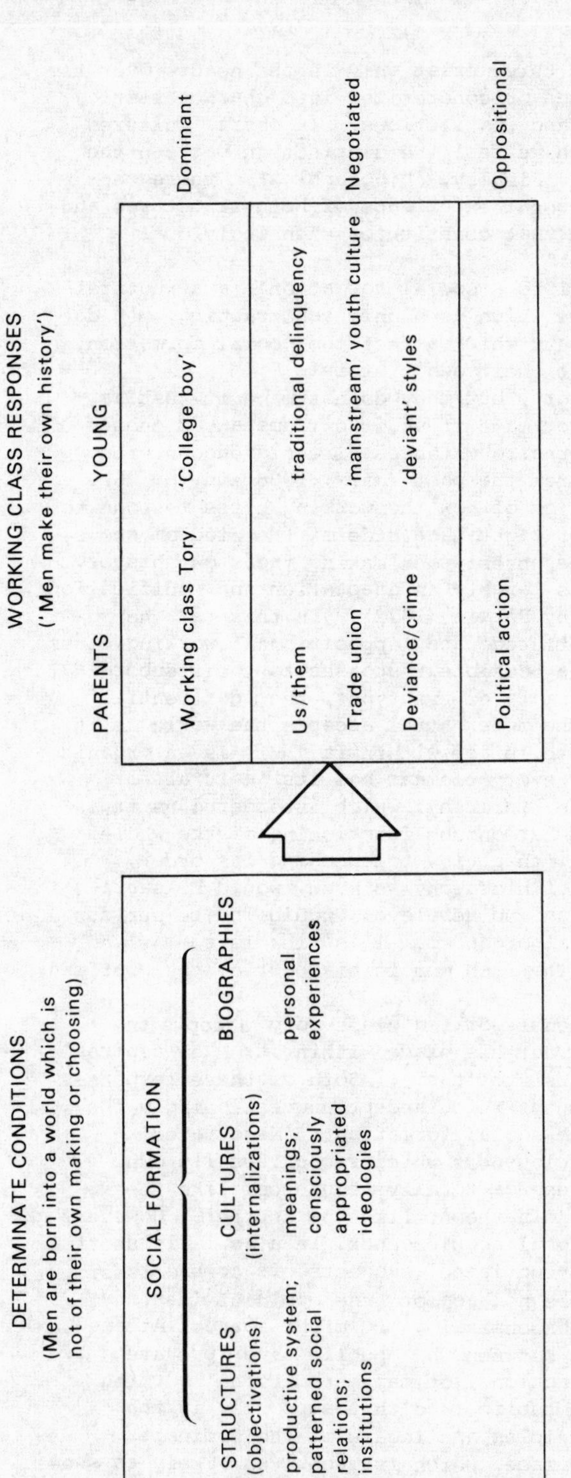

FIGURE 7.1 Reproduction of the social formation

This is not to say that cultures exist only in the head. Over time they too become objectivated or concretized into characteristic forms of social relations and institutions. In short, cultures too have structures, though we feel the distinction between the two is still worth making. Finally, 'biographies': these represent an individual's personal experience of both structures and cultures: the unique path that constitutes each individual's own life-history.

But though man is born into a social formation - a structural-cultural-biographical nexus which is highly constraining, men do, within limits respond in ways which affect the social formation, they do in this sense 'make their own history':

> Men make their own history, but they do not make it just as they please; they do not make it under circumstances chosen by themselves, but under circumstances directly encountered, given and transmitted from the past (Marx, 1968 edn, p. 96).

Now to return to the question of how the working class respond to this social formation. Our right-hand side of the diagram shows the range of observable responses: men making their own history. This part of the diagram is largely an adaptation and modification of the typology developed by Parkin (1972). In this text he talks of 'dominant', 'negotiated' and 'oppositional' working class consciousnesses: the three possible responses to their subordination. The 'dominant' form is of two types, the 'deferential' and the 'aspirational'. The deferential accepts the world as it is, and his own, subordinate, place within it. His is an organic view of the universe where every element has its 'natural' or 'ordained' place within the hierarchy, which is ordered as it is for the most efficient and harmonious functioning of the whole. To question the hierarchy with a view to changing its order, or to question the notion of hierarchy as such, would be sacrilegous on one level, and, on another level, would invite serious malfunctioning of the social organism. This view is summarized in the popular format of 'The rich man in his castle, the poor man at his gate....'

Similarly, the aspirational working class Tory accepts the social world as it is, but not his place within it: he 'aspires' to cross the divide from 'us' to 'them'. Both of these responses involve forms of consciousness which accept unquestioningly the dominant definitions of the social formation. 'Negotiated' consciousness is that consciousness which recognizes its own subordination but which does not totally acquiesce, like the deferential, nor 'seek to join them', like the aspirer. However, whilst it falls short of total acquiescence, it also falls short of total opposition. As 'negotiated' suggests, it compromises, and both 'accepts' and 'does not accept' the dominant ideology. This statement is not as nonsensical as it might sound. At one level it is the difference between the 'public' and 'private' faces, both attitudes and actions, of many traditional working class neighbourhoods: the public face that supports, in the abstract, many of the principles and ideals of the dominant ideology; and the private face, which is much less likely to show such allegiance in practice. Thus stealing, in principle, is likely to be condemned in such a neighbourhood (in public), but individual acts of pinching will probably escape such censure (in private). To give another example: diligent 'dressing up' by parents for school speech day in order to create a good impression with the school authorities is likely to be the public norm, whilst the private opinion of school might be that school is only for 'them'. We have, in short, been talking of an 'us/them' consciousness: a consciousness which fatalistically accepts and recognizes the difference between 'us' and 'them' and comes to terms with it by paying public lip service to many of the dominant class ideals, whilst actually, in private, carving out a life of a very different texture. In this way, the dominant ideology is both 'accepted' and 'not accepted' in the realm of 'negotiated' consciousness.

Trade union consciousness represents a less fatalistic view of the us/them division. Stemming from a realization of the strength of 'us', if organized collectively, it has led to the formation of unions in an attempt to redistribute some of society's wealth to their members. Typically, this takes the form of a fight for higher wages or better conditions. Conflict that arises as a result of these demands is, usually, restricted to this level. Though, in times of crisis, such as the period surrounding the General Strike, it has the potential to become a revolutionary consciousness.

A similar consciousness, in that it is less fatalistic, is that of deviance or crime. But here again the conflict is usually a restricted one; though, as Hobsbawm's examples of social banditry remind us, these too have the potential, in times of crisis, to take on a revolutionary perspective.

All of these consciousnesses (us/them, trade union, deviant/criminal) remain negotiations since they conflict with the dominant social formation only at certain points: they do not represent a total challenge to the social formation and its legitimacy. The 'oppositional' consciousness does represent such a challenge. It does not accept the legitimacy of the social formation and attempts to transform it totally, traditionally through organized political action of various kinds. It is, ultimately, subversive of the established order, though it may well recognize, as a strategy, the importance of a strong trade union consciousness.

We have worked out a similar range of possible responses for the working class adolescent. The embryonic working class Tory consciousness mirrors the parental response being either of the 'aspirational' ('scholarship boy') or 'deferential' variety. The three types of negotiated response we have identified as 'traditional' delinquency, 'main stream' youth culture and 'deviant' youth culture. Though empirically these three responses may well prove to be somewhat mixed in that, for example, a 'traditional' delinquent might well also be involved in a 'deviant' youth cultural style, we still feel the distinctions worth making, at least for the moment. The essential differences between the three would be, in 'ideal-typical' cases, as follows: the traditional delinquents would be those adolescents whose 'opposition' was limited to the extent of their delinquency or illegal activities (e.g. Parker, 1974b). These activities would largely be those fairly common, and traditional, in certain working class neighbourhoods, i.e., petty thieving, taking and driving away cars, vandalism, fighting. Though the content of such delinquency might alter with time, so that car radios would be more popular now than say thirty years ago, we believe that the form has altered little. In this sense, we believe it strongly parallels the us/them consciousness of working class adults, though perhaps being a less sophisticated version of it.

The 'main stream' youth cultural response represents, briefly, the 'incorporated' version of the 'deviant' style: the version that has been bought up, sanitized, 'made safe' and resold to the wider youth market: the 'deviant' life style become consumption style: the commercial version of the real.

The 'deviant' style represents the more 'extreme' version of the main stream response: its deviant original and progenitor. This is not to deny the role of commercial interests in the perpetuation, modification and eventual incorporation of youth styles, but it is to assert a 'moment' of originality in the formation of such a style. And it is this formative 'moment' we are most interested in when we later read the styles of the mods and skinheads. These styles remain negotiated rather than oppositional forms because they operate in one area of life only: the leisure area. Since they are not oppositional in all areas of the social formation, they cannot hope to transform it. Nevertheless we feel that these styles offer a symbolic critique of the established order and, in so doing, represent a latent form of 'non-ideological politics'. Whilst there are no fully oppositional working class adolescent groupings, we feel that deviant youth cultural styles come nearest to being such.

What we have done so far is to state the possible ranges of response in working class youth culture and how these relate to the dominated, negotiated and oppositional responses of the working class. What we must now do is take this static and a-historical model and look at the actual historical development of the 'deviant' style, and the cultural response of this section of the working class young, throughout the post-war period. Very generally, this development traces shifts in style from the teddy boy through various transitional styles to the mod, and then to the skinhead. Our focus in this analysis is on the mod and the skinhead and the various adaptations of these two dominant and clear-cut stylistic developments. Our argument at this point is in debt to Phil Cohen's analysis of youth culture as it emerged from the East End of London (1972), and, again, the concern is first to trace the connections between contradictions in the working class parent culture to the response in youth style. Again we have chosen to use a diagram to illustrate the development of this argument (Figure 7.2).

We can distinguish three elements in the working class community: the 'respectable' working class which is the staple backbone of the community; the socially mobile, élite working class leadership (the 'labour aristocracy') and the permanently outside lumpen element of the 'rough' working class. The changes in the mid-1950s in housing, employment and income caught the respectable working class in the middle of the two dominant but contradictory ideologies of the day: the new ideology of

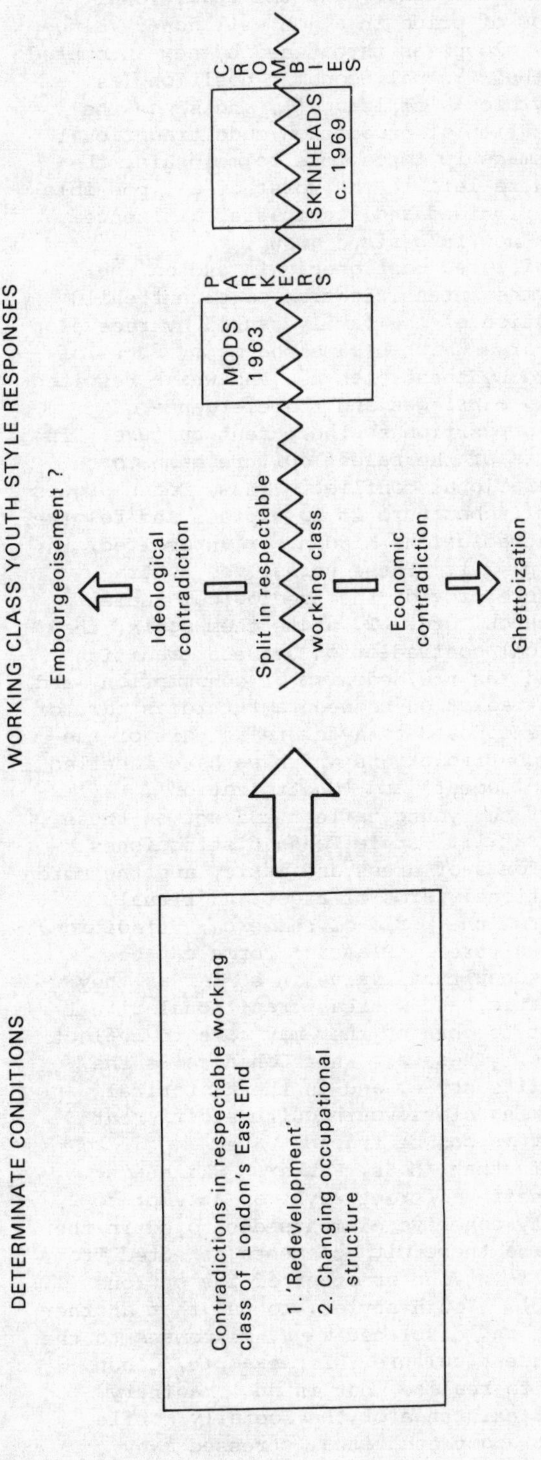

DETERMINATE CONDITIONS

Contradictions in respectable working class of London's East End

1. 'Redevelopment'
2. Changing occupational structure

WORKING CLASS YOUTH STYLE RESPONSES

Embourgeoisement ?

Ideological contradiction

Split in respectable working class

Economic contradiction

Ghettoization

MODS 1963

PARKERS

SKINHEADS c. 1969

CROMBIES

FIGURE 7.2

'spectacular consumption' and affluence, and the traditional ideology of work - the ethos of pride in a job well done. Since the bargaining power of the group was threatened by new automated techniques which weakened their actual economic position (as opposed to their largely mythical 'affluence'), and since the same changes in the organization of production made traditional pride in the job and craftsmanship impossible to maintain, the respectable working class were left in the worst of all possible worlds. The changes which promised and accompanied affluence also threatened to create a new lumpenized group.

This predicament was registered most deeply in and on the young, and was worsened by the intensification of parent/child relations due to the nucleation of the family caused by redevelopment schemes. It was this area which became the major focus of all the anxieties engendered by these changes, and which resulted in both an increase in early marriages and the emergence of specific youth cultures in opposition to the parent culture. In short, the internal conflicts of the parent culture came to be worked out in terms of generational conflict. Thus, Cohen argues that the 'latent function of subculture is to express and resolve, albeit "magically", the contradictions hidden, or unresolved, in the parent culture' (1972, p. 23). These unresolved contradictions in the parent culture provide the ideological themes which are worked on in youth culture. To state them again, they are the unresolved ideological contradiction between traditional working class puritanism and the new hedonism of consumption, and the unresolved economic contradiction between a future as part of the socially mobile élite as opposed to a future as part of the new lumpen. These are the contradictions which we have labelled in the diagram as 'Embourgeoisement' and 'Ghettoization'.

The subcultural styles of the young reflect and act on these contradictions. In looking at life-style Cohen distinguishes between the more 'plastic' forms of dress and music, and the more 'infrastructural' and traditional forms of argot and ritual. 'Plastic' forms are taken from the world of commerce; traditional forms come from the patent culture. 'Plastic' forms can be selected and invested with subcultural value in so far as they express the underlying thematic, and whereas traditional ritual and argot are more resistant to change, they may come to reflect changes in the plastic forms. These are what Cohen calls the symbolic subsystems of the life style, and in the historical development of post-war working class youth culture different adaptations of these subsystems can be traced.

Cohen's crucial insight is that 'Mods, Parkers, Skinheads, Crombies all represent in their different ways, an attempt to retrieve some of the socially cohesive elements destroyed in the parent culture, and to combine these with elements selected from other class factions, symbolising one or other of the options confronting it' (1972, p. 23). Youth styles, to put that another way, articulate, in symbolic and displaced ways, responses to the contradictions facing the parent culture. For example, Cohen sees the mods as an attempt to realize, but in an 'imaginary relation', the conditions of existence of the socially mobile white collar worker. Whilst argot and ritual stressed many of the traditional parental values, their dress and music reflected the hedonistic image of the affluent consumer. The dynamic of the mod style was derived partly from its relation to other class fractions, for example, the rockers (from the manual working class). The parkers or scooter boys - who were a transitional style between mods and skinheads - de-stressed the alien elements of music and dress and reasserted the indigenous components of argot and ritual. The skinheads, as Cohen puts it, represented an exploration of the lumpen option: an inversion, that is, of the mods. Utilizing the protest music of the West Indian ghetto poor (Reggae) and a dress that caricatured a model worker, they represented a 'meta statement about the whole process of social mobility' (1972, p. 25). They were a reaction against the contamination of the parent culture by middle class values, and a reassertion of the integral values of working class culture through its most recessive traits: puritanism and chauvinism. The puritanism crystallized in opposition to the 'hedonistic' greasers and hippies, and the chauvinism in 'queer bashing' and 'paki-bashing'. The crombies/casuals/suedes (which are post-skinhead styles) represent a further transitional phase and a move back to the mods but incorporating certain elements from middle class subcultures (e.g., dress and soft drug use from hippies), while still conserving many of the distinctive features of earlier versions of subcultures. Cohen argues that:

> If the whole process ... seems to be circular, forming a closed system, then this is because subculture, by definition, cannot break out of the contradiction derived from the parent culture, it merely transcribes its terms at micro-social level, and inscribes them in an imaginary set of relations (1972 p. 25).

In the following section we are going to attempt to fill out Cohen's work. This filling out will pay specific attention to the historical and actual development of youth style, and to the discontinuities between parent culture and youth cultures. Cohen's own scheme neglects these aspects. It does not suggest, for example, why it is that the mods appear before the skinheads; that is, the ways in which the mods and skinheads respond to quite different historical situations for the working class. Cohen suggests that both are attempts to resolve contradictions in the parent culture, but he neglects the fact that the parent culture had a substantially different problematic in the early 1960s and the late 1960s. Our analysis will therefore show how mods and skinheads were responding to different aspects of the same set of contradictions. We are adding, in short, a necessary historical dimension to the development of youth style. Second, we do not think that Cohen gives sufficient weight to the discontinuities and differences between the situation of the young and their parents. Youth are not simply resolving contradictions for the parent culture; they are responding to the specific contradictory features of the world of working class youth. There are points of similarity between young and old, but also vital differences, in the educational sphere, for example, and in the job market. These two dimensions - discontinuity and history -

help to make a more compelling analysis than the one which Cohen leaves us with.

The social situation of the working class young themselves is thus paramount in the 'reading' which follows, since our notion of style is one of 'moments' when, temporarily, the social formation, and the position of a specific group within it, becomes crystallized in specific symbolic systems which express its experiences of that formation.

III READING YOUTH CULTURAL STYLES

We now want to consider how to understand the symbolism of distinctive youth cultural styles. 'Style' we consider to be the result of a process of appropriation of disparate objects and symbols from their normal social context and their reworking by members of the group into a new and coherent whole with its own special significance. Such a process is only possible because all objects, symbols and actions possess a variety of potential meanings for social actors, and not simply single closed definitions. However in any given historical situation, each such symbol or activity has one meaning which is preferred or dominant, that meaning which it is given by the dominant culture and which represses, or conceals, its other potential meanings. What the creation of a style involves is the selection of certain symbols (clothes, hairstyles, locations and so on) which are relevant to the focal concerns of the group in question, their investment with the meanings of the group, and their use to form a distinctive whole to symbolically express that group's self-conception and focal concerns. It must be stressed that these visible symbolic elements of the style are not separate from the group who create them, but are shaped by the group and are constantly carried and reaffirmed in the group's shared activities and relations. To locate these general comments on style more specifically we have chosen to use the mods and the skinheads as examples of how to 'read' styles.

The mods

The mods are often portrayed, as we saw with Cohen, as living out the life style of the upwardly mobile affluent worker, and being dedicated to consumption for its own sake. This view, however, does not go far enough, for it misses the mods' own distinctive relation to the commodities they consumed, and the self-conscious exploitation of that style of consumption. Such an understanding cannot occur if separated from the mods' experience of their social situation and their demands on it. Being mainly unskilled or semi-skilled manual workers or in routine white collar jobs (clerks, shop assistants, etc.), their experience of the world was characterized by the recurrent themes of working class youth - routinized domination and control by others, and the threat of eternal boredom; an experience intensified by the disjuncture between it and the promises of the 'Golden Age' of affluent consumerism. The mod life style cannot be understood without this search for 'action' and the related need to escape the patronizing domination of adults. But if the daytime world was controlled by a succession of 'grey' adults, then the leisure time of nights and weekends offered the possibilities of excitement and autonomy. The style of the mods took on the forms and qualities formally approved of by the 'straight' world (notably its smartness and neatness), in an attempt to disarm adult disdain, but simultaneously subverted them by turning them into stylized qualities which seemed simultaneously 'normal', and yet incomprehensible and threatening to the adult world. As Dave Laing observed: 'They looked alright, but there was something in the way they moved that adults couldn't make out' (1969, p. 150).

This subversion of the normal characterized the mods' relation to all the commodities they consumed, and as Herman notes:

> The mod saw commodities as extensions of himself, rather than things totally independent of their maker or user and shrouded in a set of rules for their use (1971, p. 51).

Consequently, far from being the ideal passive consumer of capitalist society, consuming the commodity in the form in which it is presented, the mods raised the possibility of an active relation to the commodity. This aspect of active appropriation can be seen exemplified in the mods' use of pills:

> pills, medically prescribed for the treatment of neuroses, were appropriated and used as an end-in-themselves, and the negative evaluations of their capabilities imposed by school and work were substituted by a positive assessment of their credentials in the world of play (Hebdige, 1974a, p. 5).

This emphasis on the active role of the mods may also be seen in the Bank Holiday 'riots', where the mods' search for action led to a rejection of the passive role of consumer and spectator in favour of being an active instigator of events. Finally, the mods' relation to the media, in these and other instances, indicates the culture's preoccupation with itself as image - with their self-projection. The image of the mod life is perfectly exemplified by Denzil's description of the mod week in the 'Sunday Times' magazine (2 August 1964):

> Monday night meant dancing at the Mecca, the Hammersmith Palais, or the Streatham Locarno.
> Tuesday meant Soho and the Scene Club.
> Wednesday was Marquee night.
> Thursday was reserved for the ritual washing of the hair.
> Friday meant the Scene again.
> Saturday afternoon usually meant shopping for clothes or records. Saturday night was spent dancing and rarely finished before 9 or 10 on Sunday morning.
> Sunday evening meant the Flamingo, or perhaps, if one showed signs of weakening, could be spent sleeping.

This image - the image of themselves as style - was more significant than the mundane reality; Hebdige suggests that:

> every mod was preparing himself psychologically so that if the opportunity should arise, if the money was there, if Welwyn Garden City should be metamorphosed into Piccadilly

> Circus, he would be ready. Every mod was existing in a ghost world of gangsterism, luxurious clubs and beautiful women, even if reality only amounted to a draughty Parker anorak, a beaten-up Vespa, and fish and chips out of a greasy bag (1974a, p. 7).

The mods' victories, then, were symbolic, victories of the imagination and, in the last analysis, imaginary victories. For the mods underestimated the dominant culture's ability to exploit and incorporate the subversive and anarchic imagination.

> The magical transformations of commodities had been mysterious and were often invisible to the neutral observer, and no amount of stylistic incantation could possibly affect the oppressive economic mode by which they had been produced.
>
> The State continued to function perfectly no matter how many of Her Majesty's colours were defiled and draped around the shoulders of skinny pill-heads in the form of sharply-cut jackets (Hebdige, 1974a, p. 9).

The mods, then, were the children of affluence, but not simply its products. Their own mode of appropriation offered the possibility of a collective and active experience of consumption. Ultimately their attempted self-sufficiency and introspection (which attempted to 'magically' remove the real constraints on their situation) led to the incorporation and exploitation of their stylistic innovation - mod became 'manufactured', not 'created'.

The skinheads

We have already talked of the different social situation of the mods and the skinheads, and presented an abbreviated account of their style in Cohen's terms of its 'exploration of the downward option' of social mobility. At this point we intend to substantiate these earlier general statements with a more detailed analysis of the skinheads' style.

The connection between the skinheads and football is not, as some would suggest, fortuitous - that they could have gone anywhere but just happened to pick on football grounds. Rather, this traditional working class activity is crucial because it allows some of the skinheads' crucial concerns to be symbolically articulated. Most importantly, the support of a particular team provided a focus for the assertion of territorial loyalties, involving both a unified collective identity ('We are the Holte Enders', etc.), and an assertion of territorial rights - not those of property ownership, but of community identification. As Cohen notes:

> Territoriality is simply the process through which environmental boundaries (and foci) are used to signify group boundaries (and foci) and become invested with a subcultural value (1972, p. 27).

This assertion took place both physically, through the defending or taking of the 'home end'; and symbolically, through the sloganizing such as 'Smethwick Mob Rules here'. The emphasis on territory is a crucial one, and the 'mob' may be viewed as an attempt to retrieve the disappearing sense of community, with an emphasis on the distinction between 'us' and 'them', and the stress on mutual assistance in times of need. Thus, one fundamental rule was not to 'cut and run' from fights; as one ex-Smethwick skinhead said:

> the only real thing they'd put pressure on about was if you were the first to run and leave a fight. They'd get you for that no matter what happened.

The other major skinhead location also has strong cultural roots in the working class - the pub, which also acted as a territorial base and landmark. Here, supported not by pot or pills, but by a rather more traditional drug, beer, was the place where exploits could be discussed, plans laid, and time killed. Unlike his predecessor, the mod, the disco and the club were not the skinheads' 'natural habitat' - they were perhaps functional locations where birds could be chatted (6) or rights held with whatever opposition was available - but they were not the 'natural' resting place.

We have talked of the element of communal assertion, and another element of the style may be read as involving the 'defence' of the community - the widely-publicized activity of 'paki-bashing'. Coloured immigrants are understood as a threat to the homogeneity of the community, to its cultural and racial unity. They are also obvious scapegoats for the problems of the working class by being doubly visible. First, in a racial sense, and second by visibly competing with the white working class for limited resources (notably housing and employment) within a particular district. By comparison, the real sources of structural inequalities are obscured by geographical and ideological barriers. In addition to this, at the time of the skinheads' crystallization, such racial scapegoating was, as we mentioned earlier, being given increasingly strong public legitimation by the statements and actions of both the Labour and Conservative parties, and by sectors of the media. However, 'paki-bashing', unlike the dominant public expression which found little to distinguish between different groups of immigrants, was overlaid with a significant cultural dimension, which distinguished between Asians and West Indians. The latter were perhaps less of a threat to the cultural homogeneity of an area because many of their cultural patterns were much closer to those of working class youth than were those of the Asians whose introspective, family centred and achievement oriented way of life were closer to a middle class outlook. In addition, West Indian youths were more likely to gain respect by being willing to defend themselves physically.

However, the violence associated with the skinheads was much more closely articulated around football. Football centrally provides and allows for the expression of excitement, although its expression is supposed to take place within certain legitimate and institutionalized boundaries (e.g. those of chanting or cheering, but excluding the use of crude or vulgar language). Similarly, the legitimate source of that excitement is supposed to be the match itself, but the skinheads extended both the source and expression of the excitement (illegitimately, of course) through their own violence. (7) Fighting both expressed their involvement in the game, and was a source of excitement both directly, in the physical activity of the fight, and indirectly, in its providing a topic of conversation to dispel the continual threat of boredom in the periods between fights and other group exploits.

The violence, both actual and discussed, acted as an expression of toughness, of a specific working class self-conception of masculinity, and of particular symbolic importance here is the activity of 'queer bashing'. The skinhead definition of 'queer' extended to all those males who looked 'odd', that is to all those who were not overtly masculine looking, as this statement indicates:

'Usually it'd be just a bunch of us who'd find someone they thought looked odd - like this one night we were up by Warley Woods and we saw this bloke who looked odd - he'd got long hair and frills on his trousers.'

This emphasis on overt masculinity was visible in the most obvious areas of skinhead symbolism, most importantly, the clothes and the 'prison crop' hair style from which their name derived. The clothes, heavy denims, plain or striped button-down shirts, braces and heavy boots, created an image which was clean-cut, smart and functional - a youthful version of working clothes. The haircuts completed the severe and puritanical self-image, a formalized and very 'hard' masculinity. (It is also important to note that both the mods and the hippies had gone some way to undermining traditional stereotypes of masculine and feminine appearance and behaviour.)

Thus we would argue that by reading the skinheads' style in terms of its creators' structural and cultural context, it offers a reassertion of some elements of traditional working class culture. Certainly, it is displaced into a symbolic leisure style, but it arises in a period when the norms of that culture and its social base had been threatened by erosion and disappearance, and when social conflicts were becoming increasingly visible and demanding forms of articulation. The erosion of some expressions of working class culture, and the incorporation and quiescence of others in the 1950s and early 1960s, had removed crucial articulations of this consciousness. For the skinheads, whose experience was grounded in some of the crucial nexi of this economic and cultural conflict (e.g. housing, education and employment), their style attempted to revive, in a symbolic form, some of the expressions of traditional working class culture which could articulate their social experience. This we take to be the process behind what Cohen describes as choosing the 'downward option', a 'choice' which is grounded in, and structured by, their experiential situation.

CONCLUSION

We have not the space in this paper to deal properly with the topic of social reaction, but this should not be taken to mean that we attach no importance to it. Indeed, it is an integral part of what Taylor, Walton and Young (1973) call a 'fully social theory of deviance'. We must be content here to sketch out some elements of our view of this area.

An analysis of social reaction must deal with its structural base: with the state and with its complex institutional mediations, especially between the formal organizations of social control and the major public signifiers - the media. Second, it must deal with the cultural forms of the expression of the social reaction: that is the way in which groups and events are publicly signified. Their definition must be considered in terms of the state's attempts to mobilize public support for its actions and to tighten their support for the legitimacy of the state. Youth cultures are especially worthy of attention here because one of the consequences of the closure of the political discourse to 'consensus' politics in the post-war period was to displace the discussion of society and social change into moral terms, in which youth was a central metaphor in the articulation of such concerns (e.g., the consequences of affluence and the growth of the mass media). It is as a consequence of this displacement that Stan Cohen observes:

> The Mods and Rockers symbolised something far more important than what they actually did. They touched the delicate and ambivalent nerves through which post-war social change in Britain was experienced (1971, p. 192).

The social reaction to youth cultures cannot be fully understood without an awareness of this prominence of youth as a vehicle for the articulation of matters of public concern. The third element which must be taken into account in the social reaction to youth cultures is the element of commercial reaction which attempts to universalize, at a purely stylistic and consumption level, the innovations made by distinctive youth cultures, while simultaneously defusing the oppositional potential of the exclusive life styles.

In this paper we have been attempting to establish our view of the necessary bases for an analysis of youth cultures in relation to the situation of the working class in post-war Britain. Our main emphases are two-fold: one is the stress in the historicity of such analysis; and the second is that the analysis must relate the specific phenomenon in question to the social totality. We have attempted to do this in two ways: through the analytic distinction between the different levels of the totality which must be understood; and by our formulation of structures, cultures and biographies. This enables us to locate groups within the organization of the totality, and allows us to locate their practices in terms of their established and emergent cultural definitions of the situation. For us, this is perhaps the crucial area; for class conflict has increasingly shifted to the terrain of a struggle for the control of cultural as well as material resources. It is within this location that we see the symbolism of working class youth cultures as representing both a significant dimension, and a signification of the struggle for cultural hegemony.

NOTES

1 See, inter alia, Baran and Sweezy, 1968.
2 These arguments derive from Cohen, 1972.
3 We must also note the same oligopolistic trends in the leisure area which we commented on in the wider economy. See, inter alia, Murdock and Golding, 1974, and Hutt, 1973.
4 For more detailed comments on the changes in football, see Taylor, 1971a and b; and Critcher, 1974.
5 For an illustration of some of these processes, see Thompson, 1974, pp. 52-3.
6 See Fowler, 1972.
7 In fact, the skinheads appropriated a long tradition of collective participation in football as a leisure activity, which has been maintained through the 1960s by what Taylor (1971a and b) calls the 'subcultural rump'.

BIBLIOGRAPHY

ABRAMS, M. (1959), 'The Teenage Consumer', Press Exchange, London.
ABRAMS, M. (1961), 'The Teenage Consumer Spending in 1959, Part 2', Press Exchange, London.
ABRAMS, M. (1964), 'The Newspaper Reading Public of Tomorrow', Odhams, London.
ALLEN, J.S. and MATTOCKS, R.H. (1950), 'Industry and Prudence: a Plan for Accrington', Andrew Reid, Newcastle upon Tyne.
ALLEN, S. (1968), Some Theoretical Problems in the Study of Youth in 'Sociological Review', pp. 319-31.
AMOS, F.J.C. (1970), 'Social Malaise in Liverpool', Liverpool City Planning Department.
ASPIN, C. (1963), 'Haslingden 1800-1900', Helmshore Local History Society, Lancashire.
ASPIN, C. (1969), 'Lancashire, the First Industrial Society', Helmshore Local History Society, Lancashire.
ASPIN, C. and CHAPMAN, S.D. (1964) 'James Hargreaves and the Spinning Jenny', Helmshore Local History Society, Lancashire.
AULD, J. (1973), Cannabis: the Changing Patterns of Use, in 'New Society', 6 September.
BALDWIN, J. (1972), Delinquent Schools in Tower Hamlets - A Critique, 'British Journal of Criminology', 12, pp. 399-401.
BARAN, P.A. and SWEEZY, P.M. (1968), 'Monopoly Capital', Penguin, Harmondsworth.
BARSTOW, S. (1962), 'A Kind of Loving', Penguin, Harmondsworth.
BARTHES, R. (1972a), 'Elements of Semiology', Jonathan Cape, London.
BARTHES, R. (1972b), 'Mythologies', Paladin, London.
BENNETT, W. (1948), 'The History of Burnley 1650-1850', Burnley Corporation, Lancashire.
BERGER, B.M. (1963, 1971), On the Youthfulness of Youth Culture, in 'Social Research' (1963); reprinted in B. Berger, 'Looking for America', Prentice-Hall, Englewood Cliffs, 1971, pp. 66-86.
BERGER, B. et al. (1972), Child Rearing Practices in the Communal Family, in H.P. Dreitzel, ed., 'Family, Marriage and the Struggle of the Sexes', Recent Sociology no. 4, Collier-Macmillan, London, pp. 271-300.
BLACKWELL, T. (1974), The History of a Working Class Methodist Chapel, in 'Working Papers in Cultural Studies', no. 5, pp. 65-83.

BLUMENSTEIL, A.D. (1973) The Sociology of Good Times, in G. Psathas, ed., 'Phenomenological Sociology', Wiley, New York, pp. 187-219.
BOARD OF EDUCATION (1926), 'Report of the Consultative Committee on the Education of the Adolescent' (The Hadow Report), HMSO, London.
BOGDANOR, V. and SKIDELSKY, R., eds (1970), 'The Age of Affluence, 1951-1964', Macmillan, London.
BYTHELL, D. (1969), 'The Handloom Weavers', Cambridge University Press.
CAIN, M. (1973), 'Society and the Policeman's Role', Routledge & Kegan Paul, London.
CARTER, M. (1966), 'Into Work', Penguin, Harmondsworth.
CARTLAND, B. (1973), 'We Danced All Night', Arrow Books, London.
CARLYLE, T. (1840), 'Chartism', Fraser.
CASTLES, S. and KOSACK, G. (1973), 'Immigrant Workers and Class Structure in Western Europe, Oxford University Press.
CASTLES, S. and KOSACK, G. (1974), How the Trade Unions Try to Control and Integrate Immigrant Workers in the German Federal Republic, in 'Race', vol. 15, no. 4, pp. 497-514.
CHADWICK, E. (1852), 'Report on the Sanitary Conditions of the Labouring Population of Britain', HMSO, London.
CHAPMAN, S.J. (1904), 'The Lancashire Cotton Industry', Manchester University Press.
CICOUREL, A.V. (1968), 'The Social Organisation of Juvenile Justice', Wiley, New York.
CICOUREL, A.V. and KITSUSE, J.I. (1963), 'The Educational Decision Makers', Bobbs-Merrill, Indianapolis.
CLARKE, J. (1973), The Skinheads and the Study of Youth Culture, unpublished paper given to 14th National Deviancy Conference, University of York.
CLARKE, J. (1974), 'Subcultural Symbolism: Reconceptualising Youth Culture', University of Birmingham, unpublished MA thesis.
CLARKE, J. and JEFFERSON, T. (1974a), Down These Mean Streets: the Meaning of Mugging, 'Howard Journal', vol. 14, no. 1, pp. 37-53.
CLARKE, J. and JEFFERSON, T. (1974b), British Youth Cultures 1950-1970, 'Annali' (Sezione Germanica, Anglistica), vol. 17, nos. 1 and 2, pp. 141-75 and 87-119.
CLARKE, JOHN HALL, STUART JEFFERSON, TONY and ROBERTS, BRIAN (1975), Subcultures, Cultures and Class: a Theoretical Overview, 'Working Papers in Cultural Studies', no. 7/8, Summer 1975, pp. 9-74.
CLEMENS, J. (1973), One Nation, 'European Research', 1(6), pp. 242-6.
CLOWARD, R. and OHLIN, L. (1960), 'Delinquency and Opportunity: A Theory of Delinquent Groups', Free Press, Chicago.
COHEN, A.K. (1955), 'Delinquent Boys: the Culture of the Gang', Free Press, Chicago.
COHEN, B.G. and JENNER, P.J. (1968), The Employment of Immigrants: a Case Study within the Wool Industry in 'Race', vol. 10, no. 1, pp. 41-56.
COHEN, P. (1972), Subcultural Conflict and Working-Class Community, in 'Working Papers in Cultural Studies', 2 (Spring), pp. 5-52.
COHEN, S. (1972), 'Folk Devils and Moral Panics: the Creation of Mods and Rockers', MacGibbon & Kee, London.
COHEN, S., ed. (1971), 'Images of Deviance', Penguin, Harmondsworth.

COLEMAN, J.S. (1961), 'The Adolescent Society', Free Press, New York.
COLEMAN, J.S. et al. (1966), 'Equality of Educational Opportunity', US Government Printing Office, Washington DC.
CORRIGAN, PAUL (1975), Doing Nothing, 'Working Papers in Cultural Studies', no. 7/8, Summer 1975, pp. 103-5.
CORRIGAN, PAUL and FRITH, SIMON (1975), The Politics of Youth Culture, 'Working Papers in Cultural Studies', no. 7/8, Summer 1975, pp. 231-9.
CORRIGAN, PAUL 'The Smash Street Kids', Paladin, forthcoming.
CRAIG, D. (1973), 'The Real Foundations: Literature and Social Change', Chatto & Windus, London.
CRITCHER, C.R. (1974), 'Football since the War: a Study in Social Change and Popular Culture', unpublished MS., Centre for Contemporary Cultural Studies
CROSSLEY, R.S. (1930), 'Accrington Captains of Industry', Wardleworth, Accrington.
CUNNINGHAM, C.M. and LAWTON, R., eds (1970), 'Merseyside; Social and Economic Studies', Longman, London.
CURTIS, L.P. (1968), 'Anglo-Saxons and Celts: a Study of Anti-Irish Prejudice in Victorian Englan'', University of Bridgeport, Connecticut.
CURTIS, L.P. (1971), 'Apes and Angels', David & Charles, Newton Abbot.
DAHYA, B. (1973), Pakistanis in Britain: Transients or Settlers? in 'Race', vol. 14, no. 3, pp. 241-77.
DANIEL, S. and McGUIRE, P. eds (1972), 'The Painthouse: Words from an East End Gang', Penguin, Harmondsworth.
DANIEL, W.W. (1968), 'Racial Discrimination in England', Penguin, Harmondsworth.
DAVIES, J.G. and TAYLOR, J. (1973), Race, Community and no Conflict in J. Raynor and J. Harden, eds, 'Cities, Communities and the Young', vol. 1, Routledge & Kegan Paul, London. pp. 120-8.
DENNIS, N. et al. (1956), 'Coal is Our Life', Eyre & Spottiswoode, London.
DEPARTMENT OF EDUCATION AND SCIENCE: CENTRAL ADVISORY COUNCIL FOR EDUCATION (ENGLAND) (1967), 'Children and their Primary Schools' (Plowden Report), HMSO London.
DEPARTMENT OF THE ENVIRONMENT, (1971), 'New Life in Old Towns', HMSO, London.
DICKENS, C. (1969 edn), 'Hard Times', Penguin, Harmondsworth.
DOUVAN, E. and ADELSON, J. (1966), 'The Adolescent Experience', Wiley, New York.
DOWNES, D. (1966), 'The Delinquent Solution', Routledge & Kegan Paul, London.
DOWNES, D. (1968), Review of D.H. Hargreaves, 'Social Relations in a Secondary School', 'British Journal of Criminology', 8, pp. 316-18.
DUNNING, E., ed. (1971), 'The Sociology of Sport', Cass, London.
ELKIN, F. and WESTLEY, W.A. (1955), The Myth of an Adolescent Culture, 'American Sociological Review', pp. 680-4.
ENGELS, F. (1969 edn), 'The Condition of the Working Classes in England', Panther.
FARRINGTON, D. (1972), Delinquency Begins at Home, 'New Society', 21, pp. 495-7.

FAY, C.R. (1920), 'Life and Labour in the Nineteenth Century', Cambridge University Press.
FERRIS, T. (1973), Bowie among the Barbarians, in 'David Bowie: a Portrait', Wise Publications, London.
FLACKS, R. (1967), Liberated Generation: an Exploration in the Notes of Student Protest, reprinted in M. Kurokawa, ed., 'Minority Responses', Random House, New York, 1970, pp. 352-63.
FLACKS, R. (1971), 'Youth and Social Change', Markham, Chicago.
FOOT, P. (1965), 'Race and Immigration in British Politics', Penguin, Harmondsworth.
FOWLER, P. (1972), Skins Rule, in Charlie Gillet, ed., 'Rock File', Pictorial Publications, London.
GASKELL, E. (1970 edn), 'North and South', Penguin, Harmondsworth.
GASKELL, P. (1836), 'Artisans and Machinery: the Moral and Physical Conditions of the Manufacturing Population', Parker, London.
GASKELL, S.M. (1974), A Landscape of Small Houses: the Failure of the Worker's Flat in Lancashire and Yorkshire in the Nineteenth Century, in A. Sutcliffe, ed., 'Multi-Storey Living', Croom Helms, pp. 88-121.
GERSON, B. (1969), Record Review of 'Alladin Sane' in 'Rolling Stone', 19 July.
GILBERT, E. (1957), 'Advertising and Marketing to Young People', Printers' Ink Books, New York.
GOFFMAN, E. (1971), 'The Presentation of Self in Everyday Life', Penguin, Harmondsworth.
GOODMAN, P. (1960), 'Growing Up Absurd', Vintage, New York.
GRAMSCI, A. (1973), 'The Prison Notebooks', Lawrence & Wishart, London.
GROUP FOR THE ADVANCEMENT OF PSYCHIATRY, (1974), 'Normal Adolescence', Crosby Rockwood, Staples.
HACK, B. (1972), The Rags in Soccer Riches in '7 Days', (15) (9-15 February).
HALMOS, P. (1969), 'Solitude and Privacy', Greenwood Press, New York.
HALSEY, A.H. (1972), 'Educational Priority - Volume 1', HMSO, London.
HAMMOND, J.L. and HAMMOND B. (1919), 'The Skilled Labourer 1760-1832', Longmans, London.
HARGREAVES, B. (1882), 'Recollections of Broad Oak', Bowker, Accrington.
HARGREAVES, D.H. (1967), 'Social Relations in a Secondary School', Routledge & Kegan Paul, London.
HARLAND, J., ed. (1882), 'Ballads and Songs of Lancashire', 3rd edition, Heywood.
HARTLEY, B. (1973), Son of Alf Garnett: Riot in Leeds, paper given to Conference on Working Class Culture, University College, Cardiff, November.
HEBDIGE, D. (1974a), The Style of the Mods, mimeographed paper, Centre for Contemporary Cultural Studies, University of Birmingham.
HEBDIGE, D. (1974b), Reggie, Rastas and Rudies: style and the Subversion of Form, mimeographed paper, Centre for Contemporary Cultural Studies, University of Birmingham.
HERMAN, G. (1971), 'The Who', Studio Vista, London.
HIRSCHI, T. (1970), 'Causes of Delinquency', University of California Press.

HOBSBAWM, E.J. (1964), 'Labouring Men', Weidenfeld & Nicholson, London.
HOBSBAWM, E.J. (1969), 'Industry and Empire', Penguin, Harmondsworth.
HOBSBAWM, E.J. (1971), 'Primitive Rebels', 3rd edition, Manchester University Press.
HOBSBAWM, E.J. (1972), 'Bandits', Penguin, Harmondsworth.
HOGGART, R. (1958), 'The Uses of Literacy', Penguin, Harmondsworth.
Hollingshead, A.B. (1949), 'Elmtown's Youth', Wiley, New York.
HOPKINS, H. (1964), 'The New Look', Secker & Warburg, London.
HOPWOOD, E. (1969), 'The Lancashire Weavers' Story', Amalgamated Weavers' Association, Manchester.
HUTT, C. (1973), 'The Death of the English Pub', Arrow, London.
JACKSON, B. (1972), 'Working Class Community', Penguin, Harmondsworth.
JACKSON, J.A. (1963), 'The Irish in Britain', Routledge & Kegan Paul, London.
JAY, M. (1974), 'The Dialectical Imagination', Heinemann, London.
JEFFERSON, T. (1973), The Teds: a Political Resurrection, mimeographed paper, Centre for Contemporary Studies, University of Birmingham.
JENCKS, C. et al. (1973), 'Inequality', Allen Lane, London.
JOHNSTONE, J.W. (1961), Social Structure and Patterns of Man Media Consumption, University of Chicago, unpublished doctoral thesis.
KANDEL, D.B. and LESSER, G.S. (1972), 'Youth in Two Worlds', Jossey-Bass Inc., San Francisco.
KAY-SHUTTLEWORTH, J.P. (1970 edn), 'The Moral and Physical Conditions of the Working Classes, Cass, London.
KENISTON, K. (1971), 'Youth and Dissent', Harcourt Brace Jovanovich, New York.
KERR, M. (1958), 'The People of Ship Street', Routledge & Kegan Paul, London.
KITSUSE, J.I. and CICOUREL, A.V. (1963), A Note on the Use of Official Statistics, 'Social Problems', 11, pp. 131-9.
LAING, D. (1969), 'The Sound of our Time', Sheed & Ward, London.
LAWRENCE, D. (1974), 'Black Migrants: White Natives', Cambridge University Press.
LAWTON, R. and CUNNINGHAM, I.C.M., eds (1970), 'Merseyside Social and Economic Studies', Longman, London.
LEFEBVRE, G. (1974), 'The Great Fear of 1789', New Left Books, London.
LEWIS, O. (1967), 'La Vida', Random House, New York.
LIGHTBROWN, C. (1973), The Terraces Turn to Rock in 'Sunday Times', 28 October.
LINTON, R. (1942), Age and Sex Categories, 'American Sociological Review', 7, pp. 589-603.
MacINNES, C. (1961), 'England, Half English', MacGibbon & Kee, London.
MANNHEIM, K. (1927), The Problem of Generations, reprinted in K. Mannheim, 'Essays on the Sociology of Knowledge', Routledge & Kegan Paul, London, 1952, pp. 276-322.
MARX, K. (1968), The Eighteenth Brumaire of Louis Bonaparte, in K. Marx and F. Engels, 'Selected Works', Lawrence & Wishart, London.
MARX, K. (1974 edn), 'The First International and After', Penguin, Harmondsworth.

MATZA, D. (1961), Subterranean Traditions of Youth, 'Annals of the American Academ- of Social and Political Science', 338, pp. 102-18.
MATZA, D. (1964), 'Delinquency and Drift', Wiley, New York.
MATZA, D. (1970), Rebellious Youth: 1969, 'Youth and Society', 1(4), pp. 445-72.
MATZA, D. and SYKES, G. (1961), Juvenile Delinquency and Subterranean Values, 'American Sociological Review', 26, pp. 712-19.
MAYS, J.B. (1954), 'Growing up in the City: a Study of Juvenile Delinquency in an Urban Neighbourhood', Liverpool University Press.
MAYS, J.B. (1965), 'The Young Pretenders', Michael Joseph, London.
MEAD, M. (1972), 'Culture and Commitment: a Study of the Generation Gap', Panther, London.
MELLY, G. (1972), 'Revolt into Style', Penguin, Harmondsworth.
MILIBAND, R. and SAVILE, J., eds (1974), 'The Socialist Register 1973', Merlin Press, London.
MILLER, D. (1969), 'The Age Between', Cornmarket-Hutchinson, London.
MILLER, W.B. (1958), Lower Class Culture as a Generating Milieu of Gang Delinquency, 'Journal of Social Issues', 15, pp. 5-19.
MILLS, C.W. (1943), The Professional Ideology of Social Pathologists, 'American Journal of Sociology', 49, September, pp. 165-80.
MILLS, R. (1933), 'Young Outsiders', Routledge & Kegan Paul, London.
MILSON, F. (1972), 'Youth in a Changing Society', Routledge & Kegan Paul, London.
MITCHELL, J.C. (1956), The Kalela Dance, 'Rhodes-Livingstone Paper', no. 27, Manchester University Press.
MONOD, J. (1967), Juvenile Gangs in Paris: toward a Structural Analysis, in 'Journal of Research in Crime and Delinquency', January, pp. 142-65.
MORTON, J. (1972), Breaking the Circle, 'New Society', 9 March, no. 493, p. 498.
MORTON, J. (1973), Back to Nature, 'New Society', 31 May, no. 556, pp. 494-95.
MURDOCK, G. and McCRON, R. (1973), Scoobies, Skins and Contemporary Pop, 'New Society', 29 March, no. 547, pp. 690-2.
MURDOCK, G. and Golding, P. (1974), For a Political Economy of Mass Communications, in R. Miliband and J. Saville (1974).
MUSGROVE, F. (1969), The Problem of Youth and the Social Structure of Society in England, 'Youth and Society', 1(1), pp. 38-58.
NEWBIGGING, T. (1893), 'History of the Forest of Rossendale', Rossendale Free Press, Rawtenstall.
NUTTALL, J. (1969), 'Bomb Culture', Paladin, London.
O'CONNOR, K. (1972), 'The Irish in Britain', Sidgwick & Jackson, London.
OLIVER, P. (1972), 'The Meaning of the Blues', Collier, New York.
ORWELL, G. (1970 edn), 'Decline of the English Murder and other Essays', Penguin, Harmondsworth.
PARKER, H. (1974a), The Joys of Joyriding, in 'New Society', 4 January.
PARKER, H. (1974b), 'View From the Boys', David & Charles, Newton Abbot.
PARKIN, F. (1972), 'Class Inequality and Political Disorder', Paladin, London.

PARSONS, T. (1942), Age and Sex in the Social Structure of the United States. References here to the version reprinted in T. Parsons, 'Essays in Sociological Theory' (revised edition), Free Press, New York, 1964, pp. 89-103.
PARSONS, T. (1950), Psychoanalysis and the Social Structure. References here to the version reprinted in Parsons, 1964.
PATRICK, J. (1973), 'A Glasgow Gang Observed', Eyre Methuen, London.
PAUL, JIMMY and MUSTAFA SUPPORT COMMITTEE (1973), 'Twenty Years', The Action Centre, 134 Villa Road, Handsworth, Birmingham.
PEARSON, G. (1975a), 'The Deviant Imagination', Macmillan, London.
PEARSON, GEOFF (1975b), Does Hooliganism Make Sense?, 'Community Care', 20 August, pp. 14-17.
PEARSON, GEOFF (1975c), Vandals in the Park, 'New Society', vol. 34, no. 679, p. 69.
PEARSON, GEOFF (1976), In Defence of Hooliganism. Social Theory and Violence, in N. Tutt, ed., 'Violence', HMSO, London.
PHILLIPSON, C.M. (1971), Juvenile Delinquency and the School, in W.G. Carson and P. Wiles eds, 'Crime and Delinquency in Britain', Martin Robertson, London.
PICCONE, P. (1969), From Youth Culture to Political Praxis, in 'Radical America' 15, November.
PINTO-DUSCHINSKY, M. (1970), Bread and Circuses? The Conservatives in Office, in Bogdanor and Skidelsky (1970).
POWER, M.J. et al. (1967), Delinquent Schools? 'New Society', 19 October.
PRIDEAUX, F. (1972), Of Textiles and Tariffs, 'Race Today', vol. 4, no. 7, p. 217.
REDFORD, A. (1926), 'Labour Migration in England 1800-1950', Manchester University Press.
REICH, C.A. (1972), 'The Greening of America', Penguin, Harmondsworth.
REMMERS, H.H. and RADLER, D.H. (1957), 'The American Teenager', Bobbs-Merrill, New York.
REPORT OF THE CENTRAL ADVISORY COUNCIL FOR EDUCATION (1959), (Crowther Report), HMSO, London.
REUTER, E.B. (1936), The Adolescent World, 'American Journal of Sociology', XLIII (1), pp. 82-4.
REUTER, E.B. (1937), The Sociology of Adolescence, 'American Journal of Sociology', XLIII (3) pp. 414-27.
REX, J. and MOORE, R. (1971), 'Race, Community and Conflict', Oxford University Press.
RICKS, C. (1974), 'Keats and Embarrassment', Oxford University Press.
RIESMAN, D. (1954), 'Individualism Reconsidered, and Other Essays', Free Press, Chicago.
ROBERTS, K., WHITE, G., and PARKER, H. (1974), 'The Character Training Industry', David & Charles, Newton Abbot.
ROBERTS, R. (1973), 'The Classic Slum', Penguin, Harmondsworth.
ROCK, M. (1973), The Student Polka, in 'David Bowie: a Portrait', Wise Publications, London.
ROCK, P. and COHEN, S. (1970), The Teddy Boys, in Bogdanor and Skidelsky (1970), pp. 288-320.
ROSE, A.G. (1957), The Plug Riots in Lancashire and Cheshire, 'Transactions of the Lancashire and Cheshire Antiquarian Society, vol. 67, pp. 75-112.

ROSZAK, T. (1971), 'The Making of a Counter-Culture', Faber, London.
ROSZAK, T. (1973), 'Where the Wasteland Ends', Faber, London.
ROWBOTHAM, S. (1974), 'Hidden From History', Pluto Press, London.
ROWNTREE J. and ROWNTREE M. (1968), Youth as Class: the Political Economy of Youth, 'Our Generation', 6 (1-2), pp. 155-86.
RUDÉ, G. (1970), 'Paris and London in the Eighteenth Century', Fontana, London.
RUTTER, M. (1973), Why are London Children so Disturbed?, 'Proceedings of the Royal Society of Medicine', 66, pp. 1221-5.
SARTRE, J.-P. (1960), 'Critique de la Raison Dialectique', Paris.
SCHUR, E.M. (1973), 'Radical Non-Intervention', Prentice-Hall, Englewood Cliffs.
SEABROOK, J. (1970), Packie Stan, 'New Society', 23 April, no. 395, pp. 677-8.
SEABROOK, J. (1973), 'City Close-Up', Penguin, Harmondsworth.
SILLITOE, A. (1970), 'Saturday Night and Sunday Morning', Signet Books, London.
SINGLETON, J.W., ed. (1928), 'The Jubilee Souvenir of the Corporation of Accrington 1818-1928', Broadley, Accrington.
SMELSER, N.J. (1959), 'Social Change in the Industrial Revolution', Routledge & Kegan Paul, London.
SMITH, D.M. (1970), Adolescence: a Study of Stereotyping, in 'Sociological Review', vol. 18, pp. 197-211.
SMITH, E.A. (1962), 'American Youth Culture', Free Press, New York.
STIMSON, G. (1969), Skinheads and Cherry Reds, ' Rolling Stone', 26 July, pp. 22-3.
SUGARMAN, B. (1967), Improvement in Youth Culture, Academic Achievement and Conformity in School, 'British Journal of Sociology', 18, pp. 151-64.
SUTTLES, G.D. (1968), 'The Social Order of the Slum', University of Chicago Press.
TAYLOR, I. (1971a), Soccer Consciousness and Soccer Hooliganism, in S. Cohen (1971), pp. 134-64.
TAYLOR, I. (1971b), Football Mad: a Speculative Sociology of Soccer Hooliganism, in Dunning (1971).
TAYLOR, I., WALTON, P. and YOUNG, J. (1973), 'The New Criminology', Routledge & Kegan Paul, London.
TAYLOR, I., WALTON, P. and YOUNG, J. (1975), Critical Criminology in Britain: Review and Prospects, in I. Taylor, P. Walton and J. Young, eds, 'Critical Criminology: a Reader', Routledge & Kegan Paul, London.
TAYLOR, W. COOKE (1968 edn), 'Notes of a Tour in the Manufacturing Districts of Lancashire', 3rd edition, Cass, London.
TAYLOR, W. COOKE (n.d.), 'The Life and Times of Sir Robert Peel, Volume I', Jackson, Fisher Son & Co., London.
THOMPSON, E.P. (1968), 'The Making of the English Working Class', Penguin, Harmondsworth.
THOMPSON, E.P. (1974), An Open Letter to Leszek Kolakowski, in Miliband and Saville (1974).
THRASHER, F.M. (1927), 'The Gang', University of Chicago Press.
TUPLING, G.H. (1927), 'The Economic History of Rossendale', Chetham Society', Manchester.
TURNER, R. (1964), 'The Social Context of Ambition', Chandler, San Francisco.

TYERMAN, M. (1958), A Research into Truancy, 'British Journal of Educational Psychology', 28, pp. 217-25.
URE, A. (1861), 'The Philosophy of Manufactures', Bohn, London.
WADSWORTH, A.P. and MANN J. de L. (1931), 'The Cotton Trade and Industrial Lancashire 1600-1780' Manchester University Press.
WALLER, W. (1932), 'The Sociology of Teaching', Wiley, New York.
WARD, C. ed. (1973), 'Vandalism', Architectural Press, London.
WEBB, J. (1962), The Sociology of a School, 'British Journal of Sociology', 13, pp. 264-72.
WEINER, A. (1973), Rock to the Top, 'New Society', no. 579, 8 November.
WENNER, J. (1973), 'Lennon Remembers', Penguin, Harmondsworth.
WERTHMAN, C. (1967), The Functions of Social Definitions in the Development of Delinquent Careers in 'Juvenile Delinquency and Youth Crime', President's Commission on Law Enforcement and the Administration of Justice.
WEST, D.J. and FARRINGTON, D. (1973), 'Who Becomes Delinquent'' Heinemann, London.
WHITTAKER, J. (1909), 'Tariff Reform in Relation to the Cotton Trade', Broadley, Accrington.
THE WHO (1973), 'Quadrophenia', Track Records.
WILLIAMS, R. (1974), 'The English Novel', Paladin, London.
WILLIS, P. (1971), 'Non-Participation in Elite Culture: a Case Study of Young People and their Participation in the Culture which surrounds Popular Music', report for UNESCO.
WILLIS, P. (1972), The Motor Bike Within a Subcultural Group, 'Working Papers in Cultural Studies', no. 2, pp. 53-70.
WILLIS, P. (1973), The Triple-X Boys, 'New Society', March.
WILLIS, PAUL (1976), 'Profane Culture', Chatto & Windus, London.
WILLMOTT, P. (1960), 'Adolescent Boys of East London', Routledge & Kegan Paul, London.
WOLFE, T. (1969), The Noonday Underground in 'The Pump House Gang', Bantam Books, New YOrk, pp. 75-88.
WRIGHT, P.L. (1968), 'The Coloured Worker in British Industry', Oxford University Press.
YOUNG, J. (1971), The Role of the Police as Amplifiers of Deviancy, in S. Cohen (1971).
YOUNG, J. (1973), The Hippie Solution: An Essay in the Politics of Leisure, in I. Taylor and L. Taylor, eds, 'Politics and Deviance', Penguin, Harmondsworth.
YOUNG, J. and CRUTCHLEY, J.B. (1972), Student Drug Use, 'Drugs and Society', 2 (1), pp. 11-15.
YOUNG, M.F.D., ed. (1972), 'Knowledge and Control', Collier-Macmillan, London.